THE SIMPLE WAY TO LEARN JAPANESE

TOMOKO NAGAI

All rights reserved.

Copyright © 2019 by Tomoko Nagai

No part of this book may be reproduced or transmitted in any form or by any means, electronic or mechanical, including photocopying, recording, or by any information storage and retrieval system, without permission in writing from the publisher.

This edition contains the complete text

of the original hardcover edition.

NOT ONE WORD HAS BEEN OMITTED.

THE SIMPLEST WAY TO LEARN JAPANESE

A Bad Creative Book / published by

arrangement with the author

BAD CREATIVE PUBLISHING HISTORY

The Simplest Way To Learn French published March 2016

The Simplest Way To Learn Spanish, published March 2017

UPCOMING WORKS

The Simplest Way To Learn Dutch, 2019

ISBN: 9781075250675

Vol. 1

Vol. 2

ALSO AVAILABLE IN

- AUDIO
- HARDCOVER
- E-BOOK

FORMATS

For updates on the next book, or if you'd just like us to have a cup of coffee on your behalf, please support us on the facebook page www.facebook.com/BadCreativ3

SOCIAL #TheSimplestWay #LearnJapanese #BadCreativ3

CONTENTS

Chapter 1 - Basics
Chapter 2 - Food
Chapter 3 - Animals
Chapter 4 - Possessives
Chapter 5 - Clothing
Chapter 6 - Questions
Chapter 7 - Verbs
Chapter 8 – Preposition

Chapter 9 - Dates & Time

Chapter 10 - Family
Chapter 11 - Color
Chapter 12 - Occupation
Chapter 13 - Measures
Chapter 14 - Household
Chapter 15 - Adjectives
Chapter 16 – Determiners
Chapter 17 - Adverbs
Chapter 18 - Objects
Chapter 19 - Places
Chapter 20 - People
Chapter 21 - Numbers

Contact info

FOREWORD

While in school, we learnt stuff we probably don't use today. However, language is essential to almost every aspect of the human condition.

How do you expand your business beyond your continent for more sales? How are you going to express your love for the beautiful lady that just walked past? How do you get directions to Shibuya station? With the knowledge of language, that's how.

This book contains a lexicon of some of the most used words in everyday Japanese conversation. It makes use of the age-old learning techniques of repetition and rote memorization, to condition the brain for learning Japanese as quickly as possible. In addition, an auxiliary feature called story mode has been included to aid the reader in a test for comprehension.

Finally, it should be noted that while this book will aid in a visual recognition and comprehension of words in the Japanese language, students must also understand their proper pronunciations. To help with this, there is an accompanying audiobook that will be made available, to enable listening lessons.

And so, from the beautiful city of Tokyo, the city of sakuras and all things fashionable, we present to you, The Simple Way To Learn Japanese.

HOW TO USE THIS BOOK

1. This line is the training line (or T-Line if you prefer)

TRAINING TIME

It represents the end of a set of 25 words to memorize.

2. You are required to cover the right side of the book & attempt to translate the left side, off hand.
3. Each correct translation carries 1 point. Words after the T-line but not up to 25, are considered as bonuses.
4. Do not proceed to the next batch until you have scored twenty-five points
5. The story modes are designed to help you understand the usage of the words in sentences, so be sure to score high on the training, to fully comprehend the stories.

Now that you know the rules,

Let us begin.

Chapter 1
BASICS

Keywords : Watashi, kare, kanojo, anata, otoko, on'nanoko, otoko, josei.

No	The
Mizu	Water
Ringo	Apple
Otokonoko	Boy
On'nanoko	Girl
O toko	Man
Josei	A woman
Pan	Bread
Otoko	A man
Watashi wa otokodesu	I am a man
Watashi wa otokonokodesu	I am a boy
Josei ga ringo o taberu	The woman eats an apple
Sono shōnen wa ringo o taberu	The boy eats an apple
Kanojo wa iru	She is
Kare wa otokonokodesu	He is a boy
Kanojo wa on'nanokodesu	She is a girl
Watashi wa nomu	I drink
Anata ga nomu	You drink
Watashi wa taberu	I eat
Anata ga taberu	You eat
Kanojo wa taberu	She eats
Satō o taberu	I eat sugar
Kare wa mizu o nonde imasu	He is drinking water
Anata wa joseidesu	You are a woman

TRAINING TIME

Josei	Women
Hon	The book
Shinbun	Newspaper
Watashi wa yomu	I read
Watashi wa kakimasu	I write
Anata ga yomu	You read
Anata ga kaku	You write
Kanojo wa yomu	She reads
Kare ga yomimashita	He reads
Watashitachiha kaku	We write
Wareware wa nomu	We drink
Kare wa hon o kaita	He wrote a book
Anata wa mizuwonomu	You drink water
Watashitachiha mizu o nomimasu	We drink water
Kanojo wa nonde imasu	She is drinking
Kare wa mizu o nonde imasu	He is drinking water
Anata wa otokonokodesu	You are a boy
Watashitachiha kodomodesu	We are children
Watashitachiha danseidesu	We are men
Watashitachiha joseidesu	We are women
Watashitachiha otokonokodesu	We are boys
Anata wa otokodesu	You are a man
Gyūnyū o nomu nodesu ka?	Do we drink milk?
Gyūnyū o nomu	We drink milk
Watashitachiha mizu o nomimasu	We drink water

TRAINING TIME

No	The
Karera	They
Watashitachi, karera	We, they
Okurete	Late
Kōki gogo ni	In the afternoon
Kon'nichiwa!	Hello there!
Nihonjin	Japanese
Watashi ga itta	I said
Dōmo arigatōgozaimashita	Thank you very much
Sayōnara	Goodbye
Anata wa eigo o hanasemasu ka?	Can you speak English?
Watashi wa James desu, eigo o hanashimasu	I am James and I speak English
Hai, go yōsha kudasai	Yes, please forgive me
Watashi wa Mitsuki, watashi wa Itaria-go o hanasu koto ga dekimasu	I'm Mitsuki, I can speak Italian
Ringodesu ka?	Is it an apple?
Kare, kanojo, watashitachi	He, she, we
Karera wa danseidesu ka?	Are they men?
Karera wa joseidesu ka?	Are they women?
Karera wa danseida	They are men
Kanojotachi wa joseidesu.	They are women.
Karera wa on'nanokodesu	They are girls
Karera ga yonde	They read
Karera wa kakimasu	They write
Kanojotachi wa joseidesu.	They are women.

TRAINING TIME

Arigatōgozaimashita	Thank you
Hai	Yes
Kon'nichiwa	Hello there
Sayōnara!	Goodbye!
Konbanwa	Good evening
Ohayōgozaimasu	Good morning
Oyasuminasai	Good night
Sayōnara Salvador	Goodbye Salvador
Konbanwa Georgia	Good evening Georgia
Oyasumi Joe	Goodnight Joe
Sofia arigatōgozaimasu!	Thank you Sofia!
Īe, kekkōdesu	No, thank you
Mōshiwakearimasen	No sorry
Onegaishimasu	Please
Gomen'nasai	I am sorry
Satō de	In sugar
Watashi wa ringo ga arimasu	I have an apple
Satō o tabeta	I ate sugar
Sono shōnen wa kaita	The boy wrote
Kanojo wa satō o tabemasu	She eats sugar
Watashi wa hon o motte imasu	I have a book
Kare wa bīru o nonde imasu	He is drinking beer
Watashi wa anata ga sukidesu	I like you
Watashi wa josei ga sukidesu	I like women

TRAINING TIME

Watashitachiha joseidesu	We are women
Karera wa on'nanokodesu	They are girls
Kagi o motte imasu	I have a key
Yokunai	They are not good
Karera ga yonde	They read
Painappuru ga sukidesu	They like pineapples
Sono shōnen wa ringo o taberu	The boy eats an apple
Kono hito wa kono tegami o yomimashita	This person read this letter
Watashi wa korera no tekisuto o yomimashita	I read these texts
Shōjo wa ringo o tabete imasu	The girl is eating an apple
Kare wa korera no kotoba o yomimashita	He read these words
Kanojo wa kaite imasu	She is writing
Kanojo wa jagaimo o taberu	She eats potatoes
Karera wa banana ga sukidesu	They like bananas
Kanojo wa totemo ī-kodesu	She is very good
Karera wa nomu	They drink
Anata wa min'na on'nanokodesu	You are all girls
Hon o kaita	I wrote a book
Anata wa tegami o kaita	You wrote a letter
Watashi wa kakimasu	I write
Kare wa hon o kaita	He wrote a book

Sono shōnen wa tegami o kaita	The boy wrote a letter
Watashi wa shinbun o yonda	I read the newspaper
Karera wa honwoyomu	They read a book
Karera wa hon o kaita	They wrote a book

TRAINING TIME

Watashitachiha yonda	We read
Wareware wa nomu	We drink
Watashi wa hitorida	I am alone
Anata wa hon o yomimasu	You read a book
Shinbun o yomimasu	We read the newspaper
Kare wa, hon o yomimasu	He reads a book
Chō wa hitodesu	Cho is a person
Mitsuki wa sore o kaita, Akira wa sore o yonda	Mitsuki wrote that, Akira read it
Alberto ga honwoyomu	Alberto reads a book
Ohayōgozaimasu, ogenkidesuka?	Good morning, how are you?
Watashi wa on'nanoko de, gyūnyū o nomimasu	I am a girl and I drink milk
Anata wa mizuwonomu	You drink water
Naze watashi wa sore o iu nodesu ka?	Why do I say that?
Teki wa hoshikunai	We don't want an enemy
Kanojo wa tazunete kotaeta	She asked and answered

Dare ga kachimasu ka?	Who wins?
Watashi wa 6-ji ni okinakereba naranai	I must get up at six
Kore wa yakusokudesu	This is a promise
Botoru ni mizu o ireta	I filled the bottle with water
Kore o suru	We do this
Yatta yo	I did it
Watashi wa kiita	I heard
Watashi wa karera ga totemo sukidesu	I like them very much
Kanojo wa karera o tasukemasu	She helps them
Watashi no ani wa sorera o sagashimasu	My brother looks for them

TRAINING TIME

STORY MODE

JAPANESE

Jiro: "Riodejaneiro no senshu-tachi to pātī o suru junbi ga dekite imasu. Ashita shuppatsu shimasu"
Mitsuki: "Hitsuyōnamono wa subete sorotte imasu ka."
Jiro: "Hai."
Mitsuki: "Anata no ryokō wa dono kurai no kikandesu ka?"
Jiro: "Yaku san kara yon tsukidesu"
Mitsuki: "Kono baggu no nakami wa?"
Jiro: "Sorehodode wa arimasen. Ikutsu ka no fuku, mizu to konpyūtā."
Mitsuki: "Tōchaku ni hitsuyōnamono o kentō shimashita ka?"
Jiro: "Dōiu imidesu ka?"
Mitsuki: "Sumu basho, taberu basho, iku basho"
Jiro: "Īe, chigaimasu"
Mitsuki: "Mada basho o yoyaku shite inai baai demo, anata wa mada wāfuparesuhoteru ni taizai suru koto ga dekimasu. Chōshoku wa totemo yasuku, shinsen'na gyūnyū ga fukuma rete imasu. Tabemono ya nomimono no tame ni, anata wa akua, Sanpauro no totemo sutekina basho o hōmon suru koto ga dekimasu. Karera wa mata, anata ga suwatte iruto dansei to josei to issho ni nomu koto ga dekiru niwa o motte imasu yūgata ni wa, ' kyanberī' bīchi ni iku hitsuyō ga arimasu. Tanoshī jikan o sagashite iru shiawasena hitobito no gurūpu ga tsuneni arimasu. Saigo ni, shōhin o kōnyū shitai baai wa, Ordem māketto ni akusesu shite kudasai. Doyōbi ni eigyō shite imasuga, hotondo no torēdā wa Porutogaru-go o hanashimasu."

Jiro: "Mondainai. Porutogaru-go ga sukoshi yomeru. Watashi wa tōchaku shita toki ni mo gengo o manabu koto ga dekimasu."
Mitsuki: "Anata no imōto wa anata to issho ni ikimasu ka?"
Jiro: "Hai, watashitachiha issho ni hon o kakimasu"
Mitsuki: "Otōsan wa dōdesu ka?"
Jiro: "Īe, kare wa ie de shinbun o yomu koto ga dekirudeshou"
Mitsuki: "Sā, watashitachi no koto o wasurezu ni, odosan o mochikaette kudasai"
Jiro: "Shinpaishinaide, watashi wa anata o kōshin suru tame ni tegami o okurimasu."
Mitsuki: "Arigatō, arigatōgozaimasu."

ABCDEFGHI
JKLMNOPQ
RSTUVWXY
Z

ENGLISH

Jiro: "I'm ready to party with the players in Rio de Janeiro. We're leaving tomorrow."

Mitsuki: "Do you have everything you need?"

Jiro: "Yes."

Mitsuki: "How long is your trip?"

Jiro: "About three to four months."

Mitsuki: "What is in this bag?"

Jiro: "Not much, some clothes, water and computers."

Mitsuki: "Have you considered the necessary things for your arrival?"

Jiro: "What do you mean?"

Mitsuki: "A place to live, places to eat, places to go."

Jiro: "No, not really."

Mitsuki: "If you haven't booked a place yet, you can still stay at the Wharf Palace Hotel. Breakfast is very cheap and includes fresh milk.

For food and drinks, you can visit Acqua, a very nice place in Sao Paulo. They also have a garden where you can sit and drink with men and women

In the evening, you should go to 'Cambery' beach. There is always a group of happy people looking for a good time.

Finally, if you want to buy items, you can visit Ordem Market. It is open on Saturday, but most traders speak Portuguese."

Jiro: "No problem, I can read a little Portuguese. I can also learn the language when I arrive."

Mitsuki: "Will your sister go with you?"

Jiro: "Yes, we will write a book together."

Mitsuki: "What about your father?"

Jiro: "No, he will be able to read newspapers at home."

Mitsuki: "Well, don't forget about us and bring back some souvenirs."

Jiro: "Don't worry, I'll send letters to update you."

Mitsuki: "Thank you, I will be very grateful."

1 2 3 4 5 6 7 8 9
10 11 12 13 14 15
16 **17 18** 19 20 21
22 23 24 25 26
27 28 29 30 31

Chapter 2
FOOD

Keywords : Chokorēto, furūtsu, ninjin, shokuhin, bīru, botoru, kōhī, chōshoku, katto, taberu, ryōri suru.

Furūtsu	Fruit
Fōku	Fork
Ue	Hunger
Daietto	Diet
Asa gohan	Breakfast
Ranchi	Lunch
Dinā	Dinner
Botoru	Bottle
Garasu	Glass
Batā	Butter
Kappu	Cup
Bōru	The bowl
Kēki	Cake
Bīru	Beer
Chikin	Chicken
Tamago	The egg
Tamago	An egg
Nomimono	Beverage
Chīzu	Cheese
Ninjin	A carrot
Sōsu	Sauce
Gurēpu	Grape
Nin'niku	Garlic
Jūsu	Juice
Dorinku	Drink

TRAINING TIME

Sakana	Fish
Gyūnyū	Milk
Kōhī	Coffee
Menyū	Menu
Shokuji	The meal
Purēto	Plate
Banana	A banana
Chokorēto o taberu	I eat chocolate
Sono shōnen wa kukkī o taberu	The boy eats cookies
Watashi wa chokorētoaisukurīmu o taberu	I eat chocolate ice cream
Watashi wa chūshoku o tabete imasu	I am having lunch
Watashi wa chūshoku o tsukurimasu	I make lunch
Suppai janai	It is not sour
Jamu wa sanmi ga arimasu	The jam has a sour taste
Watashi wa niku o ryōri suru	I cook meat
Kore wa kitchindesu	This is a kitchen
Watashi wa bin o nonda	I drank a bottle
Anata wa gyūnyū o nomu	You drink milk
Anata wa kōhī o nomimasu	You drink coffee
Anata wa sakana o tabemasu	You eat fish
Kono hito wa fōku o motte imasu	This person has a fork
Furaidochīzu o taberu	I eat fried cheese
Watashitachi wa taberu	We eat
Chōshoku o toru	We have breakfast
Shefu wa batā o	The chef has butter

TRAINING TIME

Josei wa sakana o taberu	The woman eats fish
Ban gohan ga arimasu	I have dinner
Sakana wa yūshoku-yōdesu	The fish is for dinner
Watashi wa chīzu o tabemasen	I do not eat cheese
Karera wa sakana o taberu	They eat fish
Shefu ga gyūniku o kiru	The chef cuts beef
Ringo o kiru	I cut the apple
Kanojo wa ryōri suru	She cooks
Watashi wa sakana o tsukurimasu	I cook fish
Josei wa ninjin o kiru	The woman cuts carrots
Watashi wa chikin o tsukurimasu	I cook chicken
Kurīmu ga futtō shite iru	The cream is boiling
Chokorētokurīmu wa futtō shite iruzhèngzài fèiténg	The chocolate cream is boiling
Painappuru to bīru	Pineapple and beer
Pan o kiru	I cut the bread
Tabemono	The food
Kyandi	The candy
Watashi wa kudamono o tabemasu	I eat fruit
Kare wa mame o tabemasu	He eats beans
Remon	Lemon
Orenji	Orange
Kanojo wa banana o tabeta	She ate a banana
Amai kēki o tabemashita	I ate a sweet cake
Sutēki o taberu	I eat steak
Karera wa jamu o taberu	They eat jam

TRAINING TIME

Niku	The meat
Butaniku	Pork
Tamanegi	Onion
Shio	Salt
Shugā	Sugar
Sūpu	Soup
Supagetti	Spaghetti
Hakumai	White rice
Resutoran	Restaurant
Sandoitchi	Sandwich
Tomato	Tomato
Jagaimo	Potato
Jagaimo ni	I boiled potatoes
Jamu o tabemashita	I ate jam
Sono otoko wa remonēdo o nomimasu	The man drinks lemonade
Shefu ga butaniku o ryōri suru	The chef cooks pork
Hon ni reshipi ga arimasu	I have a recipe in the book
Kanojo wa abura o nomu	She drinks oil
Watashi wa abura o nomimasen	I do not drink oil
Koshō wanai	I do not have pepper
Pasuta o taberu	We eat pasta
Jagaimo ni	I boiled potatoes
Kore wa sandoitchidesu	This is a sandwich
Kare wa sarada o tabemasu	He eats salad
Ryōri hito wa sōsēji	The cook has a sausage

TRAINING TIME

Kitchin	Kitchen
Gyūniku	Beef
Wain	Wine
Furūtsujūsu	Fruit juice
Bābekyū	Barbecue
Ichigo	Strawberry
Seibun wa shiodesu	The ingredient is salt
Watashitachiha resutoran de yūshoku o torimashita	We had dinner in the restaurant
Kore wa shichimenchōdesu	This is a turkey
Josei wa resutoran de chūshoku o toru	The ladies have lunch at the restaurant
Sono otokonoko wa chūshoku o torimasu	The boy has lunch
Josei wa yūshoku o taberu	The woman eats dinner
Tomato o tabemashita	I ate a tomato
Shefu wa chūshoku o torimasu	The chef has lunch
Watashi wa u~eitāde wa arimasen	I am not a waiter
Furūtsujūsu o nomu	We drink fruit juice
Kare wa pan o kitta	He cut the bread
Kare wa menyū o yomu	He reads the menu
Kare wa banana o tabemasu	He eats bananas
Onaka hasu kimashita ka?	Are you hungry?
Anata wa ninjin ga sukidesu ka?	Do you like carrots?
Watashi wa chōri shite tabemasu	I cook and you eat
Tamago o tabemashita	I ate an egg
Kare wa bejitariande wa arimasen	He is not vegetarian
Shefu ga kinoko o ryōri suru	The chef cooks mushrooms

TRAINING TIME

Naifu	Knife
Supūn	Spoon
Nigai	Bitter
Remon	A lemon
Fāmu	Farm
Kare wa yasai o taberu	He eats vegetables
U~eitā ni wa wain ga arimasu	The waiter has wine
Kinoko o taberu	We eat mushrooms
Watashi wa sakana o tabemasu	I eat fish
Watashi wa chīzu o tabemasen	I do not eat cheese
On'nanoko wa ocha o nonde imasu	The girl is drinking tea
On'nanoko wa onaka ga suite imasu	The girl is hungry
Seibun wa jamu	The ingredient is jam
Aji wa amakunai	The taste is not sweet
Aji wa amaidesu	The taste is sweet
Kōri o taberu	You eat ice
Sono shōnen wa chīzu o taberu	The boy eats cheese
Kēki ga sukida	I like cake
Sarada to oiru ga suki	I like salad and oil
Painappuru o taberu	We eat a pineapple
Ringo o taberu	We eat an apple
Kōhī o nomimasu ka?	Do you drink coffee?
Kare wa mizu o motte imasu	He has water
Kare wa ringo o motte imasu	He has an apple
Kare wa bisuketto o tabemashita	He ate a piece of biscuit

TRAINING TIME

Shōjo wa kudamono o taberu	The girl eats fruit
On'nanoko wa koshō de pasuta o taberu	The girl eats pasta with pepper
Josei wa koshoupasuta o tanoshinde imasu	The woman enjoys pepper pasta
Anata wa poteto o tabemasu ka?	Do you eat potatoes?
Shōjo wa orenjijūsu o nonde imasu	The girl is drinking orange juice
On'nanoko wa gohan o tabemasu	The girls eat rice
Amerika to koshō no yōna dansei	Men like rice and pepper
Watashi wa hon o motte imasu	I have a book
Chokorēto ga sukida	I like chocolate
Kare wa koshō de chokorēto o tsukuru no ga sukidesu	He likes to make chocolate with pepper
Watashi wa kukkī ga sukidesu	I like cookies
Kare wa ocha o nomu no ga sukidesu	He likes to drink tea
Sandoitchi o taberu	We eat sandwiches
Gyūnyū wa futtō shite iru	Milk is boiling
Tabemono wa īdesu	Food is good
Kare wa remonēdo o nomimasu	He drinks lemonade
Kore wa shokujidesu	This is a meal
Kore wa tabemonodesu!	This is food!
Watashi wa nomimasen	I do not drink
Kare wa tanoshiku kaita	He wrote happily
Totemo yoi wain	Very good wine
Satō o taberu	I eat sugar

Yōguruto o tsukurimasu	I make yogurt
Anata wa ichigo o tabemasu ka?	Do you eat strawberries?
Sutēki ga suki	I like steak

TRAINING TIME

Īe, Ayame wa sakana o tabemasen	No, Ayame does not eat fish
Bikutoria wa Amerika o taberu	Victoria eats rice
Gyūnyū, tamago	Milk, eggs
Watashi wa sakana o tsukurimasu	I cook fish
Orenji wa isshu no kudamonodesu	Orange is a kind of fruit
Chō wa kudamono o taberu	Chō eats fruit
Īe, Han wa nomanai	No, Han doesn't drink
Kore wa tomatodesu	This is a tomato
Pasuta o taberu	I eat pasta
Pasuta ryōri wa	I cook pasta
Hai, jūsudesu	Yes, it is juice
On'nanoko wa kudamono o taberu	Girls eat fruit
Furūtsujūsu o nomu	We drink fruit juice
Hai, tomato	Yes, a tomato
Orenji, ringo	Orange, apple
Watashi wa men o tsukurimasen, watashi wa Amerika o tsukurimasu	I do not cook noodles, I cook rice
Shōjo wa ichigo o taberu	The girl eats strawberries

Īe, soreha ichigode wa arimasen, soreha tomatodesu	No, it is not a strawberry, it is a tomato
Ri wa ichigo o tabenai	Li does not eat strawberries
Aruberuto wa shōyu o tabemasen	Alberto does not eat soy sauce
Ocha, mizu, satō	Tea, water, sugar
Sandoitchi o taberu	I eat sandwiches
Ichigo o taberu	We eat strawberries
Kore wa sandoitchidesu	This is a sandwich
Sandoitchi o taberu	You eat a sandwich

TRAINING TIME

Sono shōnen wa ichigo o taberu	The boy eats strawberries
Hai, Kazuo wa bejitariandesu	Yes, Kazuo is vegetarian
Bejitarian wa bīru o nomimasu ka?	Do vegetarians drink beer?
Kazuo wa bejitariandesu, kanojo wa sakana o tabemasen	Kazuo is a vegetarian, she does not eat fish
Watashi wa bejitariandesu, watashi wa chikin o tabemasen	I'm vegetarian, I don't eat chicken
Sūpudesu	It is a soup
Remondesu	It is a lemon
Tabemonodesu	It is food
Tomato, poteto, chīzu	Tomato, potato, cheese
Watashi wa sakana o tsukurimasu	I cook fish
Tomato, tamanegi, sūpu	Tomato, onion, soup
Tamago, chīzu	Eggs, cheese

Watashi wa niku o ryōri suru	I cook meat
Ranchi	Lunch
Watashi wa chūshoku o tabete imasu	I am having lunch
Niku o taberu	I eat meat
Sakana, niku, chikin	Fish, meat, chicken
Tamago, chikin, raisu	Eggs, chicken, rice
Retasu o tabetakunai	I don't want to eat lettuce
Watashitachi no budō	Our grapes
Ninjin to ringo	One carrot and one apple
Sūpu wa Chō no tame no monodesu	The soup is for Chō
Sarada ni retasu wa iranai	I do not want lettuce in my salad

TRAINING TIME

Ninjin	Carrot
Painappuru	Pineapple
Īe, budōde wa arimasen	No, they are not grapes
Hai, kinoko wa akadesu	Yes, mushrooms are red
Kanojo wa mizu ka gyūnyū o nomu	She drinks water or milk
Sarada, kinoko, ninjin	Salad, mushroom, carrot
Alberto wa kinoko o taberu	Alberto eats mushrooms
Kagami to Mitsuki wa saishoku shugi-shadesu	Kagami and Mitsuki are vegetarians
Chō to watashi wa niku o taberu	Chō and I eat meat
Kiyoshi to watashi wa bīru o nomimasen	Kiyoshi and I do not drink beer

Kinokonosarada	I want a mushroom in a salad
Hai, soreha saradadesu	Yes, it is a salad
Painappuru o taberu	We eat pineapples
Hoshī budō wa akadesu	The grapes I want are red
Kanojo wa banana o tabeta	She ate a banana
Kēki	Cake
Motto tōmorokoshi ga hitsuyōdesu ka?	Do you need more corn?
Shitai toki ni nomu	I drink when I want to
Watashi ga ryōri o shinainara, watashi wa tabemasen	If I don't cook, I don't eat
Banana ga hoshī	I want a banana
Shiroi kēki wa watashi no mono	White cake is mine
Painappurudesu ka?	Is it pineapple?
Motto banana ga hoshī	I want more bananas
Anata ga taberu node watashi wa taberu	I eat because you eat
Sōsu, tomato, tamanegi	Sauce, tomato, onion

TRAINING TIME

Aisukurīmu	Ice cream
Kōhīaisukurīmu ga arimasu	I have coffee ice cream
Shokuji	The meal
Mame	Beans
Kinoko	Mushroom
Painappuru wa watashitachi no monodesu	The pineapple is ours
Kanojo wa banana o tabete iru	She is eating a banana
Sarada ni maguro ga hoshī	I want tuna in the salad

Shichimenchō wa watashitachi no monode wa arimasen	The turkey is not ours
Motto aisukyūbu ga hitsuyōdesu ka?	Do you need more ice cubes?
Pasuta wa tabenai	I do not eat pasta
Watashi wa yūshoku ni hanasu	I speak at dinner
Maguro, niku, chikin	Tuna, meat and chicken
Watashi wa shichimenchō ga iranai, arigatō	I do not want turkey, thank you
Shokuji-chū ni menyū o yomu	I read the menu when I was eating
Kore wa satōde wanaku kōridesu	This is ice, not sugar
Batā to oiru	Butter and oil
Abura to shio	Oil and salt
Anata wa koshō o tabemasu ka?	Do you eat pepper?
Chīzu nashi no pasuta ga hoshī	I want pasta without cheese
Nin'niku wa tabemasen	I do not eat garlic
Kanojo ga bīru o nomanakute mo, kanojo wa nomudeshou	Even if she does not drink beer, she will drink
Akira wa chīzu to Amerika o taberu	Akira eats rice with cheese
Abura ga kiiroi	Oil is yellow
Retasu	Lettuce

TRAINING TIME

STORY MODE

JAPANESE

Jiro: "Chōshoku ni wa nani ga arimasu ka"

Mitsuki: "Kyarottokēki"

Jiro: "Sore wa saradadesu ka?"

Mitsuki: "Īe, koreha hontō no kēkidesu. Sore wa ninjin de dekite imasu."

Jirō: "Sore wa oishi-sōdesu. Banana, orenji, ichigo, painappuru nado no kēki o tabetai nodesuga, ranchi wa dōdesu ka."

Mitsuki: "Gohan to maguro, gārikkusōsu."

Jiro: "Īe, shitaku arimasen. Reizōko ni hoka ni nani ga arimasu ka?"

Mitsuki: "Tomato, chikin, chīzu, tamanegi, soshite tamago dake. Watashi wa mada ikutsu ka no shōhin o kōnyū suru hitsuyō ga arimasu."

ENGLISH

Jiro: "What do we have for breakfast?"

Mitsuki: "Carrot cake."

Jiro: "Is it a salad?"

Mitsuki: "No, this is a real cake. It is made of carrots."

Jiro: "It looks delicious. I want to eat a cake made of bananas, oranges, strawberries or pineapple... how about lunch?"

Mitsuki: "Rice and tuna, garlic sauce."

Jiro: "No, I don't want that. What else do you have in the fridge?"

Mitsuki: "Nothing but some tomatoes, chicken, cheese, onions and some eggs. I still need to buy some items."

Chapter 3

ANIMALS

Keywords : Kujira, zō, ōkami, ushi, konchū, neko, hebi, ahiru, same, hae, ari, dōbutsu.

Buru	Bull
Uma	Horse
Tori	Bird
Kame	Tortoise
Raion	Lion
Inu	Dog
Neko	Cat
Zō	Elephant
Ahiru	Duck
Kumo	Spider
Kuma	Bear
Usagi	Rabbit
Buta	Pig
Monkī	Monkey
Iruka	Dolphin
Ushi	A cow
Hachi	A bee
Mushi	An insect
Kujira	Whale
Kanojo wa neko o katte iru	She has a cat
Kore wa ōkamidesu	This is a wolf
Kore wa pengindesu	This is a penguin
Dōbu~tsuen no saru	A monkey in the zoo
Anata wa toradesu	You are a tiger
Chikin wa toridesu	The chicken is a bird

TRAINING TIME

Inu wa mizuwonomu	The dog drinks water
Ushi wa gyūnyū o nomu	The cows drink milk
Neko ga mizuwonomu	A cat drinks water
Neko wa gyūnyū o nomu	The cat drinks milk
Zō wa gyūnyū o nomu	Elephants drink milk
Tori wa kudamono o taberu	The birds eat the fruit
Saru wa banana o taberu	A monkey eats a banana
Ushi wa mizuwonomu	The cows drink water
Kumo ga mizuwonomu	A spider drinks water
Watashi wa chōdesu	I'm a butterfly
Watashi wa mushidesu	I'm an insect
Hebi wa ratto o taberu	Snakes eat rats
Same o taberu	Sharks eat
Hae wa gurasu no naka	The fly is in the glass
Watashi wa hachi ga imasu	I have a bee
Kuma ga iru	I have a bear
Hachi wa satō o taberu	The bees eat the sugar
Inu wa ari o taberu	The dog eats ants
Karera wa uma ga sukide wa arimasen	They don't like horses
Kore wa nezumidesu!	This is a mouse!
Zō wa ringo o taberu	The elephant eats an apple
Shōjo wa tora ni hanashikakemasu	The girl talks to the tiger
ōkami wa on'nanoko ni hanashimasu	The wolf talks to the girl
Hebi wa kodomo ni hanasu yō ni iimashita	The snake told the child to speak
Tora wa pan o taberu	Tigers eat bread

TRAINING TIME

Furai wa pan o taberu	The fly eats bread
Ari wa honwoyomu	The ant reads a book
Dōbutsu	The animal
Neko wa gyūnyū o nomu	The cats drink milk
Uma wa mizuwonomu	The horse drinks water
Tori wa mizu o nomimasu	The bird drinks water
Uma wa dōbutsudesu	A horse is an animal
Ōkami wa gyūnyū o nomu	The wolf drinks milk
Hai, inu	Yes, the dogs
Neko ga sukidesu	I like cats
Konchū wa chokorēto o taberu	Insects eat chocolate
Hae wa chokorēto o taberu	Flies eat chocolate
Konchū wa mizuwonomu	Insects drink water
Hae wa konchūdesu	Flies are insects
Karera wa nekodesu ka?	Are they cats?
Aridesu	It is an ant
Hai, karera wa zōdesu	Yes, they are elephants
Hiroko wa kamedesu	Hiroko is a turtle
Alberto wa ahirudesu	Alberto is a duck
Hirohito wa zōdesu	Hirohito is an elephant
Zō wa mizuwonomu	The elephants drink water
Watashitachiha kamedesu	We are turtles
Karera wa kumode wa naku kanidesu	They are crabs, not spiders
Kuma wa dōbutsudesu	A bear is an animal
Tori-tachi	The birds

TRAINING TIME

STORY MODE

JAPANESE

Jirō: "Watashi o dōbu~tsuen ni tsureteitte kurete arigatō. Koko ni wa takusan no dōbutsu ga iru. Raion, -ba, zō, saru, kuma, usagi, tori ga miemasu."

Mitsuki: "Mite, sono kyodaina kumo wa taranchura to yoba rete imasu, soshite mizu nakaniha ōkina kame, ahiru, kani ya iruka ga arimasu.' Jirō: `Pengin mo imasu ka."

Mitsuki: "Pengin wa Hokkyokuken no dōbutsunanode, kōtta chiiki ni iru kanōsei ga takaidesu."

Jirō: "Anata wa dōbutsu ni tsuite takusan shitte imasu, anata wa petto o katte imasu ka?"

Mitsuki: "Mō koreijō. Watashi wa mausu o katte kara buta o kattaga, ane wa sore o tabeta. Sorekara rinjin no neko o oikakeru no ga daisukina inu ga imashitaga, soreha byōki ni nari shibō shimashita."

Jirō: "Dono dōbutsu ga anata no okiniiridesu ka?"

Mitsuki: "Watashi ga ichiban sukina dōbutsu wa, tabe tari non dari dekiru dōbutsu, tokuni niwatori ya ushidesu. Watashi ga mottomo kiraina no wa hebi to mitsubachidesu."

ENGLISH

Jiro: "Thank you for taking me to the zoo, there are so many animals here, I can see lions, horses, elephants, monkeys, bears, rabbits and birds."

Mitsuki: "Look there, that giant spider is called the tarantula, and in the water, there are big turtles, ducks, crabs and dolphins."

Jiro: "Are there also penguins?"

Mitsuki: "I doubt it, the penguin is an Arctic animal, so it's more likely to be in the frozen regions."

Jiro: "You know a lot about animals, do you have a pet?"

Mitsuki: "No more. Once I had a mouse, and then a pig, but my sister ate it. Then there was a dog that loved to chase the neighbor's cat, but it got sick and died."

Jiro: "Which animals are your favorites?"

Mitsuki: "The animals I like best are the ones I can eat or drink, especially chickens and cows. The ones I hate the most are snakes and bees."

Chapter 4

POSESSIVES

Keywords : Watashi, anata, kanojo, watashi no mono.

Watashi no monode wa arimasen.	It's not mine.
Watashi wa sandoitchi o tabemasu.	I eat my sandwich.
Watashi no neko wa gyūnyū o nomimasu.	My cat drinks milk.
Korera no inu wa watashi no monodesu.	These dogs are mine.
Kono inu wa watashi no monodesu.	This dog is mine.
Watashi no ringo wa sara no ue ni arimasu.	My apple is on the plate.
Kanojo wa watashi no kanojodesu.	She's my girlfriend.
Kono neko wa watashi no monode wa arimasen.	This cat is not mine.
Kore wa anata no monodesu ka?	Is it yours?
Watashitachi wa anata no mono o nomimasu.	We'll drink yours.
Anata no sandoitchi.	Your sandwich.
Kitchin wa anata no monodesu.	The kitchen is yours.
Kare wa anata no o sara o motte imasu.	He's got your plate.
Anata no daidokoro ni wa bōru ga arimasu.	There's a bowl in your kitchen.
Watashi wa anata o tabete imasu.	I'm eating yours.
Anata no shio.	Your salt.
Fōku wa anata no monodesu.	The fork is yours.

Sandoitchi o tabemasu.	I'll eat your sandwich.
Kanojo no pasuta wa sara no ue ni arimasu.	Her pasta is on a plate.
Okashi wa kanojo no monodesu.	The candy is hers.
Kare no uma wa Amerika o tabemasu	His horse eats rice
Watashi wa kare no bin o motte imasu.	I have his bottle.
Kanojo no fōkudesu.	It's her fork.
Anata no chō	Your butterfly.
Abura wa kare no monodesu.	The oil is his.

TRAINING TIME

Dōbutsu wa tabemono o taberu	The animal eats its food
Kore wa watashitachi no monodesu	This is ours
Watashitachi no menyū ni kaku	We write in our menu
Watashitachi no pasuta wa sara no ue ni arimasu	Our pasta is on the plate
Uma wa watashitachi no monode wa arimasen	The horse is not ours
Hachi wa watashitachi no mono	The bees are ours
Neko wa watashitachi no monodesu	The cat is ours
Kare no neko wa mausu o tabemasu	His cat eats mice
Watashitachi no ushi ga imasu	I have our cow

Kanojo wa jibun no okashi o tabemasu	She eats her own candy
Anata no naifu wa kiremasen	Your knife does not cut
Watashitachi no neko wa mizu o nomanai	Our cat does not drink water
Kare wa jibun no neko o katte imasu	He has his own cat
Josei wa anata no megane o motte imasu	The woman has your glasses
Kēki o taberu	We eat our cake
Watashi wa anata no bin o motte imasen	I don't have your bottle
Dōbutsu wa jibun no tabemono o taberu	The animals eat their own food
Sono shōnen wa jibun no kukkī o tabete iru	The boy is eating his own cookies
Anata no ahiru wa mizu o nomimasu	Your duck drinks water
Anata no dōbutsu wa yori ōku no niku o tabemasu	Your animal eats more meat
Watashinochichi wa wain o nomimasu	My dad drinks wine
Ringo wa watashitachi no monodesu	The apple is ours
Hai, kono okane wa watashi no monodesu	Yes, this money is mine
Watashi wa watashi no pan ga hoshī	I want my bread

TRAINING TIME

STORY MODE

JAPANESE

"Kono doresu wa watashi no yōna monodesu." Sono josei wa itta.
"Hotondo no fuku wa watashitachi no mise de nita yōna nyuansu o motte imasu... Mite, kore wa akai ribon de, anata no mono wa aoidesu." Ano otoko o mite kudasai.
"Kare wa mata kare no musume no tame ni nita yōna mono o kaimashita, shikashi sore wa poketto o motte imasu."
"Anata wa tadashī, watashi wa rikai shite imasu." Josei wa itta.

ENGLISH

"This dress is like mine." the lady said.
"Most clothes have similar nuances in our shop... Look, this is a red ribbon and yours is blue." The gentleman replied.
"Look at that man for example. He also bought something similar for his daughter, but it has a pocket."
"You are right, I understand." said the woman.

Chapter 5

CLOTHING

Keywords : Seifuku, juerī, -fuku, sētā, doresu.

Pantsu	Pants
Nekutai	Tie
Beruto	Belt
Irui	Clothing
Sukāto	Skirt
Shatsu	Shirt
Kutsu	Shoes
Fuku	Clothes
Handobaggu	Handbags
Bōshi	Hat
Sandaru	Sandals
Bōshi wa murasakidesu	The hat is purple
Doresu	The dress
Poketto	Pocket
Watashi no kutsu	My shoes
Kanojo no zubon	Her pants
Kare wa watashi no kōto o motte imasu	He has my coat
Watashi no shatsu	My shirt
Watashi no jaketto wa chairodesu	My jacket is brown
Watashi wa anata no beruto o motte imasu	I have your belt
Watashi no zubon	My pants
Watashi wa sukāto ga arimasu	I have a skirt
Watashi wa shatsu o motte imasu	I have a shirt
Anata no kutsu ga arimasu	I have your shoes
Naifu wa kutsu no naka	The knife is in the shoe

TRAINING TIME

Kōto	Coat
Jaketto	Jacket
Būto	Boot
Seifuku	Uniform
Sutokkingu	Stocking
Sētā	A sweater
Sūtsu	Suit
Kasa ga arimasu	I have an umbrella
Saifu wa watashitachi no monodesu	The wallet is ours
Saifu ga arimasu	I have my wallet
Watashi wa hōseki o motte imasu	I have jewelry
Kanojo wa būtsu o kau	She buys boots
Aoi kutsu	Blue shoes
Watashi no sandaru	My sandals
Tebukuro wa anata no monodesu	The gloves are yours
Otoko wa kawa no saifu o motte imasu	The man has a leather wallet
Kore wa sandarudesu	This is a sandal
Kare no kutsushita	His socks
Kore wa sukātodesu	This is a skirt
Kanojo no sukāto wa akadesu	Her skirt is red
Watashitachi no shatsu	Our shirt
Shiroi sukāto ga hitsuyōdesu	You need a white skirt
Kono doresu wa kare no	This dress is his
Kono hon wa kurodesu	This book is black
Kare wa akami no niku o taberu	He eats red meat

TRAINING TIME

STORY MODE

JAPANESE

Mitsuki: "Sorera no kutsu wa totemo utsukushīdesu, karera wa kōka ni miemasu."
Jirō: "Hai, atarashī fuku ga hitsuyōdattanode, kyō wa kaimono ni ikimashita."
Mitsuki: "Subarashī! Hoka ni nani o kaimashita ka?"
Jirō: "Saisho ni, shigoto-yō no atarashī doresu to sakunen no natsu ni sagashite ita kiiroi beruto o kaimashita. Sorekara watashi wa zubon, shiroi doresu, watashi no hahaoya no tame no kōto, soshite watashinochichi no tame no ittsui no shatsu o kaimashita. Watashi ga satta toki, watashi wa būtsu o ittsui no sukāto no shita ni mimashita, soshite sētā to tomoni anata no tame ni sorera o te ni ireru koto ni shimashita."
Mitsuki: "Arigatōgozaimashita. Arigatōgozaimasu."

"Kyō wa hijō ni kaze ga tsuyoidesu' aresshia jō wa mōru o deta toki ni itta. "Kore wa natsu ga owariwotsugeru chōkōdesu' to rōran wa kotaeta." "Watashi wa uwagi to ichi-kumi no kutsushita ga attara īnoni" `baggu no naka ni kutsushita ga aru to omoimasu' to rōran-shi wa iimashita." "Shinpaishinaide, watashi wa sonohoka no iryōhinten de sore o kau koto ga dekimasu, watashi wa mado no hanbai no tame ni ikutsu ka no yoi megane o miru koto ga dekimasu!"

ENGLISH

Mitsuki: "Those shoes are very beautiful, they seem expensive."

Jiro: "Yes, I needed new clothes, so today I went shopping."

Mitsuki: "Fantastic! what else did you buy?"

Jiro: "First, I bought a new dress for work and the yellow belt I was looking for last summer. Then I bought pants, a white dress, a coat for my mother and a pair of shirts for my father. As I left, I saw the boots under a pair of skirts, and decided to get them for you, along with a sweater."

Mitsuki: "Thank you very much, I appreciate it."

"Today is very windy." Miss Alessia said as they left the mall.

"This is a sign that summer is ending." Laurent answered.

"I wish I had a jacket and a pair of socks."

"I think I have some socks in my bag." Mr. Laurent said.

"Do not worry, I can buy one in that other clothing store, I can see some good glasses for sale at the window!"

Chapter 6

QUESTIONS

Keywords : Nan, doko, dare, naze, nango.

Shitsumon.	Question.
Dare?	Who?
Dōshite?	Why?
Doko?	Where?
Kono hiyō wa ikuradesu ka?	How much does this cost?
Nanijin no on'nanoko ga tabemasu ka?	How many girls eat?
Pan wa dore kurai tabemasu ka.	How much bread do you eat?
Dono kurai no niku?	How much meat?
Nanijin no otokonoko ga sakana o tabemasu ka?	How many boys eat fish?
Dono inu?	Which dog?
Dō yatte?	How?
Dō yatte kaku no?	How do you write?
Dare ga yomu?	Who reads?
Sorehanandesuka?	What is it?
Korehanandesuka?	What's this?
Dore?	Which one?
Hebi wa doko ni iru no?	Where's the snake?
Ryōri hito wa dokodesu ka?	Where's the cook?
Dōbu~tsuen wa dokodesu ka?	Where is the zoo?
Dono ringo?	Which apple?
Kono otokonoko wa daredesu ka?	Who is this boy?
Han wa daredesu ka?	Who is Han?
Anatahadare?	Who are you?

Anata wa nani o yonde iru?	What are you reading?
Gyūnyū o nonde iru no wa dare?	Who's drinking milk?

TRAINING TIME

Sumimasen?	Excuse me?
Anata no pengin wa doredesu ka?	Which one is your penguin?
Dono dansei ga shinbun o yomimashita ka?	Which men read the newspaper?
Dono otokonoko?	Which boy?
Watashi wa nanideshou?	What am I?
Anata no hon wa doredesu ka?	Which one is your book?
Naze kare wa okurete iru nodesu ka?	Why is he late?
Dono kame?	Which turtles?
Anata no mondai wa nanidesu ka?	What's your problem?
Kare wa sono shitsumon o yomimashita.	He read the question.
Nan-satsu no hon ga arimasu ka?	How many books do we have?
Dō shita no?	What's the problem?
Anata no shitsumon ni wa kotae ga arimasen.	Your question has no answer.
Doko ni imasu ka?	Where are you?
Itsu tabemasu ka?	When do you eat?
Watashi no kotaeha nōdesu.	My answer is no.
Kotae wa iesudesu.	The answer is yes.
Itsukara?	Since when?

Anatahadare to isshodesu ka?	Who are you with?
Kare wa nan-sai?	How old is he?
Nanijin no on'nanoko ga tabemasu ka?	How many girls eat?
Shitsumon ga arimasu.	I have a question.

TRAINING TIME

STORY MODE

JAPANESE

"Aikawa-san, kon'nichiwa. Kore wa shokuhin kenkyū no komondearu Liu Chengdesu. Kyō wa, ki ni shinai nodeareba, ikutsu ka shitsumon shitai to omoimasu."

"Wa i, tsudzukemasu."

"Arigatōgozaimashita."

"Saisho no shitsumon, anata wa tsuitachi ni sukunakutomo san-kai tabemasu ka?"

"Wa i."

"Onakagasuita-ji ga ichiban ki ni narimasu ka?"

"Asa, kore ga watashi ga chōshoku o nogashita koto ga nai riyūdesu."

"Doko de chōshoku o tabemasu ka?"

"Shokuba de."

"Tamago to niku, bejitariansandoitchi wa nani ga sukidesu ka?"

"Tamago to hamu, watashi wa saishoku shugi-shade wa arimasen." "Tamago wa ikagadesu ka? Chōri matawa age?"

"Watashi wa niru no ga sukidesu. Hoka no tokiniha, watashi wa agetaidesu."

"Dono burando no tamago o kaimasu ka?"

"SW no tamago"

"1-kagetsu ni nanpako kōnyū shimasu ka?"

"Sebun."

"-Bako wa ikuradesu ka?"

"10-Doru."

"Tamago ryōri shō o mimasu ka?"

"Hai. Tamago o tsukuru kantan'na hōhō ga sukidesu."

"O jikan o itadaki arigatōgozaimasu."

ENGLISH

"Hey, Miss Aikawa! This is Liu Cheng, an advisor on food research. Today, I would like to ask you a few questions if you don't mind."

"Yes, continue."

"Thank you."

"First question, do you eat at least three times a day?"

"Yes."

"When you feel hungry the most?"

"In the morning, this is why I never missed breakfast."

"Where do you eat breakfast?"

"At work."

"What do you like, eggs and meat or vegetarian sandwiches?"

"Eggs and ham, I'm not a vegetarian."

"How do you like eggs? Cooked or fried?"

"I like to boil. Other times, I want to fry."

"What brand of eggs do you buy?"

"SW eggs."

"How many boxes do you buy for a month?"

"Seven."

"How much is a box?"

"Ten dollars."

"Do you see any egg cooking show?"

"Yes. I like the easy way to cook eggs."

"Thank you for your time."

Chapter 7

VERBS

Keywords : Watashi wa dekimasu, aruku, okonau, sukidesu, taizai, wakarimasu.

Watashi wa nomu	I drink
Ogenkidesuka?	How are you?
Tomato no sūpu ga hoshī	I want a tomato soup
Īe, nata ga suru koto wa dekimasen	No, you can not
Dare ga resutoran ni kimashita ka?	Who came to the restaurant?
Sandoitchi o tsukuru	You make a sandwich
Kitchin ga arimasu	We have a kitchen
Karera wa hon o motte imasu	They have books
Watashi wa naifu o motte imasu	I have a knife
Karera wa danseida	They are men
Watashi wa on'nanokodesu	I am a girl
Anata wa nan-ri imasu ka?	How many of you are there?
Watashitachiha otokonokodesu	We are boys
Otoko wa satta	The man is gone
Watashi wa shiranai	I do not know
Josei wa otokonoko ni bisuketto o ataeru	The woman gives the boy biscuits
Watashi wa sono on'nanoko ga mitsukaranai	I can't find the girl
Uma wa neko o mita	The horse saw the cat
Watashi wa korera no josei o shitte imasu	I know these women

Sono shōnen wa aisatsu suru	The boy greets
Kanojo wa watashi no satō o totta	She took my sugar
Kōhī ga kite imasu	The coffee is coming
Kanojo wa hanasu	She speaks
Kare wa itta	He said
Sutēki o tanomu	I ask for a steak

TRAINING TIME

Kanojo wa watashi no kutsu o haite imasu	She is wearing my shoes
Ocha ni satō o hairenai	I don't put sugar in tea
Karera wa kangaete imasen	They do not think
Dansei wa kangaeru	The men think
Pan wa itsu todokimasu ka.	When does the bread arrive?
Riyū ga wakaranai	I don't understand why
Dōbutsu wa dōbu~tsuen ni nokoru	The animals remain in the zoo
Kono tori o kiita	We heard this bird
Kanojo wa okashi o nokoshimashita	She left candy
Kōhī wa kanmi ga arimasu	The coffee is sweetened
Doko de pan o tabemasu ka.	Where do you eat bread?
Wareware wa shinjite iru	We believe
Kanojo wa otokonoko o nokoshimashita	She left the boy
Supūn o tsukaimasu	I use a spoon

Menyū o oboete imasu	I remember the menu
Karera wa dono yō ni kurashite imasu ka?	How do they live?
Anata ga taberu	You eat
Anata wa hatarakimasu	You work
Anata wa machimasu	You wait
Anata ga nomu	You drink
Hairimashita ka?	Did you enter?
Hon o hiraku	You open the book
Kare wa yūshoku o oeta	He finished his dinner
Kēki wa dō yatte shiagemasu ka.	How do you finish the cake?
Kēki o shiagemasu	We finish the cake

TRAINING TIME

Josei wa sakana o taberu	The woman eats fish
Raion wa niku ga suki	The lion likes the meat
Watashi wa ringo o taberu	I eat an apple
Wareware wa nomu	We drink
Firippo to hanasu	You talk to Filippo
Anata wa nani ga hitsuyōdesu ka?	You need what?
Nomimono o matsu	We wait for the beverage
Watashiniha, anata ga hitsuyōdesu	I need you
Watashi wa uma ga hitsuyōdesu	I need a horse
Watashi wa hanasu	I speak
Kanojo wa kōto o hanareru	She leaves the coat

On'na ga otoko o watasu	The woman passes the man
Karera wa fuku ga hitsuyōdesu	They need clothes
Kanojo wa kōto ga hitsuyōdesu	She needs a coat
Satō ga suki	I like sugar
Shōjo wa chūshoku o matsu	The girl waits for lunch
Sara to hanasu	You talk to Sara
Anata ga hitsuyōdesu	We need you
Hanasanai	We do not speak
Kanojo wa mite yomu	She looks and reads
Kanojo wa jibun no kagi o mitsuke rarenai	She does not find her keys
Kare wa hebi to issho ni yattekuru	He arrives with the snake
Painappuru ga suki	We like pineapples
Kare wa jagaimo o motarashimasu	He brings potatoes
Kare wa pan o motte kuru	He brings bread

TRAINING TIME

Watashitachi wa anata ni shitagaimasu	We follow you
Kanojo wa aruku	She walks
Watashi wa anata o yurusu	I forgive you
Karera wa kōhī ga sukidesu	They like coffee
On'nanoko wa fuku o kite	The girl is dressed
Otoko wa kare no shita ni imasu	The man is under him
Kare wa dōbutsu ga suki	He likes animals
Kanojo wa yameta	She stopped
Kare wa yarou to shita	He tried
Watashi no kaeri wa chikaku ni arimasu	My return is nearby
Raion wa kūfuku o kanjimasu	The lion feels hungry
Karera wa supūn o mitsuketa	They found the spoon
Tōchaku suru	We arrive
Umawotomeru	Stop the horse
Menyū o miru	We look at the menu
Karera wa sono-pon o aita	They opened the book
Karera wa ringo ga sukidesu	They like apples
Akeru	I can open
Watashi wa ugoku	I move
Kare ga shiharaimashita	He paid
Sono shōnen wa henka o motarasu no o wasureta	The boy forgot to bring change
Kare wa itte shimatta	He is gone

Kanojo wa kutsu o kaimasu	She buys shoes
Kare wa kare ni kādo o watashita	He gave him the card
Kare wa nete watashi wa ryōri o suru	He sleeps and I cook

TRAINING TIME

Motteru	Have
Kakimasu	Write
Hashiru	I run
Anata ga jikkō shimasu	You run
Neru	I sleep
Karera wa shiharau	They pay
Bokutachi wa neru	We sleep
Akihiro to asobu	I play with Akihiro
Sarada wa kawanai	I do not buy salad
Karera wa asobu	They play
Uma to asobu	We play with horses
Kanojo wa hon o yonde imasu	She is reading a book
Otoko wa beruto ni kachimasu	The man wins a belt
On'nanoko wa tazunemasu	The girl asks
Watashi wa itsumo kūsō suru	I always fantasize
Peppāraisu no yōna dansei	Men like peppered rice
Watashi wa jibun no ishō o miseru	I show my costume
Kare wa kawaranai	He will not change
Kare wa nōjō o sodateta	He raised the farm

Kanojo wa hisho o shōkai shimashita	She introduced the secretary
Kare wa kono josei o shōkai shimashita	He introduced this lady
Kare wa sonzai shimasen	He does not exist
Karera wa yoru ni arawareru	They appear at night
On'nanoko wa sūpu o shiyou	The girl tries soup
Anata wa kantoku ni kōhī o sashimasu	You give coffee to the director

TRAINING TIME

Watashi wa hon o yumemiru	I dream of a book
Tamanegi o seisan suru	He produces onions
Karera wa Amerika o ajiwau	They taste rice
Gakusei wa jibun no shigoto o miseru	Students show their work
Karera wa pan o tsukurimasu	They produce bread
Kore wa totemo midjikana monodesu	This is very familiar
Kanojo wa kazoku ni tayotte iru	She relies on her family
Kanojo wa hahaoya o sagashimasu	She searches for her mother
Chūshoku wa ichi-bu-go ni hajimarimasu	Lunch starts in one minute
Kare wa kazoenai	He does not count
Watashi wa untenshu o sonchō shimasu	I respect the driver

Kutsu wa tekishite imasen	The shoes are not suitable
Shimekiri wa kin'yōbi ni shūryō	Deadline ends on Friday
Watashitachi wa anata ni tayorimasu	We rely on you
Watashi wa kyō hajimemashita	I started today
Karera wa shizen ni mieru	They seem natural
Watashitachi wa anata no sedai o sonchō shimasu	We respect your generation
Kanojo no sain	Her signature
Naze anata wa haitte konai nodesu ka?	Why don't you come in?
Kare wa Amerika o dashimasu	He serves rice
Doa ga shimaranai	The door does not close
Pātī wa kenchikka shidai	The party depends on the architect
Bebībeddo o nusunda	We stole the crib
Itsu kite mo kamaimasen	It doesn't matter when you come
Karera wa sono hon'ni shomei shita	They signed the book

TRAINING TIME

Sono shōnen wa madowoshimeru	The boy closes the window
Karera wa anata no kōzō o inpōto shimasu	They import your structure
Doko ni sain sureba īdesu ka?	Where do I sign?
Kare wa kōhī o dasu	He serves coffee

Doa wa shimatte imasen	The door is not closed
Saizu o erabimasu	You choose the size
Kare ga anata ni kiitara	If he hears you
Uchinonaka ni inu ga imasu	There is a dog in the house
Kare wa kotae o teishutsu shimashita	He submitted an answer
Yuka ni suwatte imasu ka?	Are you sitting on the floor?
Watashi no kodomo wa sugu ni manande imasu	My child is learning quickly
Sensei ni mukeru	We turn to the teacher
Anata no hanashiwokiku	I listen to you
Karera wa kiite imasen ka?	Do they not listen?
Watashi no imōto wa iro o oboemasu	My sister learns colors
Hitori no on'nanoko ga kotaeta	One girl answered
Anata ga uso o tsuite iru	You are lying
Kare wa kono gyōkai ni tsuite setsumei shimashita	He explained this industry
Anata wa ringo ya banana ga sukidesu ka?	Do you like apples or bananas?
Watashi wa uso o tsukanai	I don't lie
Watashi wa kare ni jūsu o ageru	I give him juice
Dōbutsu wa uso o tsukanai	Animals do not lie
Reizōko o ugokasu	I move the refrigerator

Otokonoko wa seichō suru	The boys grow
Akachan ga naku	The baby cries

TRAINING TIME

Dōi suru	I agree
Watashitachi wa dōi shimasu	We agree
Watashi wa utau	I sing
Watashi wa tobu	I fly
Watashi wa manabu	I learn
Kare ga waraimashita	He laughed
Ashita, watashi wa sono riyū o setsumei shimasu	Tomorrow, I explain why
Watashitachiha kazoku o kizuku	We build a family
Saibankan ni kansha	We thank the judge
Karera wa gogo ni benkyō suru	They study in the afternoon
Kanojo wa ōkina ie ni sunde imasu	She lives in a big house
Otoko ni atatta	We hit a man
Hisho ga kōhī o teikyō	The secretary provides coffee
Naifu ga kabe o utsu	The knife hit the wall
Karera wa ōkina ie ni sunde imasu	They live in a big house
Watashi wa kanojo no supagetti o teikyō shimasu	I offer her spaghetti
Naifu ga otoko o koroshita	The knife killed a man
Yaku	We bake
On'nanoko wa issho ni manabu	The girls learn together
Watashi wa sō omou	I think so

Yūbin haitatsu wa kare no musume to issho ni ryokō-chūdesu.	The postman is on a journey with his daughter
Hahaoya wa kodomo ni oshieru	The mother teaches her child
Tabemono o okuru	I send food
Josei wa megasameta	The woman woke up
Kare wa tori o mimasu	He looks at the birds
Dōi suru	

TRAINING TIME

Karera wa tēburu o settei shimasu	They set the table
Kutsu wa on'nanoko o kizutsukeru	The shoes hurt the girl
Watashi wa kyō kunren shimasu	I train today
Kanojo wa tēburu o settei shimashita	She set the table
Kare wa tabemono o teikyō suru	He provides food
Watashi wa watashi no sofu no mendōwomiru	I take care of my grandfather
Kare wa kono shōnen o kunren suru	He trains this boy
Shinshitsu de torigatobu	Birds fly in the bedroom
Akachan no yō ni naku	We cry like babies
Kare wa poketto ni kagi o ireta	He put the key in his pocket

Kare wa hiru to yoru o benkyō shita	He studied day and night
Anata wa Amerika ya pan ga sukidesu ka?	Do you like rice or bread?
Hahaoya wa akachan o mōfu de tsutsumu	The mother wraps the baby in a blanket
Kazoku wa sakka o yūshoku ni shōtai shimashita	The family invited the writer to dinner
Nani ga miemasu ka?	What do you see?
Watashitachiha ryōri shimasu	We cook
Nenai	We do not sleep
Anata wa sorera o mimasu	You see them
Karera wa chūshoku o enki shita	They postponed lunch
Īe, ikimasen	No, you don't go
Karera wa sūpu o tsukurimasu	They cook soup
Shiharawanai	I do not pay
Karera wa shippai shimashita	They failed
Nando mo shippai shimashita	We failed many times
Shippai shinakatta	I did not fail

TRAINING TIME

Karera wa doko de shio o mamoru nodesu ka?	Where do they keep the salt?
Ranpu ga taoru o Daisukesu	The lamp burns the towel
Kare wa watashitachi ga ningenda to omotte imasu	He thinks we are human

Shimai wa kagami o ugokasu	The sisters move the mirror
Kenchikka wa ranpu o ugokashimasu	The architect moves the lamp
Bin ni abura o ireta	I filled the bottle with oil
Saibankan wa shikyō o sabaku	The judge judges the bishop
Kanojo wa watashinoie ni sunde imasu	She lives in my house
Kanojo wa menyū o kaizen shita	She improved the menu
Kanojo wa hashigo o hakonde iru	She is carrying a ladder
Karera wa tamago o chōri suru	They cook eggs
Kare wa chūshoku o totta	He had lunch
Kikoenai yo	I can not hear
Karera wa hon o hakobu	They carry books
Tori wa oyogenai	Birds can't swim
Kanojo wa uma ni noranai	She does not ride horses
Kare wa dōbutsu no sewa o shimasu	He takes care of animals
Karera wa hon o motte imasu	They have books
Anata wa tabemono o teikyō suru	You provide food
Hashiranai	We don't run
Ringo ga hoshī	We want apples
Hai, watashi wa ikimasu	Yes, I go
Pan o taberu	I eat bread
Otokonoko wa mizuwonomu	The boys drink water
Shitsumon o suru	I ask a question

TRAINING TIME

Yukō	Let's go
Shite ī?	Can we?
Watashi wa dekimasu	I can
Anata wa dekiru	You can
Ahiru o chōri shimasen ka?	Don't you cook duck?
Watashinochichi wa oyogu koto ga deki, anata no okāsanha aruku koto ga dekimasu	My dad can swim and your mother can walk
Kodomo-tachi wa kuma o mimashita	The children saw the bear
Otto wa kare no tsuma ni kisuwoshita	The husband kissed his wife
Botoru ni mizu o ireta	I filled the bottle with water
Watashi wa dōbutsu o katte imasu, soreha mausudesu	I have an animal; it is a mouse
Anata wa dono doresu ga hoshīdesu ka?	Which dress do you want?
Han wa pinku no kumo ga hoshī	Han wants a pink spider
Anata wa chūshoku o harau	You pay for lunch
Īe, ikimasen	No, you don't go
Han wa nemuri, Mitsuki wa hashiru	Han sleeps, Mitsuki runs
Watashitachi wa atarashī shinbun o shinsui sa semasu	We launch a new newspaper
Inu ga asobu	The dog plays

Kodomo-tachi wa harawanai	Children do not pay
Sono shōnen wa arukanai	The boy does not walk
Kanojo wa itte shimatta, watashi wa itte shimatta	She is gone, I am gone
Otokonoko-tachi wa kiite imasu	The boys are listening
Shiharawanai	We do not pay
Sono otoko wa uma o shisa shita	The man pointed at the horse
Sōsu o tsukuru	We make sauce
Inu o mitsuketa	I found the dog

TRAINING TIME

Shitte iru	Know
Mitsukeru	Find
Gēmu	Game
Sanpuru	Sample
Ame ga futte iru	It's raining
Shitte iru	I know
Tori wa hanasanai	The bird does not speak
Tamanegi ni furenaide kudasai	Don't touch the onions
Karera wa anata no namae o sakebu	They scream your name
Chikin ni wa furenaide	We do not touch the chicken
Zō wa mizu ga hoshī	The elephant wants water
Neko wa kikoemasendeshita	The cat did not hear
Kanojo wa hanasu, karera wa hanasu	She speaks, they speak

Karera wa korera no hon o kenkyū shite imasu	They study these books
Tabemono o mitsukeru	We find food
Kodomo-tachi ga asobu	The children play
Watashi wa shiranai	I do not know
Shio nashi	No salt
Karera wa chichioya ni shitagau	They follow their father
Josei wa pan o ajiwau	The woman tastes bread
Anata wa anata no beruto o miseru	You show your belt
Watashi wa kanojo o yumemite ita	I dreamt of my girlfriend
Karera wa yoru ni arawareru	They appear at night
Watashi wa watashi no inu o sagashiteimasu	I am looking for my dog
Karera wa karera no kazoku o miseru	They show their family

TRAINING TIME

Watashitachi wa tasukemasu	We help
Modoru!	Go back!
Watashi no oba wa kodokudesu	My aunt is lonely
Mitsuki wa mado o shimeta	Mitsuki closed the window
Watashi wa anata to kare no ma ni imasu	I am between you and him
Karera wa anzendesu	They are safe
Yūshoku o tabete iru	We are eating dinner

Sobo o oboete iru	We remember our grandmother
Kanojo wa neko o sagashiteimasu	She is looking for her cat
Kanojo wa doa o shimeta	She closed the door
Dono yume?	Which dream?
Anata o omou	I think of you
Karera wa tabemono o ataenai	They don't give food
Inu wa sono hito o tasukemasu	The dog helps that person
Shefu wa niku no omo-sa	The chef weighs meat
Kanojo wa mado o mimasu	She looks at the window
Kare wa on'nanoko to isshodesu	He is with the girl
Karera wa Amerika o tamesu	They try rice
Musuko no taijūwohakaru	I weigh my son
Kare wa korera no tegami o misemashita	He showed these letters
Menyū o miru	We look at the menu
Watashi wa sofa o ukeireru	I accept the sofa
Watashi wa josei o sonchō shimasu	I respect women
Kare wa ukeiremasen	He does not accept
Kanojo wa watashi no satō o totta	She took my sugar

TRAINING TIME

Kanojo wa kazoku o hōmon shimasu	She visits her family

Karera wa nomu	They drink
Nai to omou	We think not
Kanojo wa mizu o ageru	She gives water
Watashi wa inu to issho ni modottekita	I came back with my dog
Kare wa tsuma o sonchō shimasu	He respects his wife
Kare wa isha o tazuneta	He visited a doctor
Kanojo wa bōshi o kabutte imasu	She is holding a hat
Kuma wa doa o kayotte awanai	The bear does not fit through the door
Hai, onajimi no yōdesu	Yes, it seems familiar
Kanojo wa ashita hajimemasu	She will start tomorrow
Kare wa Amerika o dashimasu	He serves rice
Beijing ni itta koto wa arimasu ka?	Have you been to Beijing?
Anata wa kazoenai	You don't count
Kongetsu wa getsuyōubi ni owarimasu	This month ends on Monday
Anata wa watashi no musume o shitte imasu	You know my daughter
Kutsu ga aimasen	The shoes do not fit
Ashita hajimemasu	I will start tomorrow
Karera wa shizen ni mieru	They seem natural
Kare wa sandoitchi o kazoeru	He counts sandwiches
Yūshoku o go yōi shite orimasu	We serve dinner
Kare wa sono hon'ni shomei shita	He signed the book

Ku getsumatsu	The end of September
Hahaoya wa kodomo o semeru	The mother blames the child
Kanojo wa kono tegami o teishutsu shita	She submitted this letter

TRAINING TIME

Kare wa kanojo ni tsuite dōomoimasuka?	How does he feel about her?
Karera wa kare no bebībeddo o yunyū shimashita	They imported his crib
Kare wa hahaoya o fukumu	He includes his mother
Kare wa daidokoro ni hairu	He enters the kitchen
Karera wa sono hon'ni shomei shita	They signed the book
Tabemono o okuru	I send food
Īe, -iro wa jūyōde wa arimasen	No, color is not important
Karera wa betsu no doresu ga fukuma rete imasu	They include a different dress
Chīzu o yunyū	I import cheese
Kare no shatsu ni sain o shimashita	We signed his shirt
Okāsan, haitte kudasai	Mom, please come in
Baai ni yorimasu	It depends
Kare wa itta	He said
Ashita wa hajimeru koto ga dekimasu	Tomorrow can begin
Kono-pon o hiraku	We open this book
Watashi no otto wa okurete imasu	My husband is late

Shigoto ga hitsuyōdesu	It needs work
Watashi wa sō iu	I say yes
Anata wa doa o akemasu	You open the door
Ashita tōchaku shimasu	We will arrive tomorrow
Nōmin wa kono moto ga totemo yoi to iimasu	Farmers say this book is very good
Itsu tōchaku suru nodeshou ka.	When will they arrive?
Kare wa motto tabemono ga hitsuyōdesu	He needs more food
Anata wa itsu kaette kimasu ka?	When will you come back?
Kawanai	I don't buy it

TRAINING TIME

Jūsu o hiraku	I open the juice
Gaka wa kare ni tayotte iru	The painter relies on him
Anata wa natsu ga sukidesu ka?	Do you like summer?
Kare wa sore o utagaimasen	He does not doubt it
Chikoku shimashita	We came back late
Kanojo wa ringo o tanomu	She asks for an apple
Watashi wa rinjin o sukutta	I saved my neighbor
Watashi wa sorera no denwa ga sukide wa arimasen	I don't like those phones
Sono shōnen wa inu o katta	The boy bought a dog

Kanojo wa bin de ippaidesu	She is filled with bottles
Watashi wa kare ga utagau koto o utagau	I doubt that he doubts
Dōbutsu o sukuu	We save animals
Kono basu wa Tianjin ni chūsha shite imasu ka?	Is this bus parked in Tianjin?
Kare wa bunsho o tsudzukemasu	He continues his document
Kare wa nijuppun-doru o kachitotta	He won twenty dollars
Kare ni kiita	I asked him
Kare wa tamanegi o mazeru	He mixes onions
Kanojo wa akai kuruma o shoyū shite imasu	She owns a red car
Kare wa tazunemasen	He doesn't ask
Watashi wa tōri ni tachimasu	I stand on the street
Karera wa jūsu to gyūnyū o mazeru	They mix juice and milk
Watashi wa machi ni sunde imasu	I live in a city
Karera wa tsudzukemasu	They continue
Anata wa takusan no okane o kasegimasu	You make a lot of money
Anata wa onaji koto o tazunemasu	You ask the same thing

TRAINING TIME

Anata wa inu o kyoka shimasu ka?	Do you allow dogs?
Dare ga usagi o uketorimashita ka?	Who received the rabbit?

Kare wa watashi ga tomodachida to omoimasu	He thinks that I am a friend
Karera wa satō o tsukau	They use sugar
Kare wa sono sūpu ni shio o kuwaeta.	He added salt to the soup.
Kono kuruma wa totemo kichōdesu	This car is very valuable
Doko ni sunde imasu ka?	Where do you live?
Watashi no pātonā wa sore o kyoka shimasu	My partner allows it
Anata wa konpyūta o tsukatteimasu	You use a computer
Karera wa watashi ga tomodachida to omou	They think I'm a friend
Kare wa Doitsu ni sunde imasu	He lives in Germany
Watashitachi wa koko ni sunde imasu	We live here
Kare wa kanojo o shitte iru	He knows her
Okane o tsukau	I spend money
Kare wa watashi o rikai shite inai	He doesn't understand me
Kanojo wa watashi ni kotaenakatta	She did not answer me
Sandoitchi wa chīzu ga fukuma rete imasu	The sandwich contains cheese
Kare wa tomodachi o yabutta	He defeated his friend
Kore wa ōku no hitobito o kyōmibukaku shimasu	This makes many people interested

Rikai dekimasen	I do not understand
Karera wa teki o taoshita	They defeated their enemies
Watashi wa tsukai sugita	I spent too much
Watashi no iu imigawakaranai	You don't understand what I mean
Ringo o kiru	I cut the apple
Tēburu o yoyaku suru	You book a table

TRAINING TIME

Yasumu	I rest
Watashi wa utau	I sing
Watashi wa janpu	I jump
Watashi wa tobu	I fly
Watashi ga unten shimasu yo	I will drive
Watashi wa kuruma o unten suru	I drive a car
Watashi wa kare o kobamu	I refuse him
Kare wa kodomo-tachi o atsukaimasu	He handles children
Kanojo wa menyū o kaizen shita	She improved the menu
Watashi wa kare o kansatsu suru	I observe him
Kare wa bōshi o kabutta	He reached for his hat
Kare wa watashi ni eikyō o ataemasu	He influences me
Dō shita no?	What happened to you?
Watashi wa jōshi ni sōdan shimashita	I consulted my boss
Musuko ga hoshī	I want a son

Kare wa tēburu o tamotta	He kept the table
Kono Ni~Tsu o issho ni sugoshimasu	We spend this day together
Kanojo wa kagi o nakushimashita	She lost her key
Sō wa omowanai	I do not think so
Kodomo-tachi wa koko o tōrimasu	Children go through here
Watashi wa watashinohaha ni wain o watashimashita	I passed the wine to my mother
Anata wa kare no shatsu o mitomemasu	You recognize his shirt
Garasu wa mizu o fukunde imasu	The glass contains water
Watashi no musume wa uma ga hoshī	My daughter wants a horse
Kare wa musume o kansatsu shita	He observed his daughter

TRAINING TIME

Ima, kare wa kore o tameshimasu	Now he will try this
Ikuradesu ka?	How much is it?
Bīru wa ikuradesu ka.	How much is beer?
Kare wa Tsuna ni sōdan shimashita	He consults Tsuna
Kare wa watashinoie ni tabemono o nokoshimashita	He left food in my home
Kare wa yoku yatta	He performed well
Karera wa tēburu o settei shimasu	They set the table

Kanojo wa menyū o tsukurimasu	She creates a menu
Tori wa tobanai	The bird does not fly
Toritachi wa tobu	Birds fly
Watashi wa koko ni iru koto ga dekimasu	I can be here
Anata wa kesshite makemasen	You will never lose
Kare wa Feng ni wa mukanai	He is not good for Feng
London andāguraundo o shiyō shite imasu	I use London Underground
Watashinonamaeha-ōdesu	My name is king
Kongetsu wa ashita de owarimasu	This month ends tomorrow
Kanojo wa oso sugiru to omou	She thinks it's too late
Kare wa watashi no imōto to issho ni aruita	He walked with my sister
Kare wa koko ni imasu	He's here
Anata wa koko ni zokushite imasen	You don't belong here
Anata wa watashi o shinjite inai	You do not believe me
Watashi wa kono shatsu o arau	I wash this shirt
Kanojo wa watashi no tomodachi to aruku	She walks with my friends
Kare wa tenraku shita	He fell
Torei o mochiageru	Lift the tray

TRAINING TIME

Kanjiru	Feel
Koko e	Go here
Shageki renshū-ba	Shooting range
Watashitachi ga kimemasu	We decide
Watashi no musuko wa anata o kiraimasen	My son does not hate you
Kare wa kutsu o kawakashita	He dried his shoes
Isha wa watashi o naoshita	The doctor cured me
Tegami wa irimasen	I don't need my letter
Karera wa yori ōku no okane o teikyō shimasu	They provide more money
Karera wa mainichi dekakemasu	They go out every day
Watashi wa mo~tsu to niku wa irimasen	I don't need more meat
Watashinohaha wa ōbun o shiyō shite imasu	My mother uses the oven
Getsuyōbi ga kiraidesu	I hate Monday
Kanojo wa nana-ji ni okiru	She gets up at seven
Shatsu o kawakashimasu	I dry my shirt
Densha wa kuji ni hassha shimasu	The train leaves at nine
Kanojo wa sore o hitsuyō to shite imasu	She needs it
Watashi wa ashita shuppatsu shimasu	I am leaving tomorrow

TRAINING TIME

STORY MODE

JAPANESE

Kyō wa haru no shonichidesu. Otokonoko, Hanabi to Naruhito wa, atarashī kisetsu o iwau tame ni kohan no bā de tomodachi ni au koto ni shimashita. Chō wa karera to issho ni ikitakattaga, kare wa sakewonomu ni wa waka sugitanode karera wa dōi shinakatta. Tochū de, otokonoko-tachi wa karera ni mukatte aruite iru kuma o mimashita. Chō ga koko ni itara, kare wa ki o ushinatta kamo shirenaiga, otokonoko wa kuma ga shizuka ni saru no o matsu. Mamonaku, shōnen-tachi wa bā ni hairi, karera no mae de giron o mimashita. `Otoko wa shiharaimasu, watashi wa odorimasu, watashi wa shiharaimasen' to Orihime wa sakebimashita. `Ryohou o motsu koto ha dekimasen, Orihime. Watashitachiha kyūryō o shiharau koto wa dekizu, soredemo nomimono ya tabemono o muryō de ataeru koto ga dekimasen.' To bā no tantōsha wa iimashita. `Mondaiarimasen, watashitachiha subete no ryōkin o haraimasu.' To Hanabi wa itta.

ENGLISH

Today is the first day of spring. The boys, Hanabi and Naruhito, decided to meet friends at the lakeside bar to celebrate the new season. Cho wanted to go with them, but they did not agree because he was too young to drink. On their way, the boys saw a bear walking towards them. If Cho was here, he may have fainted, but the boys wait for the bear to leave quietly. Shortly after, the boys entered the bar and watched the argument in front of them.

"The man pays, I dance, I don't pay," Orihime shouted.

"You cannot have both, Orihime. We cannot pay salaries and still give drinks and food free." said the person in charge of the bar.

"No problem, we will pay all the fees." Hanabi said.

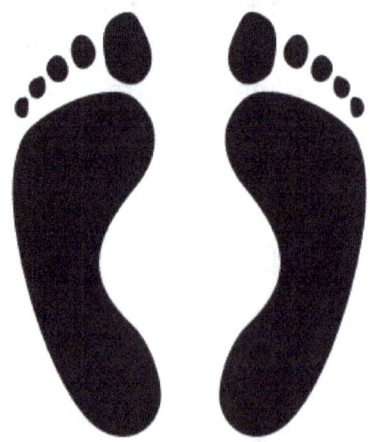

Chapter 8

PREPOSITIONS

Keywords : Kara, ni, to.

Karera wa josei ni tegamiwokaku	They write to women
Shōnen-tachi wa dansei ni yonda	The boys read to the men
Ahiru ni pan o ageru	We give bread to the duck
Kono on'nanoko wa jūsu ga sukide wa arimasen	This girl does not like juice
Dare ga dōbu~tsuen ni yattekuru no?	Who comes to the zoo?
Karera wa chūshoku o totte imasu	They are having lunch
Yūshoku o tabete iru	We are eating dinner
Watashi wa Lisa ni tsuite kangaeru	I think of Lisa
Watashi wa dōbu~tsuen ni imasu	I am at the zoo
Kare wa Mekishiko ni sunde imasu	He lives in Mexico
Dare ga kodomo o shinjite imasu ka?	Who believes in children?
Karera wa kanojo ni tsuite kaita	They wrote about her
Abura wa bin no naka ni arimasu	The oil is in the bottle
Watashi wa orenjijūsu o nomu	I drink orange juice
Watashi wa shinbun ni imasu	I am in the newspaper
Kare wa daidokoro de ryōri o suru	He cooks in the kitchen

Gohan ga hoshī megane kara nomu	We drink from glasses
Watashi wa dōbu~tsuen kara kimashita	I come from the zoo
Niku wa dōbutsu kara kuru	Meat comes from animals
Purēto no naka no tabemono	Food in the plate
Watashi ga kaita reshipi	The recipe I wrote
Gyūnyū wa ushi kara kuru	Milk comes from cows
Watashi wa uma ni ikimashita	I went to the horse
Kore wa kanojo no tamedesu	This is for her

TRAINING TIME

Itsu?	When?
Sara no ue no fōku	Fork on a plate
Satō no ari	Ants on sugar
Bin no naka no remonēdo	Lemonade in a bottle
Dansei o shinjiru	We believe in men
Sono shōnen ni yoru to, kanojo wa toriniku o tabemasen	According to the boy, she does not eat chicken
Kanojo wa resutoran kara kimashita	She comes from the restaurant
Kēki ni satō o kakeru	We put sugar on the cake
Otokonoko kara kudamono o kau	We buy fruit from the boy
Sakana wa mizu ni sunde imasu	Fish live in water
Karera wa watashitachi no ma ni iru	They are between us

Watashi wa shio o tsukatte sakana o ryōri shimasu.	I use salt to cook fish.
Kare wa anata o mite iru	He looks at you
Tamago ga sara no ue ni nai	Eggs are not on the plate
Watashi wa kare ni aruita	I walked to him
Kanojo ni yoru to, koreha-gyode wa arimasen	According to her, this is not a fish
Ahiru yurai no niku	Meat comes from ducks
Wain ni kuwaete	In addition to wine
Bīru ni kuwaete	In addition to beer
Watashi wa otoko no sara o motte imasu	I have a man's plate
Kanojo wa abura nashi de sarada o taberu	She eats salad without oil
Kare wa uma o katte iru	He has horses
Hon ni tsuite hanasu	We talk about books
Kare ni kiita	I asked him
Satō ga hoshīdesu ka.	Do you want some sugar?

TRAINING TIME

Mizu no soba ni sunde iru	We live by the water
Kumo wa kabe ni	The spider is on the wall
Korera no hon wa josei kara no monodesu	These books are from women
Yūshoku ni wain o nomimashita	We drank wine at dinner

Iro chigai nimokakawarazu, watashitachi wa mada kutsu o kaimasu	Despite the different colors, we still buy shoes
Chikin to issho ni gohan o tabemasu	We eat rice with chicken
Watashi wa ringo igai no kudamono o tabemasu	I eat fruit, except apples
Satō to kōhī ga arimasen ka.	Don't you have sugar and coffee?
Būtsu no iro wa?	What is the color of the boots?
Shōjo no neko wa shirodesu	The girl's cat is white
Orenji no ari	Ants in orange
On'nanoko no kutsu wa kurodesu	The girl's shoes are black
Kore wa ningen no fōkude wa arimasen	This is not a man's fork
Sono shōnen no inu wa mizu o nomimasu.	The boy's dog drinks water.
Watashi wa anata no ringo no hitotsu o tabemasu	I eat one of your apples
Korera no fuku ga sukina josei	Women like these clothes
Kore wa kabā no nai garasudesu	This is a glass without a cover
Dare ga sakana no aji ga sukidesu ka?	Who likes the taste of fish?

TRAINING TIME

Chapter 9

DATES AND TIME

Keywords : Shūkan, tsuki, hidzuke, jikan.

Yoru	Night
Hi	Day
Hidzuke	Date
Karendā	Calendar
Shichi gatsu kara ku gatsu	From July to September
Kyō wa shi gatsu ni owarimasu	April ends today
San gatsu wa ni gatsu kara shi gatsu no madesu	March is between February and April
Mata ashita ne!	See you tomorrow!
Watashitachi wa ichi gatsudesu	We are in January
Kore wa kinō no pandesu	This is yesterday's bread
Watashi wa ichi gatsu ni kare to yūshoku o torimashita	I had dinner with him in January
Kinō wa otokodattashi kyō wa on'nada	Yesterday it was a man and today it is a woman
Karera wa ni gatsu ni nani o tabemasu ka?	What do they eat in February?
Kyō wa san gatsudesu	March ends today
Hachi gatsudesu	It is August
Ima wa jūichi gatsudesu	It is now November
Kyō wa owaranai kamo shiremasen	May does not end today
Ashita wa mokuyōbidesu	Tomorrow is Thursday

Wareware wa jū gatsu ni karera ni tegami o kaita.	We wrote to them in October
Kore wa getsuyōbidesu	This is a Monday
Anata wa doyōbi ni hataraite imasu ka?	Do you work on Saturday?
Kayōbi ni chīzu o taberu	I eat cheese on Tuesday
Kyō wa getsuyōbidesu	Today is Monday
Kyō wa doyōbidesu	Today is Saturday
Kare wa jūni gatsu nakunarimashita	He died in December

TRAINING TIME

Haru	Spring
Fuyu	Winter
Kin'yōbi ni sutēki o taberu	I eat steak on Friday
Suiyōbi ni chīzu o taberu	We eat cheese on Wednesday
Kyō wa kin'yōbidesu	Today is Friday
Roku gatsu ni ōpun shita resutoran	The restaurant opened in June
Watashi wa kono natsu o kare to issho ni sugoshita	I spent this summer with him
Asa wa kōhī o nomimasu	I drink coffee in the morning
Kyō wa nichiyōbida	Today is Sunday
Watashi wa shōgo ni taberu	I eat at noon
Aki no yōna inu	Dogs like autumn
Kono kēki wa nichiyōbi no monodesu	This cake is for Sunday
London dewa harudesu	In London it is spring
Gogo wa chokorēto o taberu	I eat chocolate in the afternoon

Watashi wa yoru hataraku	I work at night
Kare wa mayonaka made hataraite imasu	He works until midnight
Kin'yōbi to doyōbi no yoru	Friday and Saturday nights
Kēki no jikandesu	It's time for cake
Kon'ya wa doko ni ikimasu ka.	Where are we going tonight?
Chottomatte!	Wait a moment!
Kon'ya hataraku	I work tonight
Watashi wa yoru hataraku	I work at night
Bun to jikan ga keika shimashita	Minutes and hours have passed
Konshū	Week of the month
Kayōbi wa yōbidesu	Tuesday is a day of the week

TRAINING TIME

Byō ga sugimasu	The seconds pass
Yūshokudokidesu	It is dinner time
Watashi wa sū-funkan anata o nayama seru koto ga dekimasu ka?	Can i bother you for a few minutes?
Watashi wa mō kore ijō matenai	I can not wait anymore
Maiji botoru o nomu	We drink a bottle every hour
Seiki wa ichi-nende wa arimasen	A century is not a year
Ichi-kagetsu de	In a month
Bun to jikan ga keika shimashita	Minutes and hours have passed
Kono jū-nen wa kyō de owarimasu	The decade ends today

Pātī wa ashitadesu	The party is tomorrow
Ashita wa watashi no tanjōbidesu	Tomorrow is my birthday
Kikan wa shi gatsu ni owarimashita	The period ended in April
Toshi-kagetsu ka.	Years or months?
Nanseiki mo tachimasu	The centuries pass
Karera wa nanjūnen mo hataraita	They worked for decades
Kyō wa nan'nichidesu ka?	What is today's date?
Kesa osoku tōchaku shita	You arrived late this morning
Osoidesu	It's late
Sayōnara!	Goodbye!
Watashi wa jikan ga arimasen	I do not have time
Ikkagetsumae	One month ago
Kare wa maishū watashitachi to shokuji o shimasu	He eats with us every week
Kesa nani o nomimashita ka.	What did you drink this morning?
Josei wa karendā o motte imasu	The woman has a calendar
Haru wa kisetsudesu	Spring is a season

TRAINING TIME

Bun to byō	Minutes and seconds
Sonohi no jikan	Hours of the day
Shū to tsuki	Weeks and months
Yoake	Breaking dawn
Ima shīzun	This season
Yoru ni	At night
Nanibun?	How many minutes?
Kare wa mokuyōbi ni tōchaku shita	He arrived on Thursday

Shuppatsu-ten wa dokodesu ka.	Where is the starting point?
Hachi gatsu to ku gatsu wa toshi no tsukidesu	August and September are months of the year
Watashi wa sono kikan ni hataraita	I worked in that period
Watashi wa asa aruku	I walk in the morning
Kyō wa nan'nichi?	What's the date today?
Karera wa matsuri ni ikimasu	They go to the festival
Getsuyōbi wa hatarakimasen	I do not work on Monday
Watashi wa jū gatsu ni hashirimasen	I will not run in October
Ichibu wa isshun	One minute is a moment
Natsu wa wakamono-muke	Summer is for youth
Kanojo no kinenbi wa shichigatsudesu.	Her anniversary is July.
Seiki no tanjō	The birth of the century
Shūki wa dono kuraidesu ka?	How long is the cycle?
Korera no tegami no hidzuke wa arimasen	There are no dates for these letters
Ichi-nichi no byō-sū	The number of seconds in a day
Fuyu wa nagai	Winter is long
Getsuyōbi, Kayōbi, Suiyōbi	Monday, Tuesday and Wednesday

TRAINING TIME

Watashi no musuko Cho wa ichi-saidesu.	My son Cho is one year old.
Mōikkai hitsuyō	I need a second

Senshū no doyōbi, watashitachiha niku o tabemashita	Last Saturday, we ate meat
Tokidoki hai, tokidoki īe	Sometimes yes, sometimes no
Aruberuto wa getsuyōbi to suiyōbi ni bīru o nomimasu	Alberto drinks beer on Monday and Wednesday
Hidzuke ga arimasen	We have no date
Watashi no oba Asami wa kinō kita.	My aunt Asami came yesterday
Jū gatsu to jūni gatsu wa sono-nen no tsukidesu.	October and December are months of the year
San gatsu, shi gatsu, go gatsu, roku gatsu	March, April, May and June
Watashi no sobo wa ni gatsu ni hashirimasen.	My grandmother does not run in February
Go gatsu no aru kin'yōbi	One Friday in May
Kyō genzai	As of today
Kare wa jūichi gatsu ni kaita	He wrote in November
Watashi wa hachi gatsu ni sakana o tabemasen	I don't eat fish in August
Ku gatsu kara jūni gatsu	From September to December
Fuyu wa kisetsudesu	Winter is a season
Shibaraku tabemashita	We ate for a while
Subete no pātī wa ashitade wa arimasen	All parties are not tomorrow
Watashi wa asa aruku	I walk in the morning
Hachi gatsu no kyūjitsu	Holidays in August
Watashi wa shōgo ni taberu	I eat at noon
Kyō wa kanojo to dēto shimashita	I dated her today

TRAINING TIME

STORY MODE

JAPANESE

"Ichi gatsu, ni gatsu, san gatsu wa watashi no shigoto no saikō no tsukidesu." Naze anata wa sore o iu nodesu ka? `Uki wa 1 tsuki ni owarimasu. Sore wa jimen o kirei ni suru koto ga yori kantande, kusa wa kawaite imasu. Zassō wa hayaku seichō suru koto wa dekimasen. Tetsu to semento no kakaku wa ni gatsu ni sagarudarou, soshite watashi wa motto yasui kakaku de motto kau koto ga dekiru. San gatsu ni, watashi wa mōsukoshi kasegu, soreha shigoto o supīdoappu suru no o tasukeru.' `Naruhodo, hoka no tsuki wa dōdesu ka?' Shi gatsu ni wa, -seki no kakaku ga yasuku narimashita. Shigoto wa roku gatsu chūjun ni hajimari, uki wa shichi gatsu kara hachi gatsu ni hajimarimasu. Ame wa ku gatsu to jū gatsu ki ni mottomo tsuyoku, jūni gatsu ni wa kyūkei o torimasu."

11/18/2018

ENGLISH

"January, February and March are the best months of my work."

"Why do you say that?"

"Because the rainy season is over in January. It is easier to clean up the ground and the grass is dry. Weeds cannot grow quickly.

Iron and cement prices will fall in February, and I can buy more at lower prices. In March, I earn a little more, which helps speed up the work."

"I see, what about the other months?"

"In April, the price of stone was cheaper. Work begins in mid-June, and the rainy season begins from July to August. The rain is most intense in September and October, and in December, we take a break."

Chapter 10
FAMILY

Keywords : Otōsan, haha, kodomo, oji, itoko, shimai.

Kazoku	Family
Otōsan	Father
Haha	Mother
Musuko	Son
Musume	Daughter
Ko	Child
Onīsan	The brother
Shimai	Sisters
Sofu	Grandfather
Sobo	Grandmother
Otto	Husband
Akachan	Baby
Kare to watashinohaha wa ani to imōtodesu.	He and my mother are brother and sister.
Watashi wa musuko to musume ga hoshīdesu.	I want a son and a daughter.
Watashitachiha keiteishimaidesu	We are brothers and sisters
Watashinochichi wa resutoran o motte imasu	My father has a restaurant
Ryōshin wa gohan o tabemasu	My parents eat rice
Watashi no musume wa tokei ga hoshī	My daughter wants a watch
Watashinohaha no shimai wa toriniku o tabemasen	My mother's sisters do not eat chicken
Karera wa watashi no kyōdaidesu	They are my brothers
Watashi wa imōto ga imasu	I have a younger sister
Kodomo-tachi wa gyūnyū o nomu	Their children drink milk

Watashitachiha otto to tsumadesu	We are husband and wife
Watashitachiha itokodesu	We are cousins
Kare wa watashi no itokode wanai	He is not my cousin

TRAINING TIME

Kon'nichiwa ojīsan!	Hello grandfather!
Oji no tsuma wa watashi no obadesu	My uncle's wife is my aunt
Karera wa tsumadesu	They are the wives
O bāchan no tokoro e ikimasu	We go to grandma's
Watashi wa oba to issho ni taberu	I eat with my aunt
Jūsu wa watashi no o bāchan no tame no monodesu	The juice is for my grandma
Mama to papa wa dokodesu ka	Where is Mommy and Daddy?
Sei to na ga arimasu	We have a first name and a last name
Kanojo no sei o dono yō ni kakimasu ka?	How do we write her last name?
Anata wa anata no okāsan no yōdesu	You are like your mother
Arigatō, otōsan!	Thanks dad!
Kanojo wa hahaoya no yōda	She is like her mother
Anata no myōji wa nanidesu ka?	What is your last name?
Watashi no mei wa inu o katte iru	My niece has a dog
Shōnen no inu	The boy's dog
Musuko to neko ga imasu	We have a son and a cat

Watashitachi wa kare no kodomo-tachidesu	We are his children
Anata no ryōshin wa dare?	Who are your parents?
Chō wa anata no chichioyade wa arimasen	Cho is not your father
Watashi no kodomo wa Itaria shusshindesu	My child is from Italy
Han Hebao wa watashi no musukodesu	Han Hebao is my son
Mitsuki wa watashinohahade wanai	Mitsuki is not my mother
Akira wa watashinochichide wanai	Akira is not my father
Hai, Aruberuto wa watashi no ottodesu.	Yes, Alberto is my husband.
Daisuke wa watashi no kyōdaidesu	Daisuke is my brother

TRAINING TIME

Watashi wa kare no tsumadesu	I am his wife
Karera wa watashi no ojidesu	They are my uncles
Kanojo wa watashi no obadearimasu	She is my aunt
Kanojo to watashinohaha wa shimaidesu.	She and my mother are sisters.
Anata wa watashitachi no tsumadesu	You are our wife
Īe, akachan wa imasen	No, you do not have babies
Watashinohaha wa sobodesu	My mother is a grandmother

Fumio wa watashi no sofudesu	Fumio is my grandfather
Watashi no sobo wa Hikarudesu.	My grandmother is Hikaru.
Watashi no kazoku wa Doitsu shusshindesu	My family is from Germany
O bāchan arigatō	Thank you Grandma
Aoi bōshi wa watashi no sobo no tame no monodesu	The blue hat is for my grandmother
Kare wa watashi no itokode wanai	He is not my cousin
Han Hebao wa watashi no itokodesu	Han Hebao is my cousin
Chō wa watashi no itokodesu	Cho is my cousin
Kono shiroi bōshi wa watashi no sobo ni wa tekishite imasen	This white hat is not suitable for my grandmother
Watashitachiha itokodesu	We are cousins
Aruberuto to Hinata ni kodomo ga ita	Alberto and Hinata had a child
Watashi no tsuma wa watashi no musuko no hahadesu	My wife is the mother of my son
Hanashita nochi, kare to kare no tsuma wa satta	After speaking, he and his wife left
Sūpu wa Ichirō no tame no monodesu	The soup is for Ichiro.

TRAINING TIME

STORY MODE

JAPANESE

Jirō: "Anata no shimai Yifeng wa Instagram ni shashin o okutta bakaridesu. Nakaniha takusan no hito ga ite, soreha kazoku no subarashī shōzō-ga no yō ni miemasu."

Huang: "Hai, kyō wa shashin-ka ga watashitachi no ie ni yattekimashita. Watashitachi wa watashi no sofu no tanjōbi o iwau tame ni shashin o torimashita.' `Hidarigawa ni watashi no ani to kare no tsuma ga imasu. Karera wa kekkon shite shinkon ryokō kara modotte kimashita. Soshite migigawa ni wa anata ga kazoekirenai hodo no jikan o sugoshita watashinochichi ga imasu.' `Kore wa kazoku no naka de mottomo wakai menbā, watashi no mei Suteradesu. Kanojo wa tada no on'nanokodesuga, totemo kawaīdesu.' `Watashi no sofu no tonari ni suwatte iru no wa watashi no sobo, watashinohaha, watashi no oji to watashi no bengoshideshita. Soshite yuka ni wa, watashitachi no itoko to oi ga imasu."

Jirō: "Kore wa subarashī kazoku shashindesu."

Huang: "Shitte iru, sukidayo."

ENGLISH

Jiro: "Your sister Yifeng just sent a photo to Instagram. There are many people inside and it looks like a great family portrait."

Mitsuki: "Yes, a photographer came to our house today. We took pictures to celebrate my grandfather's birthday."

"On the left are my brother and his wife, they are married and have just returned from their honeymoon, and on the right of them is my father, whom you have met countless times."

"This is the youngest member of the family, my niece Stella. She's just a girl, but she's very pretty."

"Sitting next to my grandfather was my grandmother, my mother, my uncle and my lawyer. And on the floor, we have my cousin and my nephew."

Jiro: "This is a great family photo."

Mitsuki: "I know, I like it."

Chapter 11
COLOR

Keywords : Kankitsurui, kuro, shiro, aka, ki, ao.

Iro wa midoridesu	The color is green
Kono sētā wa aoidesu	This sweater is blue
Iro no tsuita shatsu	A colored shirt
Kuroi zubon o kaimasu	We buy black pants
Kono josei wa chairo no obi o motte imasu	This woman has a brown belt
Kanojo no kutsushita wa haiirodesu	Her socks are gray
Kutsu wa aodesu	Shoes are blue
Orenji	Orange
Ūru wa murasaki	The wool is purple
Tori wa kiiroi	The bird is yellow
Watashi no shatsu wa shirodesu	My shirt is white
Kanojo wa akai zubon o shite imasu	She has red pants
Kono neko wa shiro janai	This cat is not white
Watashi no shiroi shatsu wa dokodesu ka?	Where is my white shirt?
Kanojo no fuku wa kurodesu	Her clothes are black
Kōto wa pinku	The coat is pink
Zō wa haiirodesu	The elephant is grey
Sukinairo ga wakarimasen	I don't know your favorite color
Kanojo wa akai zubon o kite imasu	She is wearing red pants
Onaji-irodesu	It is the same color
Kanojo no shatsu wa midoriirodesu	Her shirt is green
Watashi wa kuro no sukāto ga sukidesu	I like black skirts

Chapter 12

OCCUPATION

Keywords : Sagyō, piero, kyaputen, kenchikka, mekanikku, rōdō-sha, ishi, moderu, heishi, keisatsu.

Gakusei	The student
Kyaputen	Captain
Gādo	Guard
Chosha	Author
Sakka	Writer
Ātisuto	Artist
Moderu	The model
Kengen	Authority
Isha	Doctors
Senshi	Warrior
Kingu	King
Ōji	Prince
Nōmin	Farmers
Kenchikka	The architect
Kenkyūsha-tachi	The researchers
Gaka	Painter
Senmonka	The professionals
Shikyō	Bishop
Saibankan	Judge
Sensei	The teacher
Rīdā	Reader
Gakusei	The student
Daihyō	Representative
Kigyōka	The entrepreneur
Keikan	Policemen

TRAINING TIME

Kōchō	The principal
Kare wa enjiniadeari, kanojo wa kenchikkadesu	He is an engineer and she is an architect
Nōka wa ushi ya niwatori o atsukatte imasu	The farmers work with cattle and chickens
Enjinia wa nan to iimasu ka?	What does the engineer say?
Kanojo wa ryōshidesu	She is a fisherman
Kare wa anchisukiru to hanasu	He talks with the guard
Anata wa hosutodesu ka?	Are you the host?
Anata wa dōkeshidesu	You are a clown
Nōmin wa shinbun o yomimashita	The farmers read the newspaper
Watashitachi no otōto wa seibi-shidesu	Our brother is a mechanic
Keisatsu wa aoi shatsu o kite iru	The police have blue shirts
Haikan kō wa nani o tabemasu ka?	What does a plumber eat?
Watashitachiha yūbin haitatsuinde wa arimasen	We are not postmen
Anata no bengoshi wa daredesu ka?	Who is your lawyer?
Watashi no imōto wa hatarakanakatta	My sister did not work
Manējā wa dokodesu ka?	Where is the manager?
Rōdō-sha wa daredesu ka?	Who is the worker?
Watashi wa isha ni ai ni ikimashita	I went to see a doctor
Sakana wa anata no senmondesu	Fish is your specialty

Watashi no otto wa hishode wa arimasen	My husband is not a secretary
Watashi no otto wa kenkyūshadesu	My husband is a researcher
Watashi no oji to watashi no oba wa ishadesu	My uncle and my aunt are doctors
Watashi wa kenkyūsha o shitte imasu	I know a researcher
Sakusha wa kaita	The author wrote
Ryōshi wa ippai no kōhī o nomimasu.	The fisherman drinks a cup of coffee.

TRAINING TIME

Senchō no kotae ga kyō todoita	The captain's answer arrived today
Anata no otōsan wa nōkadesu	Your father is a farmer
Anata wa kenchikkadesu	You are an architect
Watashinohaha wa yūbin haitatsu o matteimasu	My mother waits for the postman
Kanojo no kyaria wa nanidesu ka?	What is her career?
Kanojo wa watashi no komondesu	She is my advisor
Kotaeha koyōdesu	The answer is employment
Kankyaku wa remonēdo o nozonde iru	The audience wants lemonade
Chōshū wa mokuyōbi ni tōchaku shimashita	The audience arrived on Thursday
Senmonka wa ō to hanasu	The expert speaks with the king
Bengoshi ga hitsuyōdesu	I need a lawyer

Kare wa keisatsu no supōkusumandesu	He is a spokesman for the police
Kare wa konseiki no rīdādesu	He is the leader of this century
Watashi wa kishade wa arimasen	I am not a reporter
Taisa to kantoku wa hanasu	The colonel and director speak
Oyasuminasai, hakushaku fujin	Good night, Countess
Watashi wa junēbu no daihyōdesu	I am a representative of Geneva
Sensei wa seito-tachi o mimasu	The teacher sees their students
Karera wa rīdādesu	They are leaders
Karera wa geijutsukadesu	They are artists
Kanojo wa kyōshidearu	She is a teacher
Anata wa moderudesu ka?	Are you a model?
Kare wa bijinesumandesu	He is a businessman
Anata wa ishada	You are a doctor
Seito-tachi wa taberu	The students eat

TRAINING TIME

Pan	Bread
Sono geijutsuka	The artist
Ōji	The prince
Supūn wa ō no tame no monodesu	The spoon is for the king
Watashinohaha to watashi no oba wa senseidesu	My mother and my aunt are teachers
Seito-tachi wa mizuwonomu	The students drink water

Kare wa gakuseidesu	He is a student
Sakka wa wain o nomimasu.	The writer drinks wine.
Kare wa isha to hanasu	He talks with the doctor
Ohayōgozaimasu sensei	Good morning teacher
Sara to kurisutīna wa keikandesu	Sarah and Christina are policewomen
Sensei wa sandoitchi o taberu	The teacher eats a sandwich
Kensatsukan wa daredesu ka?	Who is the prosecutor?
Karera wa moderudesu	They are models
Kare wa hishodesu	He is a secretary
Watashitachiha senseidesu	We are teachers
Watashi wa isha o hitsuyō to suru	I need a doctor
Seito-tachi wa pan o taberu	The students eat bread
Bosu wa nan-ri imasu ka?	How many bosses do you have?
Kanojo wa watashi no hishodesu	She is my secretary
Furedo wa keikandesu	Fredo is a policeman
Hisho ga imasu	You have a secretary
Joō wa bīru o nomimasen	The queen does not drink beer
Sensei wa ringo o taberu	The teacher eats apple
Kanojo wa watashi no jōshidesu	She is my boss

TRAINING TIME

Gaka	The painter
Nōka	The farmers
Shefu	The chef
Watashi wa kishadesu	I am a reporter
Kare wa anchisukiru to hanasu	He talks with the guard
Sono shijin wa tegami o kaita	The poet wrote a letter
Watashi no oji wa kono moto no choshadesu	My uncle is the author of this book
Watashi wa bijinesumandesu	I am a businessman
Kyōju-tachi wa yomimashita	The professors read
Watashi wa kyōjude wa arimasen	I am not a professor
Patorishia wa saibankandesu	Patricia is a judge
Heishi-tachi wa taberu	The soldiers eat
Anata wa sakkadesu ka?	Are you an author?
Watashinochichi wa shijindesu	My father is a poet
Watashitachiha kyōjudesu	We are professors
Watashi no oji wa jūgyōindesu	My uncle is an employee
Anata no bengoshi wa daredesu ka?	Who is your lawyer?
Taisa ga heishi-tachi to hanashi o suru	The colonel talks with the soldiers
Īe, Pedoro wa haiyūde wa arimasen. Kare wa shijindesu.	No, Pedro is not an actor. He is a poet.
Karera wa geijutsukadesu	They are artists
Watashi wa bengoshi ga imasu	I have a lawyer

Kare no jūgyōin wa tegamiwokaku	His employees write letters
Anjero to Zhao wa ātisutodesu	Angelo and Zhao are artists
Shefu wa niku o taberu	The chef eats meat
Watashi no imōto wa watashi no bengoshidesu	My sister is my lawyer

TRAINING TIME

Watashi wa inu no kainushidesu	I am the owner of the dog
Ējento wa daredesu ka?	Who is the agent?
Karera wa senmonkadesu	They are experts
Shirei-kan wa orenji o taberu	The commander eats oranges
Niku wa karera no senmondesu	Meat is their specialty
Ātisuto to gaka	Artists and painters
Shoyū-sha wa uma o katte iru	The owner has a horse
Watashinohaha wa tori no senmonkadesu	My mother is a bird expert
Hai, watashi wa enjinia de daikudesu	Yes, I am an engineer and a carpenter
Hai, watashi no oji Wei wa dairinindesu	Yes, my uncle Wei is an agent
Renshū wa hijō ni jūyōdesu	Practice is very important
Hai, Han wa pan-yadesu	Yes, Han is a baker
Watashi wa kyōshidesu	I am a teacher
Karera wa madoguchidesu	They are tellers
Kanojo wa watashi no kankoshidesu ka?	Is she my nurse?

Kore wa watashi no shokugyōde wa arimasen	This is not my profession
Pauro wa saishidesu	Paul is a priest
Kanojo wa pan-yadesu	She is a baker
Karera wa reji-gakaridesu	They are cashiers
Karera wa senshude wa arimasen	They are not athletes
Shisai wa bīru o nomimasen	A priest does not drink beer
Miko wa kuroi neko o katte iru	The priestess has a black cat
Watashi no musume wa u~eitoresudesu	My daughter is a waitress
Watashi no oji wa nōkade wa arimasen. Kare wa pan-yadesu.	My uncle is not a farmer. He is a baker.

TRAINING TIME

Wākā	Worker
Haikan-kō	Plumber
Yūbin haitatsuin	Postman
Piero	Clown
Shisai wa hon o kaku	Priests write books
Watashi no kanojo wa untenshudesu	My girlfriend is a driver
Watashi wa u~eitādesu	I am a waiter
Īe, watashi no kyōdai debiddo wa daikude wa arimasen	No, my brother David is not a carpenter
Kare no haigūsha wa untenshudesu	His spouse is a driver
Bao wa enjiniade wanai, kare wa kankoshidesu	Bao is not an engineer, he is a nurse
Anata no oji wa kankoshide wa	Your uncle is not a nurse. He is a chef

arimasen. Kare wa shefudesu	
Īe, Reo to Sofia wa asurītode wa arimasen	No, Leo and Sofia are not athletes
Harī wa igirisuhito enjiniadesu	Harry is a British engineer
Karurosu wa haiyūde wanai, kare wa gakuseidesu	Carlos is not an actor, he is a student
Kare wa kare no gensoku ni tsuite hanashimasu	He talks about his principles
Ī omoide ga aru	You have a good memory
Kanojo wa korera no kotoba o watashi ni setsumei shita	She explained these terms to me
Kare wa yūbin haitatsuin to shite hataraite imasu	He works as a postman
Hisho wa kōhī o nomimasu.	The secretary drinks coffee.
Watashi no musume wa keikandesu	My daughter is a policewoman
Kore ga watashitachi no senmon chishikidesu	This is our expertise
Watashi no oji wa hosutodesu	My uncle is the host
Watashitachiha yūbin haitatsuinde wa arimasen	We are not postmen
Watashi wa keisatsukandesu	I am a police officer

STORY MODE

JAPANESE

Masateru: "Ryōshin wa doko de hataraite imasu ka"
Nishimori: "Watashinochichi wa bengoshi de, watashinohaha mo bengoshidesu."
Masateru: "Soshite, anata no kyōdaidesu ka?"
Nishimori: "Watashi no ani wa gakadesuga, watashi no ane wa hisho to shite hataraite imasu"
Masateru: "Soshite, anata wa?"
Nishimori: "Watashi wa kore made ni ni-satsu no hon o shuppan shimashitanode, watashi wa jibun jishin o sakusha to yobu koto ga dekimasu"
Masateru: "Jibun ga seichō shita toki ni nanika hoka ni naritaidesu ka?"
Nishimori: "Watashi wa takusan no hito ga sukidesu. Saibankan, geijutsuka, haiyū, enjinia, ryōrijin, sarani wa heishi made. Watashi ga kodomo no koro, watashi wa kōsha to karera no jū ga sukideshita. Kore wa watashi ni totte mottomo mirikitekidesu. Shikashi, watashinohaha wa dōi shimasendeshita. Kanojo wa watashi ga isha ka daigaku kyōju ni naru koto o nozonda. Watashi wa nagaiai benkyō suru koto o sōzō dekinainode, watashi wa nani ka hoka no mono o yomimasu. Watashi ga benkyō o oeta toki, watashi no saisho no shigoto wa shisho, sorekara untenshudeshita, soshite watashi wa tsuini dairinin to shite no shigoto o mitsukemashita."

ENGLISH

Masateru: "Where do your parents work?"

Nishimori: "My father is a lawyer and my mother is also a lawyer."

Masateru: "And your siblings?"

Nishimori: "My older sister works as a secretary, while my brother is a painter."

Masateru: "And you?"

Nishimori: "So far I have published two books, so I can call myself an author."

Masateru: "Do you want to be anything else when you grow up?"

Nishimori: "I like a lot of people. Judges, artists, actors, engineers, cooks and even soldiers.
When I was a kid, I liked the latter and their guns. This is the most fascinating to me. But my mother disagreed. She wanted me to become a doctor or a university professor.
I can't imagine studying for a long time, so I read something else. When I finished my studies, my first job was a librarian and then a driver, and I finally found a job as an agent."

Chapter 13

MEASURES

Keywords : Mētoru, mairu, kiromētoru, kiroguramu.

Fuka-sa	Depth
Taka-sa	Height
Ichi kiroguramu	One kilogram
Ichi mētoru	One meter
Sokutei suru	Measuring
Kanojo wa chīsakute, watashi wa totemo ōkīdesu	She is small, and I am very big
Zō wa kyodaina dōbutsudesu	The elephant is a huge animal
Ocha ichi-guramu o shiyō	We use one gram of tea
Kanojo wa pan o sukoshi motte imasu	She has a bit of bread
Nan-senchi nokotte iru?	How many centimeters are left?
Sokutei shimasu	You do the measurement
Senchimētoru to inchi	Centimeters and inches
Boryūmu o shitte imasu	We know the volume
Satō ichi-guramu	We have one gram of sugar
Tonari no heya de	In the next room
Dono dōbutsu ga chīsai?	Which animal is small?
Watashi wa sū-jikan matta	I waited for a few hours
Amerika wa ikuradesu ka.	How much rice?
Kiromētoru shiyō	We use kilometers
Nan-kiro?	How many kilograms?

Zentai no shi-bun'no ichi	One quarter of the total
Watashi no hanbun	My half
Kore wa watashi ni tottemo onajidesu	This is the same for me
Sōsū o miru	We look at the total number
Korera wa ryōsokudesu	These are the two sides
Kiromētoru	Kilometers
Mairu wa dono kuraidesu ka?	How long is a mile?
Watashi wa daidokoro ni ichi-rittoru no abura o motte imasu	I have a litre of oil in the kitchen
Daburuesupuresso, arigatō	Double espresso, thanks
Daidokoro ni wa nanimonai	Nothing in the kitchen
Daburuesupuresso wa kanojo no tame no monodesu	The double espresso is for her
Watashi no kaban ni wa nani mo nai	There is nothing in my bag
Watashi wa sukoshi shiroi chokorēto o motte imasu	I have a little white chocolate
Doa no haba wa 80-senchidesu	The width of the door is 80 centimeters
Fuka-sa wa hijō ni jūyōdesu	Depth is very important
Ichi-ton wa sen-kiroguramu	One ton has a thousand kilograms
Anata wa watashi no hāfuappuru ga hoshīdesu ka?	Do you want my half apple?
Hachi wa yon kara ni-kai	Eight times is four times twice
Kore wa tamago no ōki-sadesu	This is the size of an egg

Heya wa seihōkeidesu	The room has a square shape
Nan-kiro no niku ga tabe raremasu ka?	How many kilograms of meat do we get?
Atarashī supīdo wa?	What is the new speed?
Watashi no chikashitsu ni wa san rippō mētoru no maki ga arimasu	There are three cubic meters of firewood in my cellar
Kore wa zen ni-kan no shōsetsudesu.	This is a two-volume novel
Seihōkei no hen wa hitoshī	The sides of the square are equal
Watashinoie no taka-sa wa nana mētoru	The height of my home is seven meters

TRAINING TIME

STORY MODE

JAPANESE

"Enjin wa dore kurai hayaku ugoku nodesu ka?" To, shirubāheāenjinia no Makkonen kyōju ga Eliseu Bridge de no kare no saishin no hatsumei o tesuto suru yō ni tanomimashita. "Jisokuyaku kyuu kiromētoru." Joshu wa kare ga ōkina supīdomētā o te ni totta toki ni itta. "Kaibatsu hachi kiromētoru no taka-sa no yōken wa nandesuka?" "Yon kara juu fīto no naga-sa, sensei." "Sate, ima, soreha mae no mono to hikaku shite dōdesu ka?" Makkōnen kyōju wa tazunemashita. "Kore wa tsūjō sono haba to gansuiryō ni izon shimasu. Kono jiten de, nitsu wa rokujuuyon-pondo kara rokujuusan-pondo made, hotondo onajidesu." To ashisutanto wa setsumei shimashita. "Hai, shikashi sore wa zen'nin-sha no kyōdo no san-bun'no ichi o shōhi shimasu, soshite sō kyori wa yori nagaidesu: Gojuu senchimētoru kara ichi mētoru no kawari ni, kyuujuu senchimētoru kara ni mētoru made, shitagatte chigai ga arimasu." To kyōju wa itta. Ashisutanto wa nōto o te ni tori, ikutsu ka no sūji o hashirigaki shita. "Osoraku, kūki rikigaku no mokuteki de, naga-sa mo hanbun ni fuyasubekidesu." "Tashika ni, u~orutā, imasugu hatarakimashou" to kyōju wa kotaemashita.

ENGLISH

"How fast does the engine run?" asks Prof. Makkonen, a silver haired engineer, to test his latest invention on the Eliseu Bridge.

"About nine kilometers an hour." The assistant said when he picked up a large speedometer.

"What is the height requirement for eight kilometers below sea level?"

"Four to ten feet long, sir."

"Okay, now, how does it compare to the previous one?" asked Professor Makkonen.

"This usually depends on its width and water content. At this point, the two are almost the same, from 64 pounds to 63 pounds." the assistant explained.

"Yes, but it consumes a third of its predecessor's intensity, and the total distance is greater: from 90 centimeters to two meters, instead of from 50 centimeters to one meter, so there is a difference." said the professor.

The assistant picked up the notebook and scribbled several numbers.

"Perhaps we should also increase the length by half, sir, for the purpose of aerodynamics."

"Indeed, Walter, let us work now." the professor answered.

Chapter 14

HOUSEHOLD

Keywords : Barukonī, isu, beddo, heya, ōbun, yane, doa, sekken, doa, kāten, tsukue, hamigakiko.

Ie	**House**
Garasu	**Glass**
Naifu	**Knife**
Denwa	**Phone**
Kappu	**Cup**
Supūn	**Spoon**
Funsui	**Fountain**
Terebi	**TV**
Potto	**Pot**
Sofā	**Sofa**
Kāten-hyō	**Curtain**
Omote	**Table**
Doa	**Door**
Kāpetto	**Carpet**
Tsukue	**Desk**
Isu	**Chair**
Beddo	**Bed**
Kitchin	**Kitchen**
Mado	**Window**
Ranpu	**Lamp**
Kī	**Key**
Hikari	**Light**
Kagami	**Mirror**
Tenjō	**Ceiling**
Chijō	**Above ground**

TRAINING TIME

Kabe	Wall
Ōbun	Oven
Shinshitsu	Bedroom
Toire	Toilet
Watashi no shanderia	My chandelier
Anata no naifu	Your knife
Watashi no denwa wa totemo ōkīdesu	My phone is very big
Watashi no supūn wa shirodesu	My spoon is white
Watashi wa basu tabu ga arimasu	I have a bathtub
Neko wa kāpetto no ue	The cat is on the carpet
Watashi wa barukonī ni imasu	I am on the balcony
Watashitachiha apāto ni sunde imasu	We live in an apartment
Watashi no mōfu ga hoshī	I want my blanket
Watashi no musuko wa midoriiro no beddo ga hoshī	My son wants a green bed
Kāpetto wa ao	The carpet is blue
Watashi no oji wa apāto ni sunde imasu	My uncle lives in an apartment
Watashi wa jibun no daidokoro ni wa kāpetto ga arimasen.	I have no carpet in my kitchen.
Mizu wa totemo kireidesu	The water is very clear
Anata wa satta, watashi wa shuppatsu shite iru.	You are gone, I am leaving.
Watashi wa isu o tsukaimasu	I use a chair
Kare wa tento o kaimashita	He bought a tent

Kyō wa hare no hidesu	Today is a sunny day
Neko wa kāpetto no ue de taberu	The cat eats on the carpet
Watashi wa tēburu no ue no hon o yomimashita.	I read a book on the table.
Anata wa doa o akemasu	You open the door

TRAINING TIME

Anata no tento ni hairimasu	We enter your tent
Kēki wa reizōko no naka	The cake is in the fridge
Kagu wa doko ni arimasu ka?	Where is the furniture?
Danbō wa arimasen	We don't have heating
Watashi wa doa no soba ni imasu	I am by the door
Kanojo wa jibun no kagi o mitsukeru koto ga dekimasen	She can't find her key
Uma wa doa ni imasu	The horse is at the door
Yokushitsu no raito wa midoriirodesu	The lights in the bathroom are green
Karera wa kagu o motte imasen	They don't have furniture
Karera wa kagi o motte imasu	They have keys
Heya ni denwa wa arimasu ka?	Is there a phone in the room?
Shanpū wa doko ni arimasu ka?	Where is the shampoo?
Shiroi makura o kau	We buy white pillows
Shanpū wa basurūmu ni arimasu	The shampoo is in the bathroom
Akai yane no ie wa watashi no ojidesu	The red roof house is my uncle's

Kagami wa doko ni arimasu ka?	Where is the mirror?
Makura ga arimasu	I have a pillow
Denwa wa ikutsu arimasu ka.	How many calls do you have?
Hashigo wa arimasu ka?	Do you have a ladder?
Yokusō no sekken	Soap in the bathtub
Sofa ga hoshī	I want a sofa
Kitchin wa anata shidaidesu	The kitchen is yours
Kabe wa aka	The wall is red
Mado o hirakimasu	We open the window
Iriguchi wa shiro	The entrance is white

TRAINING TIME

Omocha wa kāpetto no ue	The toy is on the carpet
Musuko no omocha ga mitsukaranai no wa nazedesu ka?	Why can't we find the son's toy?
Anata no kazoku wa tēburu ni imasu	Your family is at the table
Ōbun de pan	Bread in the oven
Watashinohaha wa shawā o abite imasu	My mother is taking a shower
Haha wa daidokoro ni imasu	My mother is in the kitchen
Mado wa kurodesu	The window is black
Neko wa sofa no ue	The cat is on the couch
Watashitachiha niwa de matteimasu	We are waiting in the yard
Hamigakiko wa doko ni arimasu ka?	Where is the toothpaste?
Shīto wa doko ni arimasu ka?	Where are the sheets?

Don'na kami sori ga arimasu ka?	What kind of razor do I have?
Haburashi wa arimasu ka?	Do you have a toothbrush?
Akai isu ga arimasu	I have some red chairs
Suponji wa arimasu ka?	Do you have a sponge?
Haburashi o toru	I take a toothbrush
Kare no isu	His chair
Kare wa akai denwa o motte imasu	He has a red phone
Lorenzo wa tēburu de taberu	Lorenzo eats at the table
Kappu wa arimasen!	We don't have a cup!
Nishimori wa beddo de nemasu	Nishimori sleeps in bed
Watashi wa anata no terebi o motte imasu	I have your TV
Daidokoro ni	In the kitchen
Gyūnyū ippai	A glass of milk
Kabe	The wall

TRAINING TIME

Watashi wa shinshitsu de tabete imasu	I am eating in the bedroom
Watashi wa reizōko ga arimasen	I have no refrigerator
Aruberuto wa yokushitsu o kirei ni suru	Alberto cleans the bathroom
Doraiyā ga arimasu	We have a dryer
Ano sentakuki	That washing machine
Sentakuki ga nai	I have no washing machine
Xi wa isu de nemasu ka?	Does Xi sleep in a chair?
Daisuke wa ōbun de chikin o chōri shimasu	Daisuke cooks chicken in the oven

Kare wa sentakuki ga hoshī	He wants a washing machine
Anata wa kitchin suponji ga hoshīdesu ka?	Do you want a kitchen sponge?
Sekken ga hitsuyōdesu	I need soap
Kasa wa watashitachi no monode wa arimasen	The umbrella is not ours
Shīto wa kiirodesu	The sheets are yellow
Kiiroi sekken wa arimasu ka?	Do we have yellow soap?
Sara wa sekken o taberu!	Sarah eats soap!
Kami sori wa ao	The razor is blue
Kappu ni mizu o iremasu	I fill the cup with water
Iro wa totemo shizendesu	The color is very natural
Shinbun wa saishindesu	The newspaper is the latest
Watashi wa okane ga arimasu	I have money
Tsugi no jikan	Next hour
Ocha wa shizendesu	The tea is natural
Kore wa rekishi-tekina shūdesu	This is a historic week
Tsugi wa daredesu ka?	Who is the next one?
Shinbun wa saikin no monodesu ka?	Is the newspaper recent?

TRAINING TIME

STORY MODE

JAPANESE

Jintao: "Wainserā de nani o shite imasu ka?"
Fang: "Geitaidenwa o sagashiteimasu"
Jintao: "Anata wa kono kabe no ushiro o chekku shimashita ka? Watashi wa anata ga shibaraku mae ni madogiwa ni tatte iru no o mimashita."
Fang: "Sentakuki no naka, tēburu wa itaru tokoro ni arimasu."
Jintao: "Zenkai doko de mimashita ka?"
Fang: "Watashinoheya ni oritatama reta shītsu no ue ni"
Jintao: "Anata no michi o oboete mite kudasai"
Fang: "Mā, watashinochichi ga denwa o shita toki, watashi wa yokushitsu no kagami o sōji shite imashita. Denwa ga owatta toki, watashi wa heya no tenjō kara no hikari o kae, sorekara watashi wa ame o omoidashita. Watashi wa pūru o sōji suru hitsuyō ga attanode, watashi wa kurōzetto o akete kasa o torimashita. Soshite ikutsu ka no sekken. Sonogo, watashi wa daidokoro ni modori, jūsu o nomu tame ni reizōko o akemashita. Watashi wa jibun no geitaidenwa o kappu to ikutsu ka no sara no chikaku ni oita. Daidokoro no tēburu no ue ni mo naifu ga arimasu. Watashi wa heya ni modori, sokode hirune o suru mae ni nomimono o nomu koto ni shimashita. Kore wa watashi ga oboete iru kotodesu."
Jintao: "Shinshitsu ni modorimashou."

ENGLISH

Jintao: "What are you doing in the wine cellar?"

Fang: "I am looking for my mobile phone."

Jintao: "Have you checked behind this wall? I saw you standing by the window some time ago."

Fang: "I check everywhere, inside the washing machine, the table is everywhere."

Jintao: "Where did you see it last time?"

Fang: "On the sheets folded in my room."

Jintao: "Try to remember your way."

Fang: "Well, when my dad called, I was cleaning the bathroom mirror. When the call ended, I changed the light from the ceiling of the room, then I remembered the rain. I needed to clean the pool, so I opened the closet and took an umbrella. And some soap.
After that, I went back to the kitchen and opened the fridge to drink juice. I put my phone close to the cup and some dishes. There is also a knife on the kitchen table. I went back to the room, where I decided to take a drink before I took a nap. This is what I remember."

Jintao: "Let's go back to the bedroom."

Chapter 15

ADJECTIVES

Keywords : Tsuyoku, furu, futsū, muryō, kimyō, nagai.

Mōichido?	Once again?
Yatto	At last
Watashi wa byōkidesu	I am sick
Chigaimasu	It is different
Kono josei wa totemo kireidesu	This woman is very beautiful
Kanojo wa toshioite inai	She is not old
Kore wa kanōdesu	This is possible
Karera no yunifōmu wa atarashīdesu	Their uniform is new
Kare no kotae wa watashi no to wa kotonarimasu.	His answer is different from mine.
Kore wa onajidesu	This is the same
Kare ga nozomu no wa fukanōdesu	What he wants is impossible
Ī ko ni nari nasai!	Be a good girl!
Kuni no iro wa midori to kiirodesu.	The national colors are green and yellow
Karera wa segatakaidesu ka?	Are they tall?
Kore wa ī kēkidesu	This is a good cake
Segahikuidesu	I am short
Watashitachiha kokusai-tekide wa arimasen	We are not international
Kōkade wa nai	It is not expensive
Watashi no imōto wa totemo yūmeidesu	My sister is very famous
Sakka wa yūmeide wanai	The writer is not famous

Watashitachi no hamigakiko wa hijō ni yasuidesu	Our toothpaste is very cheap
Kono pakkēji wa muryōdesu	This package is free
Kyō wa himadesu.	I am free today.
Watashi wa anata ga totemo kanemochidearu koto o shitte imasu.	I know that you are very rich.
Gaikoku no bīru wa arimasu ka?	Do you have foreign beer?

TRAINING TIME

Kore wa watashi no mainichi no pandesu	This is my daily bread
Kanojo wa gendai no hahaoyadesu	She is a modern mother
Denki guriru ga arimasu	I have an electric grill
Kanojo wa totemo ninki ga arimasu	She is very popular
Kare ni totte nani ga jūyōdesu ka?	What is important to him?
Kono uma wa benrina dōbutsudesu	This horse is a useful animal
Kore wa mi kaiketsu no mondaidesu	This is an open question
Kyōmi arimasu ka?	Are you interested?
Watashitachi wa kanpekidesu ka?	Are we perfect?
Anata wa yuiitsu no kodesu ka?	Are you the only child?
Watashi wa yūnōdesu	I am capable
Akai ringo wa tokubetsude wa arimasen	The red apple is not special
Kare wa omoshiroi ishō o kite imasu	He has an interesting costume

Anata no itoko no shigoto wa totemo omoshiroidesu.	Your cousin's work is very interesting.
Anata wa mado o shimete oku	You keep the window closed
Anata dakede wa arimasen	You are not the only one
Kanojo wa totemo tsuyoi	She is very strong
Muzukashikunai	We are not difficult
Kinoko no sūpu wa hen'na aji ga shimasu	Mushroom soup has a strange taste
Watashi no sobo wa hitorigurashidesu.	My grandmother lives alone.
Same wa kikendesu	Sharks are dangerous
Watashi no musuko wa totemo ōkī	My son is very big
Omoi būtsu o motte kuru	I bring heavy boots
Totemo nagaiyo	Very long night
Tsugi no kōhī wa anata no monodesu	The next cup of coffee is yours

TRAINING TIME

Kanojo ni totte kantan	Easy for her
Mō onaka panpan	I'm stuffed
Watashi wa marugoto chikin o tabemashita.	I ate a whole chicken.
Kanojo wa karera ni hijō ni kibishī	She is very tough on them
Watashi no sukāto wa shiro to aodesu	My skirt is white and blue
Kore wa futsū no shinbundesu	This is an ordinary newspaper
Kore wa genjitsudesu	This is real
Chōshoku wa yōi dekite iru	Breakfast is ready
Kakushin shitemasu	I am sure

Anata no kotae wa tadashīdesu.	Your answer is correct.
Kare wa futsūnohitodesu	He is an ordinary person
Kimetakara kimemashita	We decided because we determined
Anata no kotae wa meikakude wa arimasen	Your answer is not clear
Watashitachi no jikan wa mijikaidesu	Our time is short
Sūpu ga hiete iru	The soup is getting cold
Kanojo wa totemo wakaidesu, watashi wa toshidesu.	She is very young, I am old.
Kyō no tenki wa atsuidesu.	The weather is hot today.
Ni gatsu wa mijikai tsukidesu	February is a short month
Karera wa atsui sandoitchi o motte imasu ka?	Do they have hot sandwiches?
Kanojo no mondai wa muzukashī	Her problem is difficult
Kare wa yūshūna gakuseidesu	He is an excellent student
Kanojo wa sora no heya de neta	She slept in an empty room
Kāten ga yogorete iru	The curtains are dirty
Bunka shinbun	A cultural newspaper
Kare wa totemo tsuyoi	He is very strong

TRAINING TIME

Watashitachiha hitodesu	We are people
Daidokoro wa anzende wa arimasen	The kitchen is not safe
Watashitachiha se ga takakute tsuyoidesu	We are tall and strong

Watashi wa jūbun'na fuku o kite imasu	I have enough clothes
Kare wa sarani hidoi	He is even worse
Watashi wa fuku o kawakasu hitsuyō ga arimasu	I need to dry clothes
Kore wa kantan	This is easy
Dōzo, jūsu	Please, some juice
Kare wa totemo hayaku hanashimashita	He spoke very quickly
Watashi wa gaikoku hitode wa arimasen	I am not a foreigner
Mōfu wa hijō ni usuidesu	The blanket is very thin
Karera no hon wa maredesu	Their books are rare
Kare wa kotoba ga sukunai hitodesu	He is a person with few words
Kāten wa totemo usuidesu	The curtains are very thin
Watashi no musume wa usui supagetti ga sukidesu	My daughter likes thin spaghetti
Hijō ni sukunai hon	Very few books
Totemo hayaku nomu	We drink very quickly
Yuka ga yogorete iru	The floor is dirty
Kanojo no shanpū wa kōkadesu	Her shampoo is expensive
Muzukashikunai	We are not difficult
Kare wa sora no poketto o motte imasu	He has empty pockets
Aiteiruheya ga arimasu	We have a vacant room
Īe, kore wa kantandesu	No, this is simple
Kore wa fukanōda to omoimasu.	I think this is impossible.
Watashi wa zenkoku-shi o yomimashita.	I read a national newspaper.

TRAINING TIME

Kare wa sangyō kagaku-shadesu	He is an industrial chemist
Kore wa ippan-tekina kotode wa arimasen.	This is not a common thing.
Kuni no iro wa aka, kuro, kiirodesu.	The colors of the country are red, black and yellow
Kanojo no kitchin wa kōgyō-yōdesu	Her kitchen is industrial
Hai, sore wa totemo kantandesu	Yes, it's very simple
Karera wa totemo mazushī	They are very poor
Kanojo wa totemo sotchokudesu	She is very frank
Rekishi-tekina kikan wa nanidesu ka?	What is the historical period?
Remonēdo wa totemo shizen	Lemonade is very natural
Karera wa sekinin o oimasen	They are not responsible
Kabe wa towa-tekidesu	The wall is permanent
Watashi wa warui hitodakara	Because I am a bad person
Watashi wa mazushī	I am poor
Kore wa rekishi-tekina shūdesu	This is a historic week
Karera wa shizende wa arimasen	They are not natural
Sotchoku ni ieba	Frankly speaking
Watashitachiha sekinin o oimasen	We are not responsible
Jūsu wa shizendesu	Juice is natural
Kare wa totemo mazushī	He is very poor
Watashi wa utsukushī ahiru ga imasu	I have a beautiful duck
Karera wa yoi seitodesu	They are good students

Karera wa onaji sara o taberu	They eat the same plate
Anata wa totemo yoku yatta	You did very well
Anata wa bairingarudesu	You are bilingual
Kono doresu wa utsukushīdesu	This dress is beautiful

TRAINING TIME

Karera wa wakai hito-tachidesu	They are young people
Kanojo wa onaji kappu o motte imasu	She has the same cup
Kanojo wa toshiue no saibankandesu	She is an old judge
Yoi shitsumon	Good question
Onaji sūpu	The same soup
Ringo wa totemo īdesu	The apple is very good
Sore wa benridesu ka?	Is that useful?
Kore wa atarashī hondesu	This is a new book
Anata wa watashi yori mo sugurete imasu	You are better than me
Raito ga mie nikui	The lights are hard to see
Watashi no kyōdai	My brother
Watashi wa ane yori ōkīdesu.	I am bigger than my sister.
Īe, anata wa saishodesu	No, you are the first
Watashitachiha atarashī hitode wa arimasen	We are not new people
Saikōdesu	We have the best
Watashitachiha toshiue no keiteishimaidesu	We are older brothers and sisters
Kare wa minikuidesu ka?	Is he ugly?

Anata wa atarashī fuku ga hoshīdesu ka?	Do you want new clothes?
Hai, soreha honmonodesu	Yes, it is real
Anata wa akutibuna hitodesu	You are an active person
Watashitachiha saigo no katadesu	We are the last one
Hai, karera wa honmonodesu	Yes, they are real
Fukanōda yo	This is impossible
Hai, kore wa totemo jūyōdesu	Yes, this is very important
Kore ga saigo no shunkandesu	This is the last moment

TRAINING TIME

Anata wa honmonode wa arimasen!	You are not real!
Watashi no ani wa totemo jūyōdesu	My brother is very important
Kare wa akutibuna jōshidesu	He is an active boss
Sakuya wa totemo nagakatta.	It was very long last night.
Ashita wa watashi no saigo no hidesu	Tomorrow is my last day
Hādo	Hard
Kutsu ga hitsuyōdesu	Shoes are necessary
Kore wa kōkai tōdesu	This is a public party
Sakusha wa hitori de arukimasu	The author walks alone
Anata wa kodomo-tachi ni totemo ninki ga arimasu.	You are very popular with children.
Anata wa watashi to wa chigaimasu.	You are different from me.

Kore wa watashi no sen'yō denwadesu	This is my private phone
Kare wa hitori de arukimasu	He walks by himself
Kōshū yokujō	Public bath
Kangei sa rete imasen	We are not welcome
Īe, hitsuyō arimasen	No, they are not necessary
Purēto wa totemo katai	The plate is very hard
Karera wa kōmuindesu	They are public workers
Watashitachiha se ga takakute tsuyoidesu	We are tall and strong
Genshoku	Primary color
Kare wa yūnōna hitodesu	He is a capable person
Dōbutsu wa yunīkudesu	Animals are unique
Watashi wa jimoto no terebikyoku o mimasu.	I watch the local TV station.
Kore wa anzendesu	This is safe
Doa	Door

TRAINING TIME

Kanojo wa tsuyoi hitodesu	She is a strong person
Chigau	We are different
Kanojo wa anata no yuiitsu no shimaidesu	She is your only sister
Sore wa jūbunde wa arimasen	That is not enough
Kongo sū-shūkan	The next few weeks
Kare wa puro no haiyūdesu	He is a professional actor
Watashi no musuko	My own son
Kanojo wa watashi yori hidoi	She is worse than me
Fukanō wa nanidesu ka?	What is impossible?

Kono doresu wa totemo shinpurudesu	This dress is very simple
Watashi wa jibun no inu o katte imasu	I have my own dog
Watashitachiha puro no haiyūde wa arimasen	We are not professional actors
Karera wa karera jishin no pātī o hirakimasu	They have their own party
Kare wa warui hitodesu	He is a bad person
Watashi wa futsūdesu	I am normal
Karera wa sekinin o oimasen	They are not responsible
Watashi wa hon o amari yomimasen.	I don't read many books.

TRAINING TIME

STORY MODE

JAPANESE

Hayate wa, "kakkanteki seimei" to yoba reru gēmu o purei shimashou. Kono gēmu no mokuteki wa, `wa' to iu tango o 5-byō inai ni shiyō shite seimei o dasu ka, kono botoru kara nomu kotodesu. Hajimemasu' "kare wa byōkidesuga heya wa seiketsudesu."

Jirō: "Sono Moto wa kimyōdaga tokubetsuda"

Hayate: "Bin wa ōkīdesuga, nedan wa futsūdesu"

Jirō: "Furuidesuga, daunrōdo wa muryōdesu"

Hayate: "Kona wa koidesuga, junsuidesu"

Jirō: "Itsutsu ga saiteidesuga, watashi wa nitsu arimasu"

Hayate: "Chizu wa nite imasuga, mayotte shimaimashita"

Jirō: "Korera no kutsu wa īdesuga, orijinarude wa arimasen"

Hayate: "Korera no baggu wa kurashikkudesuga, sugurete iru wakede wa arimasen"

Jirō: "Kuruma wa yogorete imasuga, kanpekidesu"

Hayate: "Subarashīdesuga, yūmeide wa arimasen"

Jirō: "Motto muzukashī nodesuga, benridesu"

Hayate: "Watashi no kareshi wa amaidesuga, hidoidesu"

ENGLISH

"Hayate let's play a game called 'objective statements.' The goal of the game is to make a statement using the word 'but' in five seconds, or drink from this bottle. I will start."

"He's sick, but the room is clean."

Jiro: "The book is strange but special."

Hayate: "The bottle is big, but the price is regular."

Jiro: "It's old, but it's free to download."

Hayate: "The powder is dark, but pure."

Jiro: "Five is the minimum, but I have four."

Hayate: "The maps are similar, but I'm lost."

Jiro: "These shoes are good but not original."

Hayate: "These bags are classic, but not superior."

Jiro: "The car is dirty, but it's perfect."

Hayate: "It's brilliant, but not famous."

Jiro: "It's more difficult, but convenient."

Hayate: "My boyfriend is sweet but also terrible."

Chapter 16

DETERMINERS

Keywords : Kakujitsu, subete, ta, sorezoredesu.

Atarashī	New
Shigoto	Jobs
Akutibiti	The activity
Kanōsei	The possibility
Kanojo wa neko ga ō sugiru	She has too many cats
Subete no josei ga koko ni imasu	All the women are here
Hachi wa chōde wanai	The bee is not a butterfly
Kono moto wa taka sugiru	This book is too expensive
Kono ocha wa oishīdesu	This tea is delicious
Akai kagami ga arimasu	We have a red mirror
Korera no baggu wa akadesu	These bags are red
Kono ninjin wa totemo amai	This carrot is very sweet
Korera no hon wa atarashīdesu	These books are new
Kono kuruma wa shinsha no yōdesu	This car is like a new car
Korera futatsu no haikan kō wa itokodesu	These two plumbers are cousins
Ano hito wa watashi no ottode wanai	That person is not my husband
Kanojo wa ano kuruma ni wa mukanai	She is not suitable for that car
Shiro wa shirodesu	The castle is white

Anata wa sono hoteru o shitte imasu ka?	Do you know that hotel?
Watashi wa sorera no josei o shitte imasu	I know those women
Mura zentai de chōri suru	Cooking in the entire village
Kanojo wa hitobanjū hatarakimasu	She works all night
Watashi wa takusan no abura o motte imasu	I have a lot of oil
Boku ni wa tomodachi ga inai	I do not have friends
Koko ni wa takusan no hito ga imasu.	There are many people here.

TRAINING TIME

Anata wa sorera no toshi o oboete imasu ka?	Do you remember those years?
Kare wa maiasa gyūnyū o ichi-pon nomimasu.	He drinks a bottle of milk every morning.
Watashi wa ikutsu ka no shinbun o yomimashita.	I have read several newspapers.
Watashi wa sorera no denwa ga sukide wa arimasen.	I don't like those phones.
Ano shatsu wa kare ni wa chīsa sugiru.	Those shirts are too small for him.
Heya ni wa ikutsu ka no shatsu ga arimasu.	There are a few shirts in the room.
Kōen ni wa nan'ninka no otokonoko ga imasu.	There are several boys in the park.
Mainichi, subete no josei ga denwa o kakemasu	Every day, every woman calls

Dōbu~tsuen ni wa iroirona shurui no dōbutsu ga imasu.	There are all kinds of animals in the zoo.
Watashi wa kekkonshiki no pātī o shitaku arimasen.	I don't want to have a party for my wedding.
U~eitā wa betsu no bā de hataraku	The waiter works in another bar
Ikutsu ka no koto wa jikan to tomoni henka shimasu	Some things change over time
Kare no yō ni hatarakanai hito mo imasu	Some people don't work like him
Anata wa ikutsu ka no yoi mise o shitte imasu ka?	Do you know some good stores?
Watashi wa nan'ninka no hitobito to issho ni hatarakimasen.	I don't work with some people.
Amarini mo ōku no koto ga meikakude wa arimasen	Too many things are not clear
Kare wa wain o nomi sugita	He drank too much wine
Kare wa bīru o nomi sugita	He drank too much beer
Yasai o tabenai hito mo imasu	Some people don't eat vegetables
Takusan no koto o shitte imasu	We know a lot of things
Kōen ni wa takusan no hito ga imasu.	There are too many people in the park.
Nan'ninka no josei wa yori utsukushīdesu	Some women are more beautiful
Watashitachiha dōbu~tsuen de subete no dōbutsu o mimashita.	We saw all the animals at the zoo.

Watashitachi wa nan hyakuman mo no	We have millions
Kazoku zen'in ga nōjō de hataraite imasu	The entire family works on the farm
Don'na yasai mo hoshī	I want any kind of vegetables
Dono seki ni demo chakuseki dekimasu	Any seat can be taken
Gozonji no tōri, watashi wa kazoku ga imasen.	You know, I don't have any family.
Karera ni wa mōhitori no musuko ga imasu	They have another son
Watashi wa kare to watashinokazoku ga daisukidesu.	I love him and my family.
Ocha o mō ichi-pai nomitaidesu ka?	Do you want another cup of tea?
Korera no ringo wa totemo ōkīdesu	These apples are very big
Ryokucha o nomu josei mo imasu	Some women drink green tea
Naze karera wa anata o mite iru nodesu ka?	Why are those men looking at you?
Watashi wa sono kuroi kata ga sukidesu.	I prefer that black one.
Korera no megane wa daredesu ka?	Whose glasses are these?
Kanojo wa kareshi ga ō sugiru	She has too many boyfriends
Watashi wa betsu no musume ga imasuga, kanojo wa motto ōkīdesu	I have another daughter, but she is bigger
Mō ichi-pon bīru ga hoshī	I want another beer

TRAINING TIME

STORY MODE

JAPANESE

Hachirō: "Kono-ka ni wa ikutsu no mado ga arimasu ka. Daremoga hachi-sai to itte imasuga, watashi wa dōi shimasen."
Shen: "Watashi no yokushitsu ni wa mado ga nainode, nanatsu arimasu."
Hachirō: "Soshite, Barenshia no iedesu ka? Ikura?"
Shen: "Shi"
Hachirō: "Shi? Heya no hiro-sa o kangaeru to, kanki ga hitsuyōdesu."
Shen: "Mado no nakaniha kōkana mono ga ari, nana-ko ijō kōnyū suru no wa muzukashīdesu."
Hachirō: "Anata ga anata jishin no geitaidenwa o motte irunaraba, anata wa watashi no u~ebusaito de ikutsu ka no shashin o chekku surubekidesu. Kaku shashin no kakaku wa nanajuu doru ikadesu. Akusesu dekiru to omoimasushi, hinshitsu wa hoka no burando to onajidesu."
* Onrain kensaku*

Shen: "Mado wa, tokuni hidariue sumi ni aru 2tsu ga kireidesu. Watashi wa korera futatsu ga sukidesu."
Hachirō: "Anata ga sore o suki ni naru koto o watashi wa shitte iru, watashi wa anata ga kongetsu watashi no saisho no kokyaku ni naru koto o negatte irunode. Anata ga sore o yoyūgārunaraba, watashi wa 5-pāsento no waribiki o teikyō suru koto ga dekimasu."

ENGLISH

Hachiro: "How many windows are there in this house? Everyone says eight, but I don't agree."

Shen: "My bathroom has no windows, so there are seven."

Hachiro: "And the house in Valencia? How much?"

Shen: "Four."

Hachiro: "Four? Considering the size of the room, you need a lot of ventilation."

Shen: "Some windows are expensive, and it is difficult to buy more than 7."

Hachiro: "If you have your own mobile phone, you should check some pictures on my website. The price of each picture is less than $70. I think they can be accessed, and the quality is the same as other brands."

searches online

Shen: "The windows are beautiful, especially the two in the upper left corner. I like these two."

Hachiro: "I know you will like it, because I hope that you can be my first customer this month. If you can afford it, I can offer a 5% discount."

Chapter 17

ADVERBS

Keywords : Dai, ko, -jō, -ka.

Hai	Okay
Hotondo	Almost
Kare wa takusan no koto o tabeta	He ate a lot of things
Anata wa totemo kyōryokudesu	You are so powerful
Karera wa doko shusshindesu ka?	Where are they from?
Kore wa totemo takai	This is very expensive
Watashi wa kare ga dokokarakitano ka shitte iru	I know where he is from
Anata wa nimotsu o ikutsu motte imasu ka?	How many bags do you have?
Shusshindesu ka?	Are you from there?
Amari takakunai	It is not very expensive
Watashi wa konshū takusan hatarakimasu.	I work a lot this week.
Karera wa soko ni sunde imasu	They live there
Watashitachi wa kare ni tsuite hotondo shiranai.	We know very little about him.
Kumo wa chīzu no shita ni arimasu	The spider is under the cheese
Kono tori wa dōbu~tsuen no uedesu	This bird is above the zoo
Watashitachiha resutoran no soto ni imasu	We are outside the restaurant
Ju-nen ijō	More than ten years
Watashi wa soto de matteimasu	I am waiting outside

Harugakuru	Spring is coming
Karera wa kanojo to issho ni ikimashita	They went in with her
Kanojo wa mawari o mimawashite imasu	She looks around
Watashi wa yūshoku-go ni dekakemasu.	I go out after dinner.
Sorekara josei wa koko ni imasu.	Then the women are here.

TRAINING TIME

Watashi mo	Me too
Hoshī toki ni taberu	I eat when I want
Doyōbi wa nichiyōbi no mae ni kuru	Saturday comes before Sunday
Narubeku taberu	You eat as much as possible
Yūbin haitatsu no apāto wa kochira	The postman's apartment is here
Ryōshin ni yoku tegami o kakimasu ka.	Do you often write letters to your parents?
Fuyu ga sugiru to harugakuru	Spring is coming after winter
Anata no imōto wa aikawarazu utsukushī	Your sister is as beautiful as ever
Watashinohaha wa yoi	My mother is better
Daijōbu arigatō	Okay thank you
Hontōni mōshiwakearimasen	Really sorry
Arigatō, karera wa totemo yoidesu	Thank you, they are very good
Watashi no ani wa kesshite nomanai	My brother never drinks
Watashi wa totemo yoi	I'm very good
Sukinabasho ni idō	Go anywhere you want
Ama suginai	Not too sweet

Karera mo koko ni iru no?	Are they here too?
Hobo shōgo	Almost noon
Anata wa hitoridesu ka?	Are you alone?
Tabe suginai	I don't eat too much
Watashi wa mōsugu koko ni imasu.	I am here soon.
Watashi wa wakarimasen	I am not sure
Karera wa mata koko ni sunde imasu	They also live here
Akiraka ni, kudamono wa totemo amaidesu	Obviously, the fruit is very sweet
Dewa, naze karera wa koko ni iru nodesu ka?	Then why are they here?

TRAINING TIME

Haikan kō wa mada arimasu ka?	Is the plumber still there?
Kore wa zettai ni fukanōdesu	This is absolutely impossible
Kare wa mada koko ni imasu	He is still here
Kanzen ni midoridesu	It is completely green
Taimurīna	Timely
Kono uma wa mada totemo wakai	This horse is still very young
Doko demo kon'na kanjidesu	Everywhere is like this
Mō roku gatsudesu	We are already in June
Kodomo wa imasu ka?	Do you have children?
Kore wa totemo omoshiroidesu	This is very interesting
Shikashi, hidzuke wa sadakade wa arimasen	But the date is not certain

Sukunakutomo karera wa shokutaku de shokuji o shite iru	At least they are eating at the table
Watashi wa niku o tabemasenga sakana o tabemasu.	I don't eat meat, but I eat fish.
Izure ni seyo, kore wa jūyōde wa arimasen	In any case, this is not important
Mō kin'yōbi?	Already Friday?
Neko o katte	Have a cat
Anata wa anata no okāsan no yōdesu	You are like your mother
Watashitachiha ima shuppatsu shite imasu	We are leaving now
Dōshite watashitachiha fōku sae motte inai nodesu ka?	Why don't we even have a fork?
Watashi wa maitoshi hon o kakimasu.	I write a book every year.
Issho ni ikou?	Let's go together?
Tēburu no ue ni ringo ga arimasu	There is an apple on the table
Sore wa tada no mausudesu	It's just a mouse
Watashi wa omoni sorera ni tsuite hanashimasu.	I mainly talk about them.
Kyō wa kitto	Today, I am sure

TRAINING TIME

Hijō ni tōku	Very far
Tsūjō	Usually
Īe, madadesu	No, not yet
Saigo ni	Finally
Jā matane	See you later
Sayōnara	Goodbye
Mochiron, sore wa hontōni karedesu.	Of course, it is really him.
Kakushin shitemasu	I am sure

Shi gatsu wanaku sangatsu	Maybe March, but not April
Tabun sore wa chokorētochippukukkīdesu	Maybe it's chocolate chip cookies
Tabun kanojo wa yūshoku o tsukurudarou	Maybe she will cook dinner
Tabun kore wa hontōdesu	Maybe this is true
Kanojo wa soko ni iru	She is there
Ippantekini wa shiro	Generally, it is white
Anata wa watashitachi no tame ni gutaitekini kakimasu	You write for us specifically
Saigo ni, kin'yōbidesu.	Finally, it is Friday.
Anata wa takusan nemashita ka?	Have you slept a lot?
Anata wa totemo utsukushīdesu	You are very beautiful
Watashi no imōto wa kesshite nomimasen	My sister never drinks
Kore wa kanzen ni seijōdesu	This is completely normal
Watashi wa issoku dake kutsu ga arimasu	I only have a pair of shoes
Kanojo wa arukimawatte imasu	She is walking around
Kare wa totemo yoku hanashimashita	He spoke very well
Watashi no ani wa kesshite nomanai	My brother never drinks
Kore wa zenzen chigaimasu!	This is totally different!

TRAINING TIME

Kanzen ni	Completely
Machigainaku	Undoubtedly
Sonotōri!	Exactly!
Watashi wa oyogimasen	I never swim
Anata wa hontōni ī hitodesu.	You are really a good person.
Hai, sugu ni ikimasu	Yes, I will go immediately
Ō sugiru kamo	Maybe this is too much
Mata sayōnara	Again, goodbye
Kare wa kyō tsuita no kamo shirenai.	He may have arrived today.
Tēburu no shita ni	Under the table
Susumu	We move on
Anata wa hotondo watashi no kyōdaidesu	You are almost my brother
Mōichido, arigatō, isha	Again, thank you, doctor
Tabun kore wa kanōdesu	Maybe this is possible
Watashi no neko wa sofa no shita de nete imasu	My cat is sleeping under the sofa
Buta wa tēburu no shita ni arimasu	The pig is under the table
Karera wa hitoshiku sekinin ga arimasu	They are equally responsible
Karera wa sugu ni tōchaku shimasu	They arrive right away
Kare wa pasuta o taberu dake	He only eats pasta
Kore wa mattaku kanōdesu	This is entirely possible
Kanojo wa omoni satō o tabemasu	She mainly eats sugar
Kare wa mōhitori no hitodesu	He is another person

Hai, saikin	Yes, recently
Kanzen ni midoridesu	It is completely green
Kanojo wa kudamono o taberu dake	She only eats fruit

TRAINING TIME

Watashitachi wa koko ni iru	We are here
Omoni satōdesu	It is mainly sugar
Anata wa kanzen ni yūnōdesu	You are fully capable
Saikin hanashimashita	We have talked recently
Wakai, nachuraru	Young, natural
Totemo hayaku nomu	We drink very quickly
Kore wa watashi no zō ni chigainai	This must be my elephant
Uma wa totemo hayakuhashiru	A horse runs very fast
Seikaku ni wa nanidesu ka?	What exactly are they?
Watashi wa zettai ni kakushin shite imasu	I am absolutely sure
Hai, anata wa machigainaku sugurete imasu.	Yes, you are definitely better.
Jūsu, mochiron	Juice, of course
Suiyōbi, tsūjō	Wednesday, usually
Kare wa totemo yukkuri aruku	He walks very slowly
Fuyō	Unnecessary
Kanojo wa yomi yasuidesu	She is easy to read
Motto warui kamo	May be worse
Kare no musuko wa karōjite hanasu	His son barely speaks

Kore wa hikakuteki atarashīdesu	This is relatively new
Kare wa yukkuri tabemasu	He eats slowly
Tsūjō, nan'nen mo kakarimasu	Usually, it takes years
Senshū	The past week
Reizōko wa totemo yasuidesu	The refrigerator is very cheap
Anata wa otokonoko janai	You're hardly a boy
Kanarazushimo hitode wanai	It is not necessarily a person

TRAINING TIME

STORY MODE

JAPANESE

Saigo ni, kin'yōbi ni kurabu ni kimasu ka?' Emiko wa itta. `Osoraku.' Shen wa kotaemashita. `Iri tte ikanakereba, anata wa sore o nogasudeshou. Nomimono ya yūmeijin ga irudeshou.' `Sore wa subete watashi no imōto shidaidesu. Kanojo ga sarunaraba, watashi wa sarudeshou. Sono zen ni, watashi wa mada kimete imasen.' Shen wa kotaemashita. `Anata wa ima kimenakereba narimasen. Emiko-san wa tsudzukemashita. " Watashi wa mada chūcho shite imasu." Shen wa itta. `Yōyaku ki ga kawatta baai wa, oso sugiru kamo shiremasen. Okiniiri no ātisuto ni au kikai wa mōnidoto arimasen' to Emiko wa iimasu.

ENGLISH

"Finally, will you come to the club on Friday?" said Emiko.
"Possibly." Shen replied.

"If you don't go in, you will miss it. There will be drinks and celebrities."

"It all depends on my sister. If she leaves, I will leave. Before that, I have not decided yet." Shen replied.

"You have to decide now; the VIP part is one of the best parts of the world." Emiko continued.

"I am still hesitating." Shen said.

"If you finally change your mind, it may be too late, and you will never have the chance to see your favorite artist again." said Emiko.

Chapter 18
OBJECTS

Keywords : Kuruma, kikai, bokkusu, kushi, hoīru, bōru.

Mōtā	Motor
Pen	Pen
Chizu	Map
Botoru	Bottle
Konpyūtā	Computer
Ressha	Train
Jitensha	Bicycle
Tama	Ball
Kī	Key
Kuruma	A car
Sono kake-ra	The piece
Musen	Radio
Ano hikōki	That plane
Kamera	Camera
Denchi	Battery
Bakku pakku	Backpack
Hasami	Scissors
Kādo	Card
Kono fune	This ship
Ashi	Foot
Takusan no mono ga hoshī	I want a lot of things
Kore wa furui kotodesu	This is an old thing
Watashi wa kuruma ga arimasu	I have a car
Biggu koin	Big coin
Watashi no geitaidenwa	My cell phone

TRAINING TIME

Kī	The key
Okane	Money
Zasshi	The magazine
Shinbun	Newspaper
Beru	The bell
Kappu	Cup
Maindo	Mind
Hashi	The bridge
Gōrudo	Gold
Kusari	Chain
Kami	Paper
Doru	The dollar
Korera no koto	These things
Firumu	The film
Dokyumento	The document
Geitaidenwa	Mobile phone
Gamen	Screen
Anata wa nikki o tsukemasu ka?	Do you keep a diary?
Anata wa mada burashi o motte imasu ka?	Do you still have a brush?
Nikki mo arimasu.	I also have a diary.
Karera wa konpyūta o motte imasu ka?	Do they have a computer?
On'nanoko no kushi	The girl's comb
Watashi wa sudeni fūtō o motte imasu	I already have an envelope
Hako wa tēburu no ue ni oka remasu	The box is placed on the table
Watashitachiha kukkī no hako o motte imasu	We have a box of cookies

TRAINING TIME

Koin	Coin
Hata	Flag
Biru	Bill
Kuruma	Car
Hoīru	Wheel
Ude	Arms
Migakimasu	Brush
Enberōpu	Envelope
Kushi	Comb
Nikki	Diary
Shashin	Photo
Buki	The arms
Gazō	The image
Ha	Leaf
Kare wa ikutsu ka no akai megane ga hoshī	He wants some red glasses
Natsu ni wa atarashī fan ga imasu.	We have new fans in the summer.
Kare wa kenkōda	He is in good health
Watashi wa kanpekina okurimono o shite imasu	I have the perfect gift
Kore wa chīsana sakuhindesu	This is a small piece
Watashi wa kībōdo o mimashita	I saw a keyboard
Kyō, watashi wa raisensu o emashita.	Today, I got the license.
Purezento ga hoshī	I want a gift
Raisensu ga mitsukarimasen.	I can't find my license.
Watashinochichi wa furūto to baiorin o motte imasu.	My father has a flute and a violin.
Kanojo wa itsumo onaji koto o itta	She always said the same thing

TRAINING TIME

Enjin	Engine
Arukōru	Alcohol
Handobaggu	Handbag
Watashitachi no bin	Our bottle
Hashikko	The edge
Kin wa watashi no monodesu!	The gold is mine!
Watashi wa shiroi kami ni kaite imasu	I am writing on white paper
Watashi wa sharin to enjin o motte imasu	I have a wheel and an engine
Anata wa jūyōna koto o suru jikan ga nai	You never have time to do important things
Kore wa hakushidesu.	This is a blank sheet of paper
Kuruma wa oiru-giredesu	The car is out of oil
Watashi wa jibun no kuruma no tame ni batterī o kaitaidesu.	I want to buy a battery for my car.
Dare ga kono gakki o motte imasu ka?	Who has this instrument?
Kono fune wa totemo furuidesu	This ship is very old
Watashi no itoko no kuruma wa totemo atarashīdesu.	My cousin's car is very new.
Watashitachiha-sha o motte imasu	We have a car
Senchō wa fune ni tsuite hanashite imasu.	The captain is talking about the ship.
Kore wa watashi no kurumadesu	This is my car
Watashi wa kōdo o motte iru	I have a code

Anata wa kikaidesu ka?	Are you a machine?
Kore wa koramudesu	This is a column
Ima shinbun o yomimasu	We read the newspaper now
Kare wa itsumo zasshi o yomimasu	He always reads a magazine
Kono on'nanoko wa takusan no pēji o kaita	This girl wrote a lot of pages
Kanojo wa reizōko no ichibu ga hitsuyōdesu	She needs a part of the refrigerator

TRAINING TIME

Batterī	The battery
Kanojo wa chēn-ten o motte imasu	She has a chain store
Kanojo wa ittsui no aoimoku o shite iru	She has a pair of blue eyes
Shinbun o yomimasu	We read the newspaper
Bōru no naka no buttai wa nanidesu ka?	What is the object in the bowl?
Kanojo no fuku wa yunīkudesu	Her clothes are unique
Kore wa itsumo yoi kotodesu	This is always a good thing
Kare wa sukoshi okane ga aru	He has a little money
Kanojo wa kami o motte imasu ka?	Does she have paper?
Bōru ga arimasu	I have a ball
Watashi wa kuruma ga arimasu	I have a car
Julio wa kare no ashi ni batā o okimasu	Julio puts butter on his feet
Watashi no sūtsukēsu wa kiirodesu	My suitcase is yellow
Tekisuto ga arimasu	I have text
Terebi ga takai	TV is expensive

Tokei wa taishōdesu	The watch is an object
Kare wa gogo ni nomimasu	He drinks in the afternoon
Kare wa dansei ni okane o watashimashita	He gave the money to the men
Neko wa inu no ue de nemasu	The cat sleeps on the top of the dog
Kare wa kōkana mono o tsukurimasu	He produces expensive items
Karera wa doru o haratta	They paid a dollar
Doggufūdo wa kōkadesu	Dog food is expensive
Keitai arimasu ka?	Do you have a cell phone?
Watashi no ane no sūtsukēsu wa totemo ōkīdesu.	My sister's suitcase is very big.
Anata wa koin o motte imasu ka?	Do you have a coin?

TRAINING TIME

Shashin	Photo
Gamen	Screen
Me	Eye
Atama	Head
Hata	Flag
Sōsu	Source
Enjin	Engine
Ude	Arms
Hoīru	Wheel
Paudā	Powder
Kikai	Machine
Danpen	Fragment
Bokkusu	Box
Botoru	Bottle
Denchi ga hitsuyōdesu	I need a battery

Watashi wa sono koto ga sukide wa arimasen.	I don't like that thing.
Bengoshi ga ronbun o happyō shimashita	The lawyer published a paper
Dare ga fairu o motte imasu ka?	Who has the file?
Hoka ni dare ga notte imasu ka?	Who else is on board?
Kamera o motte imasu ka?	Do you have a camera?
Watashi no bōto wa aoi	My boat is blue
Anata wa udedokei o motte imasu ka?	Do you have a watch?
Shinbun wa saikin no monodesu	The newspaper is recent
Kono fairuni wa ōku no pēji ga arimasu	This file has many pages
Watashi wa chīzusandoitchi to koppuippai no mizu ga hoshīdesu.	I want a cheese sandwich and a glass of water.

TRAINING TIME

Heiwa	Peace
Bumon	Department
Idō	Movement
Kono chōsa	This survey
Yōryō	Capacity
Hitsuyō-sei	Necessity
Kōka	Effect
Kōdo	Code
Kādo de shiharaimasu	I pay by card
Kore wa okane no minamotodesu	This is the source of money
Pen wa arimasu ka?	Do you have a pen?
Kore wa berudesu	This is the bell

Rājiobujekuto	A large object
Tokei janai	It is not a clock
Watashi wa eigo no zasshi ga hitsuyōdesu.	I need an English magazine.
Watashi-mono	Personal items
Kore wa dorudesu	This is the dollar
Kore wa watashi no kurumadesu	This is my car
Kare wa basu de shigoto ni ikimasu ka?	Does he go to work by bus?
Jitensha ga arimasu	We have bicycles
Taisa wa bakudan o motte imasu	The colonel has a bomb
Pen o motte imasu	I have a pen
Ōgata disupurei	Large display
Kore wa memo ga haitta bindesu	This is a bottle with notes
Bīru wa nōmin no tame no monodesu	Beer is for farmers

TRAINING TIME

Buki	The arms
Sebone	The spine
Anata wa kikaidesu ka?	Are you a machine?
Kanojo wa kisoku ni shitagau	She obeys the rules
Kanojo wa totemo kashikoi	She is very smart
Sakusha wa mōtā o yomimashita	The author has read the motor
Kore wa warui kotodesu	This is a bad thing
Sharin wa shirodesu	The wheels are white
Bakudan wa hidoi	The bomb is terrible

Kare wa kuruma o motte iru	He has a car
Dono kutsu ga anata ni pittaridesu ka?	Which shoe is right for you?
Kanojo wa anata ni shinbun o miseta	She showed you a newspaper
Watashi wa atode anata ni au yō ni narudeshou.	I will come to see you later.
Kare wa watashi o forō shimashita	He followed me
Watashi wa anata ga hoshīdesu	I want you
Anata wa ringo o tabemashita	You ate an apple
Korera no kutsu wa watashi no tamede wa arimasen.	These shoes are not for me.
Anata wa watashi ni shitagaimasu	You follow me
Kare wa anata o mite iru	He looks at you
Orenji o tabemashita	We ate an orange
Anata wa karera to hanasu	You talk to them
Karera wa kashikoidesu ne.	They are smart, aren't they?
Watashi no kutsu wa kōkadesu	My shoes are expensive
Kanojo wa watashitachi o hinan suru	She blames us
Ranpu wa kōkadesu	The lamp is expensive

TRAINING TIME

STORY MODE

JAPANESE

Masahiko: Kyō wa bōdo-jō no shashin kara mono ni tsuite manabu koto ni shimasu. Hidari kara migi ni, anata wa sorezore bōdo-jō no 7tsu no obujekuto ni namae o tsukete, sorera no tsukaikata o hanashiaimasu. Zeng! Anata kara hajimemashou. Hajimete kudasai."

Zeng: "Appuru, bōru, batterī, jitensha, tokei, botoru, bako"

Rikuto: "Karendā, kamera, geitaidenwa, tokei, konpyūtā, magukappu"

Kim: "Doru, hata, kagi, chizu, pen."

Li: "Gazō, rajio, hasami, bōto, sūtsukēsu, densha, sharin."

ENGLISH

Masahiko: "Today we will learn about objects from the pictures on the board. From left to right, each of you will name seven objects on the board and discuss their use.

Zeng! Let's start with you. Please start."

Zeng: "Apple, ball, battery, bicycle, clock, bottle, box."

Rikuto: "Calendar, camera, car, mobile phone, clock, computer, mug."

Kim: "Dollars, flags, houses, keys, maps, paper, pens."

Li: "Image, radio, scissors, boat, suitcase, train, wheels."

Chapter 19

PLACES

Keywords : Ken, shoten, gekijō, seika, kyūden,-bashi,-kaku, kōen, sūpāmāketto, basho, keimusho.

Hoteru	Hotel
Resutoran	Restaurant
Kazoku	Family
Gakkō	School
To shōkan	Library
Kūkō	The airport
Yama	The mountain
U~ebusaito	Website
Hashi	The bridge
Kōnā	Corner
Sentā	Center
Fīrudo	Field
Banku	Bank
Kyōkai	Church
Shiro	Castle
Ichiba	Market
Hiroba	The square
Kono chiiki	This area
Gekijō	Theater
Bā	The bar
Nakaniwa	Courtyard
Eria	The area
Ofisu	The office
Tatemono	The building

TRAINING TIME

Keimusho	Prison
Pāku	Park
Hakubutsukan	Museum
Chīsai shima	Small island
Teien	Garden
Jichitai	Municipality
Abenyū	Avenue
Raunji	Lounge
Rejidensu	Residence
Kōhī	Coffee
Chīsana machi	Small town
Dōro	Road
Bīchi	Beach
Shihon	Capital
Saibansho	Court
Watashi wa shiro o mimashita	I saw the castle
Watashitachi wa onaji hoteru ni imasu ka?	Are we at the same hotel?
Dare ga hon'ya ni haitta no?	Who entered the bookstore?
Watashitachi no pan'yasan wa chīsaidesu	Our bakery is small
Tatemono wa kyodaidesu	The building is huge
Kanojo wa pan-ya kara pan o kau	She buys bread from the bakery
Hon'ya-san wa dokodesu ka?	Where is the bookstore?
Dono hon'ya ga kare no hon o utte imasu ka?	Which bookstore sells his book?
Atarashī tatemono wa totemo ōkī	The new building is very large
Yane kara watashitachiha-jō o mimashita	From the roof we saw the castle

TRAINING TIME

Watashinochichi wa bā o motte imasu	My father has a bar
Kore wa Yamanomachidesu	This is a mountain city
Kono kazoku wa hata de hataraite imasu	This family works in the fields
Yūgata, watashitachiha sumi no bā ni ikimashita	In the evening, we went to the bar at the corner
Watashi wa machi o totemo yoku shitte imasu	I know the city very well
Kanojo wa hata de hashitte iru	She is running in the field
Kitchin wa ie no chūō ni arimasu	The kitchen is in the center of the house
Hiroi chiiki ni sunde iru	We live in a large area
Watashi no ibasho wa dokodesu ka?	Where is my location?
Kōen no iriguchi ga miemasu ka.	Do you see the entrance to the park?
Doko ni ikitaidesu ka?	Which place do you want?
Watashi wa anata no tokoro ni ikimashita	I went to your place
Karera wa sutajiamu ni imasu	They are at the stadium
Zen'iki	The entire area
Kokusai shakai no namae wa nanidesu ka?	What is the name of the international community?
Atarashī sūpāmāketto wa kochira	The new supermarket is here
Ashita, watashi wa mura ni ikimasu	Tomorrow, I am going to the village
Gekijō wa totemo ōkīdesu	The theater is very big

Dono tōri ga machi ni tsūjite imasu ka?	Which street leads to the city?
Korera no machi wa chigaimasu	These towns are different
Watashi wa tōri ni ikimasu	I am going to a street
Eki kara tsukimashita	We arrived from the station
Kare wa mise de hataraite imasu	He works in a store

TRAINING TIME

Hiroba	The square
Shinshitsu	Bedroom
Minato	Port
Chīsai shima	Small island
Kinjo no	Nearby
Ken	The province
Tawā	Tower
Kazoku	Family
Dōro	Road
Toshokan	The library
Sutajiamu	Stadium
Tōri	Street
Gekijō	Theater
Eki	Station
Shiti	City
Watashitachiha rinjin no yama ni sunde imasu	We live in the mountains of the neighbors
Kare wa furui ressha shiki-sha no seifuku o kite	He has an old train conductor uniform
Kon'ya kyūden o mimashita	We saw the palace tonight
Rinjin no josei wa totemo kireidesu	The neighboring women are very beautiful

Kyō, watashitachiha kyūden de tabete imasu	Today, we are eating in the palace
Watashinoie no chikaku no pātī	Party near my home
Kare wa jūyōna kyūden ni sunde imasu	He lives in an important palace
Kyōkai no machidesu	It is the city of the church
Jirō wa resutoran de taberu	Jiro eats at the restaurant
Kare wa tochi ga hoshī	He wants land

TRAINING TIME

Koronī	Colony
Gyararī	Gallery
Hondo	The mainland
Kare wa sono shisetsu o hōmon shita	He visited the institution
Kore wa watashi no chiikidesu	This is my area
Watashi no resutoran e yōkoso	Welcome to my restaurant
Hoteru e yōkoso	Welcome to the hotel
Jo wa bīchi no ue o aruku	Jo walks on the beach
Nobuyuki wa niwa ni imasu niwa	Nobuyuki is in the yard
Jirō wa niwa ni imasu	Jiro in the garden
Tiananmen hiroba e no densha wa dokodesu ka?	Where is the train to Tiananmen Square?
Watashi wa arayuru kuni ni ie o motte imasu	I have a house in every country
Kono basho wa totemo ōkī yōdesu	This place seems very big
Kore wa kare no chiikidesu	This is his area

Watashi wa kono machi ni imasu	I am in this city
Watashinoie ni wa yane ga arimasen	My house has no roof
Ichi wa yokunai	The city is not good
Korera no basho wa chīsaidesu	These places are small
Subarashī tatemono	Great building
Nobuyuki wa kōen de asobu	Nobuyuki plays in the park
Hakubutsukan wa dokodesu ka?	Where is the museum?
Kore wa jūyōna hōhōdesu	This is an important way
Afurika wa kunide wa arimasen	Africa is not a country
Hiroba o aruita	We walked on the square
Hiroba wa totemo utsukushī	The square is very beautiful

TRAINING TIME

Kuni	Country
Korera no chiiki	These areas
Chikei	Terrain
Watashi no oji wa Itaria ni ie o motte imasu.	My uncle has a house in Italy.
Komyuniti wa eigo o hanashimasu	The community speaks English
Kanojo wa daigaku ni ikimashita	She went to college
Kanojo wa ginkō ni tsuite yoku shitte iru	She knows a lot about the bank
Korera no bun'ya ni tsuite hanashimashita	We talked about these areas
Watashitachi wa kyodaina komyunitidesu	We are a huge community

Watashitachiha-dō no waki o aruite imasu	We are walking on the side of the road
Ginkō wa shirodesu	The bank is white
Kore wa totemo yoi byōindesu	This is a very good hospital
Kaigan de	On the coast
Kore wa jūyōna minatodesu	This is an important port
Watashi no imōto wa kenkyūjo ni ikimashita	My sister went to the institute
Kokunai de saikō no kikandesu	It is the best institution in the country
Totemo hirobiro to shita oheyadesu.	These rooms are very spacious
Korera no kikan wa watashitachi ni tayotte imasu	These institutions rely on us
Kore wa ōkina ryōdodesu	This is a big territory
Anata no ie wa kyūdendesu	Your house is a palace

TRAINING TIME

STORY MODE

JAPANESE

Angelo: "Ienikaeru mae ni, rirakkusu suru tame no atarashī basho ga hitsuyōdesu. Nanika teian wa arimasu ka?"

Nobuyuki: "Kore wa mondaide wa arimasen. Shinai ni wa takusan no basho ga ari, sonōchi no ikutsu ka wa bijutsukan, bijutsukan, shūritsu toshokan, shoppingusentā, soshite ōku no bā to resutoran o fukumimasu. Anata ga shizen ga sukinara, anata wa kokuritsu kōen ni iku koto ga dekimasu."

Angelo: "Sore wa doko?"

Nobuyuki: "Dai roku chiku no ryōri gakkō to kūkō no sugu sobadesu. Daigaku no mon to byōin no tatemono kara nishi e sū burokku."

Angelo: "Watashinoie no chikaku ni wa basho ga hitsuyōdesu. Kono kyori wa watashiniha tō sugimasu."

Nobuyuki: "Matawa, Tokugawa shiro o hōmon suru koto ga dekimasu. Jimusho kara sorehodo tōkunai shizukana basho, aruiwa tokugawa ke ga shoyū suru Tokugawa rizōto-nai ni arimasu. Mata, bā to chīsana puraibētobīchi mo arimasu."

Angelo: "Dō yatte soko ni tsuku nodesu ka?"

Nobuyuki: "Soreha toshi kaihatsu kenkyūjo no ushiro no ni-banme no tōridearu Shinjuku-eki no chikakudesu."

ENGLISH

Angelo: "Before I go home, I need a new place to relax. Do you have any suggestions?"

Nobuyuki: "This is not a problem. There are many places in the city, some of which include museums, art galleries, state libraries, shopping centers and many bars and restaurants. If you like nature, you can go to the national park."

Angelo: "Where is it?"

Nobuyuki: "It's just around the cooking school and airport in the sixth district. A few blocks west of the university gate and hospital building."

Angelo: "I need a place close to my home. This distance is too far for me."

Nobuyuki: "Or, you can visit Tokugawa Castle. It is in a quiet area not far from the office, or even the Tokugawa Resort owned by the Tokugawa family. It also has a bar and a small private beach."

Angelo: "How do I get there?"

Nobuyuki: "It is close to Shinjuku Station, the second street behind the Urban Development Institute."

Chapter 20

PEOPLE

Keywords : Otona, kodomo, ningen, hito.

Hito	People
Kono josei	This lady
Joō	Queen
Shimin	The citizen
Rinjin	Neighbor
Soboku	Naive
Gisei-sha	Victim
Shūjin	Prisoner
Kojin-tekina	Personal
Dōryō	Colleague
Watashitachiha tomodachi no gurūpu ga arimasu	We have a group of friends
Watashitachiha otona to kodomo ni nani o ataemasu ka?	What do we give to adults and children?
Watashi wa fianse ga daisuki	I love my fiance
Karera wa onaji nenreidesu	They are the same age
Watashi no kodomo-tachi wa ie de totemo segatakaidesu	My children are very tall at home
Gunshū wa kotae o matsu	The crowd waits for the answer
Watashitachiha kojindesu	We are individuals
Anata wa ima otonadesu	You are an adult now
Tsugi no kōhī wa anata no monodesu	The next cup of coffee is yours
Watashi wa gesutode wa arimasen	I am not a guest

Kare wa watashi no pātonādesu	He is my partner
Keisatsu wa kiken'na hito o sagashimasu	The police search for a dangerous person
Yūmeina kekkonshiki wa raishū kaisai sa remasu	A famous wedding will be held next week
Watashitachi wa tsugi no	We are next
Kumiai wa totemo ōkī	The union is very big

TRAINING TIME

Watashi no musuko wa tada no tīn'eijādesu	My son is just a teenager
Kono toshi wa jinkō ga ōi	The city has a large population
Tsugi wa donatadesu ka?	Who is next?
Watashi wa kodomodesu	I am a child
Kanojo wa watashi no fiansede wa arimasen!	She is not my fiancee!
Hitobito wa dōomoimasuka?	What do people think?
Taishū wa kare no kotae o kiita	The public listened to his answer
Shin sedai no rikai	A new generation of understanding
Watashi wa futsūnohitode wa arimasen	I am not an ordinary person
Kanojo wa seikaku ga tsuyoi	She is strong in character
Oyasumi, shinshi shukujo.	Good night, gentlemen and ladies.
Kare no chichi wa hanayome ni atta	His father met the bride

Watashitachiha dōryōde wa arimasen	We are not colleagues
Watashitachiha shiminde wa arimasen	We are not citizens
Watashi wa oba to tokubetsuna kankei ni arimasu	I have a special relationship with my aunt
Kanojo wa watashitachi no rinjindesu	She is our neighbor
Josei wa kanarazushimo joseide wa arimasen	Women are not always ladies
Anata no tsuma wa itariahitodesu	Your wife is Italian
Kakumei to wa nanidesu ka?	What is a revolution?
Gārufurendo ga imasu	I have a girlfriend
Kanojo wa hitodesu	She is a person
Kore ga watashi no bunkadesu	This is my culture
Watashitachi wa ī hitodesu	We are good people
Kare wa kumiai ni ikimashita	He went to the union
Jinrui wa yunīkudesu	Humanity is unique

TRAINING TIME

Nōka	Farmer
Shimin	Citizen
Watashi no chīmumeito	My teammate
Shōnen-tachi wa sutajiamu de densha	The boys train in the stadium
Kanojo ni wa teki ga imasen	She has no enemies
Kodomo wa gurēpujūsu o nomimasu	The child drinks grape juice
Dare ga tīn'eijādesu ka?	Who is a teenager?

Kono josei wa sekinin ga arimasu	This lady is responsible
Kanojo wa seikaku o motsu joseidesu	She is a woman with character
Chōshū wa kiita	The audience heard
Anata no imōto wa watashi no hanayomedesu	Your sister is my bride
Ningen wa niku o taberu	Humans eat meat
Gunshū wa ō no iken o kikimashita	The crowd listened to the views of the king
Anata wa yoi shūkan o motte imasu	You have good customs
Kekkonshiki wa itsudesu ka?	When is the wedding?
Shimin to wa nanidesu ka?	What is a citizen?
Gesuto mo shigoto	Guests also work
Naoki wa hitodesu	Naoki is a person
Hito ga miru	People watch
Bunka ga arimasen	You have no culture
Karera wa ī hitodesu	They are good people
Inu wa otoko no shin'yūdesu	The dog is man's best friend
Watashitachiha peadesu ka?	Are we a pair?
Kare wa jibun no nenrei o shiranai	He doesn't know his age
Nante yoi shūkan	What a good habit

TRAINING TIME

Chīmu wa byōin o hōmon shimashita	The team visited the hospital
Karera wa atarashī rinjindesu	They are new neighbors
Kakumei wa ima hajimatta!	The revolution is now beginning!
Kare wa watashi no shigoto no dōryōdesu.	He is a colleague of my work.
Kare wa watashi no rinjin no hitoridesu	He is one of my neighbors
Watashitachiha, majime ni hataraku	We work hard
Neko wa totemo ī dōbutsudesu	The cat is a very good animal
Watashi no oji wa ryokō ni tsuite no kiji o kakimashita.	My uncle wrote an article about travel.
Kōrei-sha wa hijō ni jūyōdesu	The elderly are very important
Īe, kare wa watashi no bōifurendode wa arimasen.	No, he is not my boyfriend.
Kanojo wa totemo omoshiroi hitodesu	She is a very interesting person
Ippan no kata e	For the general population
Kare wa watashi no rūmumētodesu	He is my roommate
Karera wa chīsana otonadesu	They are small adults
Anata wa gisei-shadesu ka?	Are you a victim?
Kore wa kojindesu	This is an individual
Anata wa mō otonadesu	You are already an adult
Kanojo wa on'nanoko o mimasu	She looks at the girls
Kore wa ningen ni totte yokunai	This is not good for humans

Watashi mo sōde wanaidesu	Neither do I
Anata wa teki ga imasu ka?	Do you have an enemy?
Karera wa kankō o manabimasu	They study tourism
Karera wa yakuindesu	They are officers
Watashi wa teki ga iru	I have an enemy

TRAINING TIME

Kyōkai ga arimasu	We have an association
Mata, mokugeki-sha wa imasen	In addition, we have no witnesses
Kare wa itsumo shinshi ni narudarou	He will always be a gentleman
Watashi no itoko wa mihon'ichi ni ikimashita.	My cousin went to the fair.
Watashi wa wain ga hoshiku arimasenga, watashi wa mizu o nomitaidesu.	I don't want wine, but I want to drink water.
Watashi wa mokugeki-shadesu	I am an eyewitness
Naze wakamono wa manabanai nodesu ka?	Why don't young people learn?
Kore wa yoi kekkonde wa arimasen	This is not a good marriage
Watashi wa tomodachi ni okane o haratte imasen.	I don't pay for my friend.
Watashitachi wa koko no gisei-shadesu	We are the victims here
Watashi no pātonā wa sore o kyoka shimashita	My partner allowed it

Isha wa ashita kekka o uketorudeshou	The doctor will receive the results tomorrow
Sensei wa watashitachi no tame ni hon o yonda.	The teacher read a book for us.
Kare wa sutaffu o totemo yoku atsukaimasu	He treats his staff very well
Watashitachiha san no kotonaru basho o motte imasu	We have three different places
Watashinochichi wa kanojo o totemo aishiteimasu.	My father loves her very much.
Shimin shakai wa hijō ni jūyōdesu	Civil society is very important

TRAINING TIME

STORY MODE

JAPANESE

Kisha: "Kotoshi no kānibaru ni wa hijō ni ōku no hito ga imasu. Watashi wa rinjin to dōryō to hata o mimashita. Watashi wa nōmin chiiki ni iki, soko ni iru nan'ninka no hitobito to hanashi o shimashou.' `Minasan, kon'nichiwa. Dai nijuuyon-kai gurīnkānibaru e yōkoso. Kyō wa ogenkidesuka?"

Tsūrisuto 1: "Watashitachi wa totemo umaku itte imasu, watashitachi wa kono tenran-kai o tanoshinde imasu."

Kisha: "Watashi wa anata no fuku ni tsuite anata ni tazuneru koto ga dekiru koto o shitte totemo ureshīdesu ka? Tēma wa nandesuka?"

Tsūrisuto 1: "Watashitachiha Porutogaru kokumin, jinkō ichi, hyakuman-ri no kunideari, watashitachiha dokuji no bunka o motte imasu. Anata no ni-banme no shitsumon ni kotaeru tame ni, kotoshi no watashitachi no tēma wa `jinrui kankō'desu."

Tsūrisuto 2: "Watashitachi zen'in ga harikēn no hakai-tekina chikara o manoatari ni shitanode, watashitachiha ishiki o takame, gisei-sha ni kifu o suru koto o kesshin shimashita."

ENGLISH

Reporter: "There are so many people at this year's carnival. I have seen my neighbor and a colleague with a flag. Let me go to the peasant area and talk to some people there."

"Hello everyone, welcome to the 24th Green Carnival, how are you today?"

Tourist 1: "We are doing very well; we are enjoying this exhibition."

Reporter: "I am very happy to know that I can ask you about your clothing? What is the theme?"

Tourist 1: "We are Portuguese citizens, a country with a population of 11 million, and we have a unique culture. In answering your second question, our theme this year is "humanity tourism."

Tourist 2: "We have all witnessed the destructive power of the hurricane, so we decided to help raise awareness and make donations for the victims."

Chapter 21

NUMBERS

Keywords : Sū, ichi, ni, san, yon, go, roku, nana, hachi, kyuu, juu, nijuu, nijuuichi, hyaku.

Ichi	One
Ni	Two
San	Three
Yon	Four
Go	Five
Roku	Six
Nana	Seven
Hachi	Eight
Kyuu	Nine
Juu	Ten
Juuichi	Eleven
Juuni	Twelve
Juusan	Thirteen
Juuyon	Fourteen
Juugo	Fifteen
Juuroku	Sixteen
Juunana	Seventeen
Juuhachi	Eighteen
Juukyuu	Nineteen
Nijuu	Twenty
Nijuuichi	Twenty-one
Hyaku	One hundred
5 peeji me	Fifth page
8 peeji arimasu	We have eight pages
Watashi wa 4-doru motte imasu.	I have four dollars.

TRAINING TIME

Nijuu	Twenty
Sanjuu	Thirty
Yonjuu	Forty
Nanbaawan wa daredesu ka?	Who is the number one?
Sanban-me wa sosuudesu	The third is the prime number
Kare no oba wa san-biki no neko o katte iru	His aunt has three cats
Kanojo wa watashi no san-banme no gaarufurendodesu	She is my third girlfriend
Machimasu.	I will wait.
Kare wa kanojo no saisho no kodomodesu	He is her first child
Eki wa koko kara ni meetoru no kyoridesu.	The station is 2 meters away from here.
Anata wa gohan no nihaime ga iranai	You don't want the second bowl of rice
Kare no saisho no pinku no shatsu	His first pink shirt
Kare wa nananin chuu roku-banmeno kodomodesu	He is the sixth of seven children
Roku-nin bunno reshipi	Recipes for six people
Kare wa roku-ji mae dewanaku roku-ji choudo ni koko ni kimashita.	He came here at six o'clock instead of before
Yonsara-me ga kare ni fusawashī.	The fourth dish is suitable for him.
Yonin no booifurendo wa nani o tabemasu ka?	What do four boyfriends eat?
Doumo arigatougozaimasu!	Thank you very much!
Gojuu ka yonjuu?	Fifty or forty?

Watashi wa juuhattou no uma o katte imasu.	I have eighteen horses.
Zero kara juu made	From zero to ten
Kare wa kono kazoku no kyuunin-me no otokonokodesu.	He is the ninth boy in this family.
Watashi no musuko wa jussai desu.	My son is ten years old.
Watashitachi wa juuichinin desu	We are eleven people
Kare ni wa juuninin no musuko ga imasu	He has twelve sons

TRAINING TIME

Hanbun	Half
Meetoru	Meter
Okanenara tashou arimasu	I have some money
Kare ni wa hachinin no mago ga imasu.	He has eight grandchildren.
Watashi wa juusan-biki no neko o katte imasu	I have thirteen cats
Juuyonin no itoko	Fourteen cousins
Watashi wa juugo-sai deshita	I was fifteen years old
Tsugi no juuni-jikan	The next twelve hours
Naze anata wa watashitachi no rokkai-me no tanjōbi ni konakatta nodesu ka?	Why didn't you come to our sixth birthday?
Gonin-you no teburu wa arimasu ka?	Is there a table for five people?
Zenbu de yattsu arimasu	We have a total of eight
Watashitachi wa jukkashome ni tasshimashita	We reached the tenth place
Juppun	Ten minutes

Taryou	High quantity
Kare wa mada juunana-sai desu	He is only seventeen years old
Watashi wa hachiji kara juuichiji made benkyō shimasu	I am studying from eight to eleven
Gogo sanji koro ni ocha o nomimasu.	I drink tea around three in the afternoon.
Juuni-sai, inu wa oite imasu	Twelve years old, a dog is old
Watashi wa juuyon-mai no shiroi shatsu o motte imasu.	I have fourteen white shirts.
Watashi wa juuichi-ji ni nemashita.	I slept at eleven o'clock.
Watashitachi ni wa nijuttou no uma ga imasu	We have twenty horses
Karera wa ikutsu ka no ringo o tabemashita	They ate some apples
Roku-bun'no ichi wa san	One sixth is three
Juu-ji han desu	It's half past ten
Go-banme no hashi wa bijutsukan ni tsuujite imasu	The fifth bridge leads to the museum

TRAINING TIME

Hyakuman	Million
Yonin	Four people
Issoku no kutsu	A pair of shoes
Nanajuu-ippon no ninjin	Seventy-one carrots
Kore wa hyakuman-dorudesu	This is one million dollars
Watashi no oba wa yaku yonjussai desu.	My aunt is about forty years old.
Watashi wa senkyuuhyaku-hachijuu nendai desu.	I am in the 1980s.

Watashi wa kyuujuppun-kan yomimashita.	I read for 90 minutes.
Keki o oobun ni rokujuppun-kan irete okimas	The cake is kept in the oven for 60 minutes
Ichi meetoru	One meter
San-ban	Third
Kyou wa mikka-me desu	Today is the third day
Kore wa anata no hanbun desu	This is half of you
Genzai, kare wa hachi-i desu	Currently, he is ranked eighth
Watashitachi wa yaku rokujuu-nen matte imasu.	We have been waiting for about sixty years.
Watashi wa hobo nanajussai desu.	I am almost seventy years old.
Nanajuunin no dansei ga chikin o tabemasu	Seventy men eat chicken
Kare wa nanajuu-nendai o oboete imasu	He remembers the seventies
Raishuu wa watashi no saigo no shuudesu.	Next week is my last week.
Kotae ga arimasen.	I don't have any answers.
Hakubutsukan wa kuji ni akimasu	The museum is open at nine
Karera wa sukunakutomo hyakuman o youkyuu shimasu	They demand at least one million
Go meetoru	Five meters
Suu sen-kiro	Thousands of kilometers
Nana ga kanojo no suuji desu	Seven is her number

TRAINING TIME

Sorera no hyaku wa totemo yoidesu	One hundred of them are very good
Gonin no sensei	Five teachers
Anata wa sennin no tomodachi ga imasu	You have a thousand friends
Kare wa watashi no nenrei no ni-baidesu	He is twice my age
Koko ni wa takusan no hito ga imasu.	There are many people here.
Anata wa kare yori dore dake ookii desu ka?	How much are you bigger than him?
Watashi no oji no kuruma wa chiisaidesu	My uncle's car is small
Juu hiku yon wa roku	Ten minus four equals six
Kare no ani wa go-sai-mimandesu	His brother is less than five
Juubun'na jikan ga arimasu	We have enough time
Kanojo wa ikutsu ka no fuku o kaimashita	She bought a few clothes
Naze ooku no hito ga shinu nodesu ka?	Why do many people die?
Watashitachi wa hanbun no pan o tabemashita	We ate half of the bread
Kare wa takusan no sakana o tabemashita	He ate a lot of fish
Kare no kutsu wa aoi desu	His shoes are blue
Watashi wa kuji ni yuushoku o torimasu.	I have dinner at nine.
Ima, kanojo wa juuhassaidesu.	Now she is eighteen years old.
Motto ookina mono wa arimasu ka?	Do you have something bigger?
Shuu no nanoka-me wa doyoubi desu	The seventh day of the week is Saturday
Tsuki no dai-go nichiyoubi	The fifth Sunday of the month

Go-dai no shiroi kuruma	Five white cars
Shefu wa yonjukkiro no niku o motte imasu	The chef has forty kilograms of meat
Kanojo no kyuu-kai-me no suupaamaaketto	Her ninth trip to the supermarket
Sanjuu-nen-go, watashitachi wa onaji machi ni imasu	Thirty years later we are in the same city
Nijussetai ga koko ni sunde imasu	Twenty families live here
Ajia-san no sanjuuroku shurui no orenji	Thirty-six kinds of oranges from Asia
Maria ni wa yonjuuyon-hiki no pengin ga imasu	Maria has forty-four penguins
Itaria shusshin'no sanjuugo-nin	35 people from Italy
Han wa yonjuusan-biki no doubutsu o katte imasu	Han has forty-three animals
Kono dansei wa rokujuu-sai desu.	This man is sixty years old.
Watashi no kanojo wa juukyuu-sai desu	My girlfriend is 19 years old
Kon'ya, kare wa nana-i desu.	Tonight, he is ranked seventh.
Gogo wa sukoshi koohii o nomimasu.	I have a little coffee in the afternoon.
Watashi no musuko wa juuroku-sai desu	My son is sixteen
Kanojo wa ni sen-satsu no hon o motte imasu	She has two thousand books
Kore wa yoi issoku-no kutsu desu	This is a good pair of shoes
Kono machi no jinkou wa nihyaku man-nin desu	The city has a population of 2 million

TRAINING TIME

STORY MODE

JAPANESE

"Kinō mananda koto o oboete imasu ka? Jo" to mitsuki wa iimashita. "Dekireba, watashi no shigoto no hanbun ga owarimasu. Dekinai nonara, shiken ni gōkaku shitai nodeareba, motto doryoku surubekidesu." `Hai, dekimasu' to Xu wa iimashita. Subarashīdesu! Tsudzukemashou. "2 tasu 2 wa 4, 3 tasu 1 wa 4, 1 tasu 3 wa 4 ni hitoshii, 8 waru 2 wa 4." `Hijō ni yoi desu. 6-Banme kara hajimete kudasai, ima yori ōku no chūi o haraimashou. Mitsuki wa iimashita. `6 tasu 1 wa 7, 6 tasu 3 wa 9, 6 tasu 4 wa 10, 7 tasu 6 wa 13, 6 tasu 6 wa 12, 6 tasu 4 wa 10 ni hitoshī' " yoku dekimashita Jo. Sā, kono mondai ni kotaete kudasai. Snapchat ni 14-nin no fanga ite, 15-nin no fan ga iru baai, korera futari no fan no gōkei wa dō narimasu ka?' " 29-nin no fan," Jo wa kotaemashita."

ENGLISH

"Can you remember what we learned yesterday, Xu?" said Mitsuki.
"If you can, half of my work will end. If you can't, you should work harder if you want to pass the exam."
"Yes, I can." Xu said.
"Great! Let's continue."
"Two plus two is four, three plus one is four, one plus three equals four, eight divided by two equals four."
"Very good, let us pay more attention to them now, starting with the sixth. Can you tell me about the sixth?" Mitsuki said.
"Six plus one equals seven, six plus three equals nine, six plus four equals ten, seven plus six equals thirteen, six plus six equals twelve, six plus four equals ten."
"Good job Xu. Now answer these questions. If I have 14 fans on Snapchat, and you have fifteen, what is the sum of these two fans?"
"Twenty-nine fans," Xu replied.

**10 20 30 40 50
60 70 80 90 100**

END OF BOOK ONE

For the complete experience, please get the second and third book in the series

#THESIMPLEWAYTOLEARNJAPANESE

For updates on the next book, we're available on twitter as the @BadCreativ3, and on facebook
www.facebook.com/BadCreativ3

OTHER BADCREATIVE BOOKS

The Simple Way To Learn French

The Simple Way To Learn Spanish

The Simple Way To Learn Italian

Thank you for reading, and we hope you'd be kind enough to drop us a review on our amazon page.

www.ingramcontent.com/pod-product-compliance
Lightning Source LLC
Chambersburg PA
CBHW072010110526
44592CB00012B/1261

www.ingramcontent.com/pod-product-compliance
Lightning Source LLC
Chambersburg PA
CBHW072007110526
44592CB00012B/1234

A Word from the Publisher

Destinée Media publishes both fiction and nonfiction and aims to bring a fresh perspective to spirituality and culture.

At Destinée Media we seek to operate by faith in God within a Biblical/Christian worldview. We hope to inspire 'culture making' by promoting ideas that will contribute to Christ being understood as Lord of the whole of life, which is to be marked by redemption and renewal.

We are committed to reflecting carefully on vital matters for the church, academy and society, while aiming to keep a personal and intimate dimension of the Christian life in view.

We thank you for your interest in our materials and hope that you find them both relevant and challenging. Please share your thoughts with us: www.destineemedia.com

January
Week 1 *A Word of Gratitude* (Portrait of CS Lewis) Public domain

February *Introduction to February* (Heart in the snow) Pixabay
Week 2 *Valentine's Day* (Candies) Pixabay

March
Week 1 *Emergency Lane* (Car with policeman) CC BY-SA, author unknown
Week 2 *Esteem* (Girl with outstretched arms) Pixabay
Week 4 *Eye on the Sparrow* (Two sparrows) CC BY-SA, author unknown.

April
Introduction to month of April (Three Crosses) Pixabay

May
Week 1 *Floating with God's Will* (Man floating in Dead Sea) CC BY-SA, author unknown

June
Introduction to June (Daisys) Pixabay
Week 2 *The Flint and the Fire* (Campfire) Reshot

July
July introduction page (Sparklers-923029_1920) Pixabay
Week 1 *First Independence Day* (Statue of Liberty) Pixabay
Week 2 *First days in heaven (Older man looking up)* Pixabay

August
Week 2 *Venus fly trap* Pixabay
Week 3 *Just So Many Days* (Heaven's stairway) CC BY-SA
Week 4 *Green Tomatoes* Pixabay

Additional Articles
Introduction to Additional Articles (Girl reading a devotional) Pixabay
Week 1 *Oak Tree* Pixabay

Photo Credits and Meaning

Public Domain- This photo is free to download and can be used for commercial purposes.
CC BY-SA (Creative Commons)-This license allows users to distribute, remix, adapt, and build upon the material in any medium or format, so long as attribution is given to the creator. If author is unknown, then attribution is not necessary. The license allows for commercial use.
Pixabay -This picture is free to download, it is unrestricted in its use, and the author of the picture may or may not be credited.
Reshot- This is a free photo download, free for commercial use and unlimited digital use.

Book cover (USS Jason) Public Domain, unrestricted use by the Department of Navy

September
Week 3 *Never Deserted* (Elephant Island) CC BY-SA, unknown author
Week 4 *Wolf and the Blade* (Wolf) Public Domain Picture

October
Week 1 *Boll Weevil (Statue)* Public Domain
Week 3 *One River, Two Seas* (Dead Sea) Pixabay

November
Week 1 *Ready, Willing, and Able* (USS Jason repairing USS Randolph) Public Domain, US Federal Government, free of restrictions
Week 2 and 3 *Shipwrecked and American Colony,* Portraits of Annie, Maggie, Bessie, and Tanetta Spafford, ca. 1873 From Spafford family photograph album. American Colony in Jerusalem collection, Manuscript division, Library of congress Part I, Box 1, Folder 1. http//hd.loc.gov/loc.mss/mamcol.001. Group portrait of Bertha, Grace, and Anna Spafford, Jerusalem, ca. 1890s. From album of studio portraits of American colonists and friends. Visual materials of John D. Whiting Papers Prints and Photographs Division, Library of Congress. http//www.loc.gov/pictures/ote/2008676305

December
Week 2 Bethlehem Star (3 wisemen) Pixabay

Dear Kent,

The best thing that I can give to you is my love, my intense pride in your achievement at the U. of Wyoming, and not the least your genuine religious convictions.

With all my love, Dad

Epilogue

I hope you have found some encouragement, restoration, and perspective in these fifty-two devotional articles. I pray many will stay with you throughout your life, especially when hard times come.

As a young boy, I had some difficult times as I needed and missed my dad, but encouragement did come later. With the final year of graduate school at the University of Wyoming approaching, I was a bit discouraged because I had a thesis to write, and the library at the university did not have the references I needed.

My dad invited me to come down during my summer break and check out his library at church. When he took me into his library, there were three rows (floor to ceiling) of over a thousand books. My dad was a vociferous reader, which helped him very much in his sermon preparations. Amazingly, I found all the references I needed.

After graduating, my dad told me how proud he was of me, which meant the world, for I was no different than any other child needing affirmation from a dad. I loved it, even at age 22.

Now I am beyond his age when he died, with children and grandchildren of my own. My soul purpose is to always encourage and be there for them all the days of my life, however long that will be.

Scripture References

Matthew 27:5 *And Judas threw the pieces of silver into the temple sanctuary and departed, and he went away and hanged himself.*

Luke 22:31-32 *31 Jesus said, 'Simon, Simon, behold, Satan has demanded permission to sift you like wheat; 32 but I have prayed for you, that your faith may not fail; and you, when once you have turned again, strengthen your brothers.'*

Luke 22:60-62 *60 But Peter said, 'Man, I do not know what you are talking about.' Immediately, while he was still speaking, a rooster crowed. 61 The Lord turned and looked at Peter. And Peter remembered the word of the Lord, how He had told him, 'Before a rooster crows today, you will deny Me three times.' 62 And he went out and wept bitterly.*

John 21:17 *He said to him the third time, 'Simon, son of John, do you love Me?' Peter was grieved because He said to him the third time, 'Do you love Me?' And he said to Him, 'Lord, You know all things; You know that I love You.' Jesus said to him, 'Shepherd my people (sheep).'*

6th Trial
(John 18:39-40; John19:1-16; Matthew 27:24-26)

Jesus returns to Pilate for his last trial. Pilate still tries to get out of executing Jesus by giving the Jews the choice to crucify Jesus or a thief and murderer, Barabbas. Surely the people would choose Jesus, but they didn't at the urging of the religious leaders. Hence, Pilate had Jesus crucified, even though this decision greatly troubled him.

Last Thoughts

When you suffer an unexpected trial, do not be surprised if you are treated unfairly. Jesus was wrongly accused and slapped around, yet He did not respond in kind.

Not all who claim to be spiritual leaders are, so take note of how they live the Christian life, over and above their official positions. Jesus certainly took note of this when confronting the Pharisees who were judging Him. Realize when you are going through a trial where Satan is the prime mover, hypocrisy and cover-up will characterize those following his lead. However, like Jesus, stick with the truth, give simple answers, and hold on knowing that one day all will be made right.

During a trial, look for those who are observing, listening, and wanting to know the truth of the matter. They may be candidates for the kingdom. I believe Jesus did this with Pilate; in fact, he opened up more with Pilate than any of the supposed spiritual leaders of His day.

Trials tend to be long and repetitive, especially when Satan is controlling events and people. During the trials you encounter, continue praying for strength to sustain and realize that often when a trial is at its worst, it is almost over. It was for Jesus the second time around with Pilate.

In your trials, there may be those who have great sympathy for you. However, put all your hope in the Lord and not them. Pilate had some compassion for Jesus, but in the end, he decided for his own benefit to crucify him.

When going through a trial, of course, you would like to succeed as Jesus did during his trials, but whether you succeed or not, hold onto your faith. Be assured that afterward, God will not only restore you but will have built a new measure of faith within you. A level you have never had before.

3rd Trial
(Luke 22:66-71)

In this trial the sun had finally risen, which made it a legal trial. Jesus was asked again, "Are you the Son of God?" He said, "Yes, I am." They now had their evidence and wanted to put Him to death according to Jewish Law but could not because they were under Roman rule. Thus, they had to defer to the Romans

4th Trial
(John 18:28-38; Luke 23:5-7)

Jesus is taken to Pilate, the Roman Governor. As they approached Him, their deceitful ways had not lessened. In their continuing effort to put Jesus to death, they told Pilate he was an evildoer as well as one who stirred up the people. Calling Jesus an evildoer had no impact on Pilate but identifying Him as a sort of rabble-rouser amongst the people did. Romans did not like rebellion of any kind, and their resolve was to crush any uprisings before they got started. So, Pilate took Jesus into a separate chamber to question Him. Unlike the previous three trials, Jesus talked with Pilate, answering his questions and explaining that His kingdom was not of this world. Evidently, this moved Pilate, who then pronounced Jesus innocent.

In response to Pilate's determination, the entire Sanhedrin leaders who had accompanied Jesus to this Roman court were upset at his findings and pressured him to execute Jesus. Instead of "sticking to his guns," so to speak, Pilate tried to escape the matter by sending Jesus to Herod, another Roman sanctioned authority in the area. Jesus was a Galilean, and Herod oversaw the Galileans, so away went Jesus to the next trial.

5th Trial
(Luke 23:8-12)

The Jewish leaders hated Herod but were willing to openly accept him for the moment if he would put Jesus to death. In this court appearance, Jesus received the same treatment, being questioned, mocked, beaten, and humiliated. However, unlike His time with Pilate, Jesus said nothing, which brought a quick end to the meeting.

During the trials we encounter, Satan is often, but not always, the culprit behind many of them. If he is directly involved, his goal is to dissuade us from believing and trusting in God. For example, Satan was successful with Judas during Jesus' trials, because he never did have any faith as the Scripture reports. The conclusion was that he not only betrayed Jesus but committed suicide afterward.

On the other hand, Peter, who also betrayed Jesus, had a faith that God had given him upon his belief. A conviction, when all was said and done, Satan could not penetrate. After it was all over, Peter was forgiven, recovered, and went on to do great things for the kingdom.

Finally, before we go into each of Jesus' six trials, remember God allows each of us to go through our own set of trials, not to hurt us, but to build our faith as was the case with Peter and the other disciples.

1st Trial
(John 18:12-14; 19-24)

This was a preliminary hearing before the powerful religious leader, Annas. Jesus was asked about His teaching. He answered, *"I have spoken openly to the world; I always taught in synagogues and in the temple, where all the Jews come together; and I spoke nothing in secret. Why do you question Me?"* He was then struck by a soldier standing near and promptly sent off to the next court hearing.

2nd Trial
(Matthew 26:57, 59-68)

The second trial was more official. It had a charge, testimony, witnesses, judge, jury, and verdict. It was still illegal, though, as it was held at night with no official representation for Jesus. During most of this trial, Jesus kept silent. Because of this, the witnesses called could not get their stories straight. After some on-sight coaching, they were able to get at least two witnesses to collaborate on the same story. This trial ended with the High Priest asking Jesus if He was the Christ, the Son of God. Jesus did not deny it, only quoting *Psalm 110*, a messianic prophecy. He was slapped around some more, mocked, and spit on, not quite what would be expected from educated and spiritual leaders.

Additional Article 4

(Sculpture of Jesus praying in Gethsamne)

Jesus' Six Trials
Supplemental Easter message

Be of sober spirit, be on the alert. Your adversary, the devil, prowls about like a roaring lion, seeking someone to devour. I Peter 5:8

As you celebrate Easter, remember that toward the end of this treasured week Jesus went through a series of trials that led Him to be crucified on the cross. Had He not done this, our sins would not have been forgiven. For Jesus, death on the cross was the sacrifice required to pay for our sins, all of them. Jesus did as God asked, even though it would be painful and cause Him to suffer much.

The beginning of His terrible suffering started with six trials Jesus had to endure during that first Easter week. We should realize that trials come to all of us from time to time, and they can be difficult and painful. The pandemic of 2020, for example, was a trial that we all experienced in one degree or another. For some, it was an inconvenience, isolation from others, or loss of work, and for others, it was being sick, hospitalized, or even losing a loved one.

Yet, just as there was a beginning and an ending to Jesus' trials, so there will be to the trials we are going through. Jesus' ending was the cross, resurrection, and the salvation of mankind. Our endings will be different, but they will all be orchestrated by God, as Jesus' were during that first Easter week.

Scripture References

John 12:12-13 *12 On the next day the large crowd who had come to the feast, when they heard that Jesus was coming to Jerusalem, 13 took the branches of the palm trees and went out to meet Him, and began to shout, 'Hosanna! Blessed is He who comes in the name of the Lord, even the King of Israel.'*
Proverbs 3:5-6 *5 Trust in the Lord with all your heart and do not lean on your own understanding. 6 In all your ways acknowledge Him, And He will make your paths straight*
.

Some of those miracles included healing the sick, bringing back to life those who had died, feeding thousands with only a few baskets of food, and even quieting a storm.

It is little wonder they demonstrated such confidence in Jesus that day. However, Jesus did not come to deliver them from the Romans, but from sin, which was keeping many of them out of His kingdom and heaven as well. A week later, Jesus did that when He gave up His life on the cross for all our sins.

Palm Sunday was not a victory celebration from Jesus' view, but rather a last big gathering to ready the people to move from where they were in their lives with God to where they needed to be.

The following is a simple illustration of God's wisdom to move everyone He has created to where they need to be with Him. Whether this is for those who threw palms down before His feet 2000 years ago or any of us today.

A farmer happened to be drawn one morning to a bird that was vigorously building a nest for her coming family. Unfortunately, the spot the mother bird chose was in a heap of dead branches to be set ablaze the following day. Knowing this, the farmer relocated the nest. The next day the persistent mother tried again to rebuild her nest in the same spot, and for a second time, the farmer thwarted her efforts. On the third day, the bird finally accepted the new spot, a limb near the farmer's kitchen window. A place that was safe, and a place where he could watch the mother bird and her new family. And should she need any further assistance or help, he would be close by to give it.

Last Thought

As you might surmise, God is the farmer, and you are the mother bird in this illustration. Like the farmer, God knows what is best for you, for He sees what you cannot always see. He moves you, not only for your sake but for the sake of others, like the little birds in this illustration that were going to hatch.

Additional Article 3

(East Gate in Jerusalem)

Palm Sunday
Supplemental Easter message

The Best Spot for a Nest

For I know the plans that I have for you, declares the Lord, plans for welfare and not for calamity to give you a future and a hope. Jeremiah 29:11

A few years ago I walked down the road where Jesus walked on Palm Sunday. To the left was the garden of Gethsemane, and in front at a distance was the East gate of Jerusalem. Jesus walked through that gate on Palm Sunday over 2000 years ago on the way to the Temple. He will do that again when He returns for a second and last time. I am confident He will come again as many prophetic events have come to pass, like the return of Israel as a nation in 1948.

When Jesus rode into Jerusalem on Palm Sunday the multitudes were thrilled, lining the streets to celebrate and usher Him in as their deliverer. Too long had they been under the iron hand of Rome; now it looked like that Roman reign could be over. Those who threw palms on the ground in His honor had either heard Jesus teach, or seen Him do some incredible miracles.

Jerusalem, so, too, does the Lord surround us during our most difficult moments and refuses to leave even after all is okay.

The mention of Jerusalem and its mountains in this Psalm has particular meaning because I have been there. Old Jerusalem as a city is quite small and compact. In my younger days I could have jogged around it in about 35 minutes. The city is special, though, for Scripture refers to it as God's city, and, of course, Jesus spent much of His time there. The Mount of Olives, Mount Zion, and Mount Moriah are the mountains that surround it.

I guess the next time I visit Jerusalem, I will take special note of these mountains. However, if I do not return, I will keep in mind how they encircle and protect Jerusalem.

Last Thought

Just as God surrounded Jerusalem with mountains, and the young mother and her toddler in this story, so He will do the same for you; just lift your eyes to Him when encountering troubling circumstances

Scripture Reference

Psalm 121:1-8 *1 I will lift up my eyes to the mountains; from where shall my help come? 2 My help comes from the Lord, Who made heaven and earth. 3 He will not allow your foot to slip; He who keeps you will not slumber. 4 Behold, He who keeps Israel Will neither slumber nor sleep. 5 The Lord is your keeper; the Lord is your shade on your right hand. 6 The sun will not smite you by day, nor the moon by night. 7 The Lord will protect you from all evil; He will keep your soul. 8 The Lord will guard your going out and your coming in from this time forth and forever.*

Footnotes

Patricia Raybon, *Surrounded by God*, Daily Bread, (Thursday, March 28, 2019)

Additional Article 2

(Mountains around Old Jerusalem)

Surrounded

As the mountains surround Jerusalem, so, the Lord surrounds His people from this time forth and forever. Psalm 125

This is a story of a young mother in a busy airport struggling with her toddler, who was throwing a tantrum. Have any of us ever been in that kind of situation, either looking on or right in the middle of it? This little toddler was screaming, kicking, and refusing to board the plane. This young mother, who was also very pregnant with another child, was burdened tremendously. In frustration, she gave up and started crying, covering her face with both hands.

Then out of the blue, six women travelers, all strangers to the young mother, formed a circle around her and the child and shared their snacks and water with them. They spoke gentle words of comfort and encouragement and even sang a familiar nursery song to the child. This brought great calm to the mother and child, which allowed them to board the plane peacefully, without any further strain or stress.

The six women boarded the plane and took their seats, knowing that what they had done helped this young mother in her moment of stress.[1]

This incident illustrates a beautiful truth and lesson that comes from Psalm 125, which states that as the mountains surround the people of

Last Thoughts

Can you put too much of a load on the Lord? Hardly, for like the great oak, He can handle every burden, fear, or anxious thought you will experience when storms come your way in this life. And when you are so thirsty for answers to life's many dilemmas, without hesitation, God allows us to quench our thirst through the Scriptures He provides just for us

Therefore, cling to God and drink of His Word, for it is the path to make you more beautiful to Him and others while quenching your thirst at the same time.

Scripture References
Psalm 63: 8 *My soul clings to You; Your right hand upholds me.*
Isaiah 62:3 *You will also be a crown of beauty in the hand of the Lord, and a royal diadem in the hand of your God.*
John 4:14 *Whoever drinks of the water that I will give him*
shall never thirst, but the water that I will give him will become in him a well of water springing up to eternal life.

Additional Article 1

The Oak and the Vine

Come to Me, all who are weary and heavy laden, and I will give you rest. Matthew 11: 28

    The oak tree has long been praised for its legendary strength, longevity, and exceptional wood properties. Oak trees adapt well in the natural forests, suburban yards, and even our nation's inner cities.
    At my wife's childhood home, there was a beautiful oak tree in her front yard. On that tree were numerous green vines that made it look all the more beautiful.
    Even though the vines added to this great oak's attractiveness, they also created a higher wind load on its trunk and branches during storms. During the dry seasons, the vines would also compete with the oak for water. Yet, through the years, my wife's oak tree never seemed to lose any of its strength or grandeur, even when she continually swung on its branches as a little girl.
    Similarly, we are like the vines on a grand and majestic oak tree, in that we need God to help us survive the storms of this life. The tighter we can wrap ourselves around Him during such storms, the better chance to endure.
    Of course, we can pray that God will remove storms when they come our way, and sometimes He does. But for the most part, He does not because He knows we are at our best and most beautiful when we cling to Him, just as the vines did on that great oak.

Additional Articles

(brings the total to 52)

The Oak and the Vine
Surrounded
Palm Sunday
Jesus' Six Trials

to. What we ask for is good, but like un-ripened tomatoes, our prayers sit there with little or no change.

Like a gardener, we do everything possible with our requests before God; we prepare the soil of our lives with faith, we plant ourselves where we believe He wants us, we water ourselves with His Word, and finally, weed out our old sinful habits. Yet still no answer from God, no ripened tomatoes appearing. So, we begin to panic and freak out and decide to take things into our own hands. The waiting is over as far as we are concerned and acting on this thought we end up with an answer that we are hardly ready for, one that needed a little more time to ripen.

Immediately we know we have made a colossal mistake, one that seems relatively irreversible. In disgust with ourselves for being too impatient, we start to throw away what we had prayed and hoped for, until God intervenes and says, "Let me see what I can do with what you have done." God then takes our prayers and puts them into His box so that they can ripen for a while. Time passes, and we move onto other things, almost forgetting what we had prayed for so hard. But God does not forget and proves it when He brings that prayer and hope back into our lives, all ripened, matured, and ready to be received.

Last Thought

God always answers your prayers according to His timing and not yours. Will you learn from this on the next go around with another prayer request or hope? Sure hope so, for it is better to wait on God's timing, no matter how long it takes, then to force something to happen ahead of time, like picking a tomato that is not quite ready to be picked.

Scripture References

Psalms 27:14 *Wait on the Lord: be of good courage, and he shall strengthen thine heart: wait, I say, on the Lord.*

Psalms 37:7-9 *Rest in the Lord and wait patiently for him: fret not thyself because of him who prospers in his way, because of the man who brings wicked devices to pass.*

Isaiah 40:31 *But they that wait upon the Lord shall renew [their] strength; they shall mount up with wings as eagles; they shall run, and not be weary; [and] they shall walk, and not faint.*

August
Week 4

Green Tomatoes

Be patient brethren… for the farmer waits for the precious produce of the soil, being patient about it. James 5:7

One of my past and present hobbies is to grow tomatoes every spring. Usually, I have been successful, especially when I lived in Arizona. On the other hand, in Boise, Idaho, it has been a bit of a challenge due to the changing weather, I believe. Nevertheless, I planted some tomatoes plants here a couple of years ago, but it seemed to take forever for them to ripen.

After a couple of months of waiting, I began checking them every day during the summer to see what was going on. Then at the end of the summer, none of the plants were ready. As early fall began, I decided I would pick them anyway. Maybe they were ripe but did not look like it on the outside. What a big mistake! They were not ripe at all.

As I was getting ready to toss them away in frustration, a neighbor came by and suggested that I lay them in a box on paper towels, and then put them in the darkest part of the house, perhaps a closet. I did and then forgot about them. A few weeks afterward, when going to get a coat, there they were. I opened the box, and the tomatoes were all red on the outside and quite ripe. They were great eating!

The illustration of the tomatoes is like when we ask for certain things from God in our lives, and yet they do not come about when we expect them

As much as we all want to control how many days we have on earth, we cannot do this ourselves, for this is totally in God's hands. Some live longer than others, and we all die in different ways. I mentioned my college friend who died of a stroke when he seemingly should have had more years to live, but I have known others much younger than him who died early.

There was a junior high school student in one of my youth groups, for instance, who drown in a canal on one of my spring retreats. It was tragic and incredibly heartbreaking, as can be imagined. How does one tell a mother that her son will not be coming home, not ever coming home? But God has his reasons why one lives longer than another or dies in one way or another, which will not be fully known until we get to heaven to see things from His perspective.

Last Thoughts

What will you do until that day finally comes? What kind of relationship will you have with your families, friends, and all those whom God put in your path while in this world? Most importantly, what kind of relationship will you end up with God, Himself?

As you ponder this, which I have done many times, please take a moment to be joyful and relieved that you are still alive. Yet do not forget that you are only alive because God has ordained it. If you need to, while still breathing, consider making things right with Him. Then move on and do the same with others as well.

If after surveying your life, all is okay with God and others, then enjoy the rest of the day and plan for tomorrow. And if God should call you home tomorrow, what a day that will be! You will be amazed what will be awaiting you.

Remember, you have just so many days on earth, but an innumerable number of joyous days in heaven, countless days with no more death, crying, or pain.

Scripture References

Revelation 21:4 *God will wipe away every tear from their eyes, and there will no longer be any death and no more mourning, crying, or pain.*
Revelation 7:17 *for the Lamb in the center of the throne will be their shepherd, and will guide them to springs of the water of life; and God will wipe every tear from their eyes.*

God, in His omniscience, knows everything about us, and He alone determines our last day on earth. He knows what we have done in this life, what we are doing at the moment, and what we will do in the years to come. He knows about our faith too, when it began, what it has been like, what it is today, and what it will be like before He brings us to heaven. Yet if we live a life of faith and faithfulness unto Him, then in many cases, not all, our days on earth can be lengthy because of what God can do through us.

> *Respect given to the Lord prolongs life, but the years of the wicked will be shortened. Proverbs 10:27*

> *Do not forget my teaching, but let your heart keep my commandments; for the length of days and years of life and peace will be added to you. Proverbs 3:1-2*

> *If you walk in My ways, keeping My statutes and commandments, ...then I will prolong your days. Proverbs 3:1-2*

Only in a few cases, though, has God ever changed the ending of a person's life due to their request. Hezekiah, for example, one of Israel's greatest kings, asked God to extend his life. The Lord granted his wish giving him 15 more years. Unfortunately, those extra years were full of conflict and turmoil. I bet if Hezekiah could have a do-over, he would have passed on that request for extra life. *(Isaiah 38:1-5)*

> *In those days Hezekiah became mortally ill. And Isaiah, the prophet, came to him and said, 'Thus says the Lord, 'Set your house in order, for you shall die and not live.' Then Hezekiah turned his face to the wall and prayed to the Lord and said, 'Remember now, O Lord, I beseech You, how I have walked before You in truth and with a whole heart, and have done what is good in Your sight.' Hezekiah wept bitterly. Then the word of the Lord came to Isaiah, saying, Go and say to Hezekiah, 'Thus says the Lord, I have heard your prayer, I have seen your tears; behold, I will add fifteen years to your life.' Isaiah 38:1-5*

August
Week 3

Just So Many Days

For You formed my inward parts and have woven me in my mother's womb. I will give thanks to You, for I am fearfully and wonderfully made. And in Your book were all written the days that were ordained for me to live, when as yet there was not one of them. Psalm 139:13, 14, 16

A few years ago I experienced a sobering event, a loss of an old college friend. His death was sudden and unexpected, caused by a blood clot and subsequent stroke—a similar clot to the one I had in my leg during the summer. But thankfully mine was caught in time, praise God! I don't know where my old friend was with God; we were just beginning to talk about this aspect of his life. However, he was gone, and so was the opportunity to further speak with him about his faith.

As I pondered his death during the week that followed, I realized once again that we have just so many days to live here on earth. Solomon, one of Israel's most successful kings, writes about this reality before his own life came to an end. Jesus shares a similar thought in the Sermon on the Mount, as recorded in the book of Matthew.

There is an appointed time for everything. There is a time for every event under heaven, a time to give birth and a time to die; a time to plant and a time to uproot what is planted. Ecclesiastes 3:1, 2, 11

Who of you by being worried can add a single hour to his life? Matthew 6:27

can thwart and rescue us from any temptation. The closer we get to God, the farther away we get from a particular temptation.

A second strategy when dealing with temptations is to look for an escape route before it completely sucks us into its lethal nectar again. The Scripture says there are escape routes God provides with every temptation. Our job is to look for them and take these routes as quickly as possible. We need to be like the surviving bugs that flew away from the Venus flytrap when its sweet nectar was put forth. This may take some serious dedication. So, we need to practice an escape route God has placed on our hearts to take. This practice should be done long before the temptation arrives again. We can best discover these escape routes through prayer, reading applicable Scriptures, and gathering advice from other Christians who have been similarly tempted.

A third strategy is to take a victory lap every time we win out over a temptation. God indeed celebrates; He loves it when we win. In the application of this, I log every victory over temptation in my daily journal. This really helps later on, especially when struggling with a new one that has arrived. I sometimes will read and reread these journaled victories for extra motivation not to give in or give up the fight.

Last Thought

There will be losses when striving against temptation, as you well know. However, unlike the bugs that fall into the Venus Trap and perish, you will never perish. For God will never leave nor forsake you no matter what, even when falling again into the same temptation. He will simply reach down and pull you out of temptation's poisonous grasp, clean you up with His forgiveness, and start you off again. Perhaps a little shaken and scarred, but able to fly.

Scripture References

Ephesians 6:10-11 *Finally, my brethren, be strong in the Lord and in the power of His might. Put on the whole armor of God, that you may be able to stand against the temptations of the evil one.*

II Peter 2:9 *The Lord knows how to rescue the godly from temptation.*

August
Week 2

Venus Fly Trap

No temptation has overtaken you but such as is common to man; and God is faithful, who will not allow you to be tempted beyond what you are able, but with the temptation will provide the way of escape also, so that you will be able to endure it. I Corinthians 10:13

It takes about five to ten days for a Venus flytrap to dissolve an insect, entirely depending upon the bug's size. When an unsuspecting insect pursues the attractive smell of the plant and then crawls onto it, the leaves quickly close, trapping it. Within a few seconds, the digestive nectars of the plant begin to consume and dissolve the bug.

In a way, the Venus flytrap is very much like the various temptations we sometimes face in this life, especially those that cause us to fall again and again. However, there is no reason for this to keep happening from God's perspective, because He said that He would not allow us to be tempted beyond what we are able to understand. Yet, God cannot do His protective work unless we partner with Him and do what He lays on our hearts to do.

One strategy is to separate ourselves as far as we can from an old temptation. In other words, do not go near it, or let it linger in our minds and hearts. This may take some discipline, but if we ask for God's help, He will help; He always does.

Sometimes God sends others to help with our discipline. Being accountable to another for what we do puts a good kind of pressure on us from His perspective. Although this human accountability will not entirely free us from an old or chronic temptation, it can move us closer to God, who

Of course, these words and lyrics mean much to our son and his family who live on the front line as missionaries. They reside in a small rural community where the villagers are very appreciative, but the language is challenging to learn, and the conveniences of America difficult to come by.

Mission work is tough, and it takes a lot of God-given vision to handle the waiting, patience, and defeats that often accompany a ministry in a foreign country.

In some cases, sad to say, significant pain and even death may result in a missionary's effort, as was the case with those who lost their lives trying to reach the Auca Indians in Ecuador several years ago. Five of the key men in this mission were murdered by the very tribe they were trying to reach for the Gospel. The wives of these men were devastated as you can imagine, and counseled to leave the field.

As some said, "This tribe will never be reached, so let them go." But Elizabeth Elliot, one of the wives, and some others too, went right back into the fray, just because of the vision God had given them. In the end, the tide turned, and the Auca Indians came to know Christ as their Lord.

Last Thoughts

The next time you hear the song, *Be Thou My Vision* in church or on a Christian radio station, think of the missionaries who daily work hard to bring about the Gospel. Be a supportive chorus to them in any way possible. And please don't try and convince them to come home when times get tough, but instead increase your prayers, support, and encouragement for these families. Perhaps this is the vision God has for you for them.

> *"He is no fool who gives what he cannot keep, to gain that which he cannot lose. And wherever you are, be all there! Live to the hilt every situation you believe to be the will of God."* Jim Elliot

Scripture Reference

1Thessalonians 5:11 *Therefore encourage one another and build up one another, just as you also are doing.*

Roman 12:12-13 *12 Rejoice in hope, persevere in tribulation, devote yourself to prayer, 13 and contribute to the needs of the saints.*

August
Week 1

(My son envisioning the possibilities on his mission field)

Vision

Where there is no vision, the people perish. Proverbs 29:18

There is a classic story of two shoe representatives from a company who were sent to a remote region of the world to see if there could be any potential for sales there. The first called back and left a voice mail saying, "Coming home soon, there is no interest in our shoes here." The second representative wired, "Send a boatload of shoes, for the possibilities are great with the people here." The same could be said of two different Christians, one with no vision, and the other with nothing but a vision.

There is a song about vision among the old hymns, titled *Be Thou My Vision*. It was an old Irish hymn; one my wife and I love to hear when sung in church. There are particular phrases of that song that mean a lot to us, especially as we think of our son and his family's ministry in a small village in the Republic of Georgia in Eastern Europe.

> Be Thou My vision, oh Lord of my heart,
> Be Thou my wisdom,
> Be Thou my best thoughts, by day and night,
> Be thou my victory.
> And riches I heed not, nor man's empty praise
> For Thou art mine inheritance, now and always.

August

**Vision
Venus Fly Trap
Just So Many Days
Green Tomatoes**

delirium to say, "Prayer, yes, prayer is the answer, Kent." Then he died to be with the Lord.

Last Thought

What can you gain from this story? I know what Pap's Sunday School teachers took from it. But what about you? Maybe the resolve to do all you can to help others find Christ during their lifetime. And in doing this, you may have to go through a quagmire of marshy circumstances to get some of them into the kingdom. Yet, wouldn't it be worth it to know others made it to heaven because of your rescue efforts.

Scripture Reference

Luke 15:4-7 4 What man among you, if he has a hundred sheep and has lost one of them, does not leave the ninety-nine in the open pasture and go after the one which is lost until he finds it? 5 When he has found it, he lays it on his shoulders, rejoicing. 6 And when he comes home, he calls together his friends and his neighbors, saying to them, 'Rejoice with me, for I have found my sheep which was lost!' 7 I tell you that in the same way, there will be more joy in heaven over one sinner who repents than over ninety-nine righteous persons who need no repentance.

hardly make it much further, thinking that his own life was also about to come to end.

On my end as I walked deeper into the marsh, mile after mile, and hour after hour, and regularly yelling out at the top of my lungs, 'Luis, where are you? Luis, where are you?' Then I heard a small faint voice off in the distance, it came from Luis, who was trying to yell back as best he could. 'I am here, I am here, oh brother, I am here!'

When I pushed on toward him, I could hardly recognize Luis, for his face was so swollen due to all of his mosquito bites. I immediately embraced him, and then picked Luis up and carried him back to camp. The other man with me also helped in carrying him. On the way back, Luis kept saying over and over again, 'I knew you would come and save me; I just knew you would.'"

After telling this story to the Sunday School teachers, Pap ended by saying, "I loved my brother and would have done anything to save him. Perhaps in your teaching this year, you might have the same feeling of love and commitment toward the children you will be serving at Sunday School each week. And maybe, just maybe, you might visit them in their homes, helping them invite their friends to your class. If just one of those found Christ by your extra efforts, wouldn't that be worth it. Like my brother Luis, who was lost, worth going after, and found." The Sunday School teachers responded, and more came to Sunday school than ever before."

Before I end this story about Pap and what he shared with his Sunday School teachers, I happened to be with Pap when Luis the older brother he saved died years later. He had a stroke, which put him in a wheelchair for several months, and then in the hospital. As my grandfather visited him one last time, he held his hand as he passed away. It was a precious time.

Many years after that, while at school in seminary, a message came to me while in class, "Your grandfather does not have long to live, you need to come as soon as possible." He had been in the hospital for several days. I arrived and was at Pap's bedside, much like what he had been with Luis. He was delirious, for his cancer had gotten to his brain. But when I took his hand and said to him, "Pap, I am praying for you," he came out of his

telephone rang and on the other end of the line was my younger brother who told me that Luis, our older brother, and another man, were missing from a hunting trip they had gone on. He wondered if I could join in to search for the two of them. In those days there were no search and rescue teams, everyone was pretty much on their own.

All, I remember saying was, 'I am leaving right now, where can I meet up with you,' for I loved my older brother very much. As I arrived at the site of the camp where the other hunters were, only one of them knew the marsh area where Luis and the other man could have gotten lost. I said to my younger brother, 'Stay here, I will go out with this man and find our brother. Pray that he is still alive.' And so, we went off into the marsh which was a quagmire of filthy water, reeds, and thickets, which came up to our waists as we trudged through it. It was difficult to make much progress, but I was determined, my brother was not going to die.

Meanwhile, what had happened to Luis, is that both he and his other hunting partner got cut off and separated from the rest of their hunting group and had lost their way. They tried shooting their guns off in the air so they could be heard and located, but both guns jammed and became useless. While trying to make their way, Luis and his partner went further in the wrong direction, ending up deeper in the wet and mucky marsh. Exhausted, they tried to sleep when night fell, but found this impossible standing in water up to their arm pits. When morning came, Luis was able to see better and discovered they had been going in the wrong direction, but when he turned to his hunting partner to tell him, he had died during the night. It could have been his heart, or just the bite of a venomous snake, which were everywhere. Nevertheless, he was dead. According to Luis' account he tried to carry his partner for a mile or two but finally ran out of energy and could go no further. Luis then placed their two guns into the marshy ground and placed his friend's shoulders and head on top of them so that he could be found later. He was eventually found when others on horseback saw and retrieved his body. Luis continued on but was so beat that he could

July
Week 4

(My grandfather, Pap, after he saved his brother)

Lost in the Marsh

Rejoice with me, for I have found my sheep which was lost! Luke 15:6

In 1955, my grandfather whom I always called Pap, recorded the following account at the end of a book he wrote for Bresee church located in Pasadena, California, which was once a flag ship church for the Nazarene denomination.

Pap was a highly successful businessman, retiring at a young age to spend time with my brother and me after our family breakup. Yet amid his many business affairs he made time to lead Bresee's large Sunday School program. And in trying to make an important point with his Sunday School teachers before the new year kicked off, he shared the following personal story with them. When I read it by chance a few years ago I was greatly moved, for I never knew this story about my grandfather. Here's Pap's story.

"*On November 1, 1925 at one o'clock, I was on duty at the Magnolia Petroleum Company in Beaumont, Texas. The*

offering prayer with joy in my every prayer for you all, for I am confident of this very thing, that He who began a good work in you will perfect it until the day of Christ Jesus. For it is only right for me to feel this way about you all, because I have you in my heart.

Philippians 2:1-2 *Therefore if there is any encouragement in Christ, if there is any consolation of love, if there is any fellowship of the Spirit, if any affection and compassion, make my joy complete by being of the same mind, maintaining the same love, united in spirit, intent on one purpose.*

I Thessalonians 5:11 *Therefore encourage one another and build each other up.*

Many years ago when I was young, I used to run in long distant races to keep fit. In my first marathon which was 26.2 miles, I trained hard for two months with a friend named Mark. A week before the marathon we were running 10 and 15 miles to make sure we would be ready for the race. However, on the weekend of the race, I did some foolish last things, like refereeing three basketball games the day before the marathon and skipping breakfast that morning, feeling two cups of coffee was all I needed. As I found out later during the race, these were not wise decisions to say the least.

As the race begun Mark and I ran a surprisingly good pace, but around mile 14 I began to run out of gas. I told Mark to go on without me that I would catch up later. As I struggled to get to the 18-mile marker, I was all but done, very discouraged, and ready to quit. As I slowed to a walk, a young college girl running her first marathon ran by me. She stopped, and said, "Come on, you can make it, I will run with you the rest of the way." Encouraged, I began to run again, and she was true to her word, and stayed with me until the finish line. I thanked her and introduced this young girl to Mark and my family who were awaiting me at the end.

I never saw this girl again, but what she did was so supportive and selfless. She could have had a much better running time but decided cheering me on to the finish was a far better goal. In the years to come when it came time for me to encourage others, I would remember her along with other Christians I knew who were also great encouragers. And, of course, there was Paul, perhaps one of the greatest encouragers in the Scripture, who not only uplifted the discouraged, but inspired them to do likewise with others.

Last Thoughts

If you ever have the opportunity to share an encouraging word with another don't hesitate and do it, for it may make a huge difference in that person's life. Kind, uplifting, affirming, and reassuring words can go a long way with all of us.

Below are some Scriptures Paul was inspired to write about encouraging others, take them to heart and do as he did.

Scripture References

Philippians 1:3-7 *I thank my God in all my remembrance of you, always*

July
Week 3

The Rawhide Marathon

Encourage the exhausted and strengthen the feeble. Isaiah 35:3

    Some years ago, I was listening to a sermon on encouragement when the pastor broke into a joke, saying, "What has helped me the most when discouraged is a file I put together with all of the upbeat comments I had received from others over the years. When I get down about the things in this life, I just read those comments. I must have reread those two comments from my mother and wife over and over again." Of course, I and others laughed for what he said was kind of funny, but I thought such a folder was not a bad idea.

    Subsequently, I put together a folder of my own, and sure enough when things go *south* in my life, I get out that folder and read some of the comments. It really helps, for God uses these catalogued comments to encourage me when my life needs reassurance. I suggest making such a folder for yourself, for it could help when criticisms roll in or adverse circumstance hit in your life.

    Let me share with you an experience I had several years ago, one where I received an important encouragement during a difficult challenge. What I got from it not only helped me get through the challenge, but inspired me to encourage others as well.

have no hope. For if we believe that Jesus died and rose again, even so them also that are fallen asleep in Jesus will God bring with him.
Psalm 34:7 *The angel of the Lord encamps around those who respect Him and rescues them.*
Psalm 91:11 *For He will give His angels charge concerning you, to guard you in all your ways.*
Hebrews 1:14 *Are angels not all ministering spirits, sent out to render service for the sake of those who will inherit salvation?*
1Corinthians 13:12 *For now we see in a mirror dimly, but then face to face; now I know in part, but then I will know fully just as I also have been fully known.*
II Corinthians 5:6-8 *6 Therefore, being always of good courage, and knowing that while we are at home in the body, we are absent from the Lord. 7 For we walk by faith, not by sight. 8 And we are of good courage, I say, and prefer rather to be absent from the body and to be at home with the Lord.*
Romans 7:18-24 *18 For I know that nothing good dwells in me, that is, in my flesh; for the willing is present in me, but the doing of the good is not. 19 For the good that I want, I do not do, but I practice the very evil that I do not want. 20 But if I am doing the very thing I do not want, I am no longer the one doing it, but sin which dwells in me. 21 I find then the principle that evil is present in me, the one who wants to do good. 22 For I joyfully concur with the law of God in the inner man, 23 but I see a different law in the members of my body, waging war against the law of my mind and making me a prisoner of the law of sin which is in my members. 24 Wretched man that I am! Who will set me free from the body of this death? 25 Thanks be to God through Jesus Christ our Lord! So then, on the one hand I myself with my mind am serving the law of God, but on the other, with my flesh the law of sin.*
Romans 8:1 *Therefore there is now no condemnation for those who are in Christ Jesus.*
Luke 9: 28-31 *28 Some eight days after these sayings, He took along Peter and John and James, and went up on the mountain to pray. 29 And while He was praying, the appearance of His face became different, and His clothing became white and gleaming. 30 And behold, two men were talking with Him; and they were Moses and Elijah, 31 who, appearing in glory, were speaking of His departure which He was about to accomplish at Jerusalem.*

Maybe others will assist God Himself as Moses and Elijah did at the Transfiguration. (*Luke 9:28-31*) It could also be that some will nurture the children who died early in their lives, or even the millions that were aborted. Regardless of what each of us ends up doing, it will be incredibly helpful, significant, and critical to God's kingdom.

7th experience in heaven
(Final celebration)

At just the right time, and nobody knows, God will call an end to everything on earth by the return of Jesus. It will be a triumphant, celebratory, and glorious event. Those on earth who refused to believe will fall on their knees and confess Him as Lord when this happens. *(Romans 14:11-12)* However, it will be too late for them to enter heaven.

On the other hand, the believers on earth during Jesus return will join together with those already in heaven, and together all will surround Jesus with joyous song, celebration, and worship. After which all will return to heaven for eternity to carry out what is next in God's plan.

> *For this we say unto you by the word of the Lord, that we that are alive, that are left unto the coming of the Lord, shall in no wise precede them that are fallen asleep. For the Lord himself shall descend from heaven, with a shout, with the voice of the archangel, and with the trump of God: and the dead in Christ shall rise first; then we that are alive, that are left, shall together with them be caught up in the clouds, to meet the Lord in the air: and so shall we ever be with the Lord. Wherefore comfort another with these words.*
> *I Thessalonians 4:15-18*

Last Thought

God speed and see you in heaven if I don't see you again here on earth. It should be quite a reward and new beginning for you.

Scripture references

I Thessalonians 4:13-14 *But we would not have you ignorant, brethren, concerning them that fall asleep; that ye sorrow not, even as the rest, who*

5th experience in heaven
(New relationships with those with whom we struggled)

    I assume that after a good self-look from God's perspective, then the next experience in heaven is to settle any wrongs, hurts, disputes, or misgivings we had with other believers while in this world. How many of these there will be, or how long it will take to make things right, is different for each of us. This is a must, though, from God because we no longer have sin or a sin-nature to deal with anymore. Therefore, restoration with other believers will be natural, easy, loving, unifying, and genuine.

> *And forgive us our debts, as we also have forgiven our debtors. Matthew 6:12*

> *I do not ask on behalf of these alone, but for those also who believe in Me through their word; that they may all be one; even as You, Father, are in Me and I in You. John 17:20-21*

6th experience in heaven
(New responsibilities)

    As we are in heaven, resting in His love and peace, there is still lots to do until God brings an end to the world. This means for each of us there will likely be new responsibilities to accomplish before Christ returns. And amidst the joy of being with God, loved ones, and others with whom we've been restored, there are some important assignments for all of us to complete. What those will be cannot be known until we get to heaven. Perhaps some of us will help the angelic realm do their various jobs, for there is still a war going on in heavenly places with evil forces as Paul indicated in his Ephesian and Galatian letters.

> *Finally, be strong in the Lord and in the strength of His might. Put on the full armor of God, so that you will be able to stand firm against the schemes of the devil. For our struggle is not against flesh and blood, but against the rulers, against the powers, against the world forces of this darkness, against the spiritual forces of wickedness in the heavenly places. Ephesians 5:10-12*

4th experience in heaven
(An honest view of yourself)

A 4th experience in heaven is to grapple with what we did on earth, both the good and the bad. During this session God will bring before us the good things we contributed to the kingdom, as well as those that didn't. This includes everything, even the loving or hurtful relationships we had with others. How long this reflection will be is once again not known, but it doesn't matter, because time is never an issue with God as I shared earlier. Especially when it comes to getting each of us ready for the next part of our lives in His eternal plan. Did you think that God would have so much purpose and plan for you on earth, but not in heaven to come? Hardly, for each of us have only just begun our lives with God, there is so much ahead.

During this time of self-reflection with God there won't be any need to explain, justify, or argue for what we did or didn't do, because our sin-nature, which once plagued us, will be gone. *(Romans 7:18-24; Romans 8:1)* With it gone and in the history column, perhaps for the first time we will truly see ourselves as God has always seen us. And praise to His name, those things that were bad, sinful, and selfish, will be burned out of our memories forever as this session comes to an end. Those things that were good, righteous, and loving will remain forever. So as long as each of us is still breathing we still have the time and opportunity to add to those good things that will last forever.

> *For we must all appear before the judgment seat of Christ, so that each one may be recompensed for his deeds in the body, according to what he has done, whether good or bad." II Corinthians 5:10*

> *Now if any man builds on the foundation with gold, silver, precious stones, wood, hay, straw, each man's work will become evident; for the day will show it because it is to be revealed with fire, and the fire itself will test the quality of each man's work. If any man's work which he has built on it remains, he will receive a reward. If any man's work is burned up, he will suffer loss; but he himself will be saved, yet so as through fire. Do you not know that you are a temple of God and that the Spirit of God dwells in you? I Corinthians 3:12-16*

2nd experience in heaven
(New bodies)

Simultaneously to seeing God face to face for the first time comes an immediate gift of a brand-new body. Not like the one we had on earth, for this new body will be without deterioration, shortcomings, ugliness, or limitations. It will also be one that is indestructible, strong, beautiful, and well equipped for heaven. What a joy this will be, especially for those afflicted with disease, paralysis, disfigurement, or the maladies of old age while on earth. How each of us will appear with our new bodies, I do not know. I can only surmise or imagine that these bodies will be many times greater than our greatest expectations or dreams.

> *God shall fashion anew the body of our humiliation, that it may be conformed to the body of His glory.... Colossians 3:21*

> *If there is a natural body, there is also a spiritual. There are heavenly bodies, they are imperishable bodies. I Corinthians 15:44, 40*

3rd experience in heaven
(Rejoicing with family and friends)

A third experience is time set aside to be reunited with all believers. This likely will begin with the loved ones and friends with which we shared life during our time in this world. What a glorious time this will be to see loved ones and friends again, to hear their voices, and be able to touch, kiss, and embrace as never before. I think of my grandparents in this regard, who stepped in to help me so much during my youth. What a great joy it will be to see them again. This is perhaps another reason why we should keep presenting Christ to loved ones and friends who have not yet embraced Him as Lord. For we do want them in heaven, don't we?

> *But I would not have you misunderstand, brethren, concerning those who have passed away, for if they believed in Jesus, who died and rose again, God will take care of them in heaven. I Thessalonians 4:13-18*

chats on heaven. As the Scripture teaches, when we set our minds on things above, an unsurpassable peace comes, even when facing death.

> *If you were raised together with Christ, seek the things that are above, where Christ is seated on the right hand of God. Set your mind on the things that are above, not on the things that are upon the earth. Colossians 3:1-2*

Bob died a few weeks later, but based on several Scriptures, here are seven possible first experiences he encountered when entering heaven. The following order may not be exactly how it will be, for we will not truly know this until we get there ourselves.

1st experience in heaven
(Meeting with God)

The first experience for Bob was to see and hook up with God the Father, Son, Spirit, and even some of the angelic realm who had been assigned to him while on earth. I say some because there are a multitude of angels in heaven. As with Bob, this will be a joyful celebration for us as well, and perhaps carried out by the same angels who rejoiced when each of us made our decision to accept and follow Christ. *(I Thessalonians 4:13-14; Psalm 34:7; Psalm 91:11; Hebrews 1:14)*

> *Even so, I say unto you, there is joy in the presence of the angels of God over one sinner who repents. Luke 15:10*

Although this first experience of heaven may be different for each one of us, what it does bring to all is great comfort, understanding, peace, and happiness. How long this first meeting is between us and God, is not known, yet keep in mind that the Father, Son, and Spirit are never in a hurry to rush their time with any of us. For God's time is not based on a schedule, but an eternal timetable, without beginning or end. *(I Corinthians 13:12; II Corinthians 5:6-8)*

> *But forget not this one thing, beloved, that one day is with the Lord as a thousand years, and a thousand years as one day. II Peter 3:8*

July
Week 2

First Days in Heaven

Rejoice and be glad, for your reward in heaven is great. Matthew 5:12

Throughout my lifetime I have had the opportunity to talk and minister to several Christians who were dying. Some were members of churches for which I worked, some were friends, and others were family members.

To give them comfort, there was no need to share Jesus' message of salvation, for all had put their faith in Him. But what I could share was what was ahead, especially during their first days in heaven.

There was Bob, a friend of mine who was terminal and only had a few weeks to live. He had been given every pill, medicine, and treatment possible to extend his life, but to no avail. Day by day he was moving ever closer toward the end of his earthly life. Some of his friends and pastors had come by and prayed that God would miraculously heal him. However, for whatever reason, God wanted Bob in heaven. So, when I and another friend came to visit Bob during those last days, we focused on his first days in heaven, and nothing else. Amazingly, Bob exclaimed during one of our talks that he had never felt more at peace, and that not even previous hopes for a miracle gave him as much calmness and assurance as he felt after our

backslide in our morals and spirituality. A slide that may take years from which to recover, if ever.

Perhaps in our idealism, we believe our voting for this candidate or that will make a difference. But are there candidates out there with the same moral and leadership fiber as a George Washington, John Adams, or Abraham Lincoln? I don't think so, at least I haven't seen many men or women so far that compare to these great leaders of the past.

Last Thoughts

If this moral decline is true, and I hope it isn't, then your resolve must be to ask God to intervene and save us as a nation before it becomes too late.

Maybe through your prayerful pleas, He will hear your requests and raise up new leaders: men and women who not only love the people of this nation but love God, too. Men and women who put others before themselves, even if it causes them to lose an election.

Therefore, suggest in this year's Independence Day celebration to include a time of prayer with all that you do.

Footnotes

1. Thomas George [editor], *God governs the Affairs of Men, Benjamin Franklin*, (The Greatest Message of All-time, Great-messages.com).
2. William J. Johnson, *George Washington the Christian* (New York, Forgotten Books/ Abingdon Press, 1919), pages 28-31.
3. Natalie Nichols, *Is America a Christian Nation? More Quotes from Our Founders: John Adams,* (Internet, Americana, May 10, 2010) *Note-Two quotes are combined into one.
4. Franklin Graham, Quote *by Abraham Lincoln* (Washington D.C., Inaugural Invocation of President George W. Bush, January 20, 2001)
5. L.H. Butterfield, editor, *Letters of Benjamin Rush*, (Princeton: The American Philosophical Society, 1951), Volume I page 414.
6. Why-the-bible.com, *Daniel Webster*, (Internet, The Bible-Quotes from Famous Men).
7. Christian Quotes, *James Madison Christian Quote about Learning,* (Published in Christian Education Quotes, February 12, 2012).

"O blessed Father, let thy Son's blood wash me from all impurities, and cleanse me from the stains of sin that are upon me. Give me the grace to lay hold of Your merits; that they may be my conciliation and atonement. May I know my sins are forgiven, by Your Son's death and resurrection?" [2] *President George Washington*

"The Declaration of Independence laid the cornerstone of human government upon the first precepts of Christianity, for I have examined all religions, and the result is that the Bible is the best book in the world." [3] *President John Adams*

"We have been the recipients of the choicest bounties of heaven. We have been preserved these many years in peace and prosperity. We have grown in numbers, wealth, and power as no other nation has ever grown. But we have forgotten God. It behooves us then to humble ourselves before the offended powers, to confess our national sins and to pray for clemency and forgiveness." [4] *President Abraham Lincoln*

"Let the children who are sent to those schools be taught to read, write, and above all, let both sexes be carefully instructed in the principles and obligations of the Christian religion. This is the most essential part of education." [5] *Benjamin Rush (Signer of Declaration of Independence)*

"Education is useless without the Bible." [6] *Daniel Webster*

"Cursed be all learning that is contrary to the cross of Christ." [7] *President James Madison*

It is amazing what a majority of our early leaders believed when forming our laws, policies, and visions. Not quite what many of our current political, judicial, and educational leaders hold to when establishing our laws, policies, and visions of today. What a difference, what a contrast, and what a disappointment.

The way our country is digressing in its values and principles right now, relying less and less on God for guidance and strength, the more we

July
Week 1

First Independence Day

Blessed is the nation whose God is the Lord, the people whom He has chosen for His own inheritance. Psalm 33:12

In 1775, the people in and around New England began fighting the British for independence. The war lasted until 1783 when the British finally surrendered. During this time, a makeshift Congress formed and secretly voted on July 2, for complete independence. The vote passed, and two days later, on July 4, 1776, the final wording of the Declaration of Independence was approved and published.

The commemoration of that special day, July 4, evolved into an annual celebration of our freedom as an independent nation. The designation of Independence Day came later in 1791.

Here are what many of our early Founding Fathers believed and said during that time in our history. It is too bad we do not have more leaders like these today. What a moral difference that would make for us.

"I've lived, sir, a long time, and the longer I live, the more I am convinced that God governs in the affairs of men. And if a sparrow cannot fall to the ground without the Lord's notice, how is it possible that a nation can rise without His aid? For without the Lord building the house, all who labor, do so in vain." [1] *Benjamin Franklin*

July

**First Independence Day
First Days in Heaven
Rawhide Marathon
Lost in the Marsh**

Last Thought

Give in to the Spirit, who shows up every day to prune away your sins and old sinful tendencies, which the Scripture calls sanctification. Not so much to become sinless, for that will only occur when you get to heaven, but to sin less by obeying the leading of the Spirit.

Scriptures References

Galatians 5:16, 25 *16 But I say, walk by the Spirit, and you will not carry out the desire of the flesh. 25 If we live by the Spirit, let us also walk by the Spirit.*

Ecclesiastes 7: 20 *Indeed, there is not a righteous man on earth who continually does good and who never sins.*

1Thessalonians 4:3,7, *3 For this is the will of God, your sanctification, 7 For God has not called us for the purpose of impurity, but in sanctification.*

After breakfast we both walked around the yard that morning seeing more and more of what had been hidden. It was kind of embarrassing to us that we had waited so long to have all of this needed pruning done, but as they say, "Better late than never." Now we do this regularly at our new home. For as we learned there is no good reason to just let things go, all this does is make things ugly when they were meant to look beautiful, alive, and thriving.

In a way this whole pruning experience with our old and new homes, is akin to what God, our master gardener, wants to do with our Christian lives on a daily basis. Instead of letting overgrown bushes and lifeless tree branches personify us, which are brought on by old selfish and sinful behaviors, God wants to regularly cut away those and throw them into the green trash bin. He does this for many reasons, one of which is for us to always see just how beautiful we are to Him without the presence of selfishness and sin. A beauty that is not only seen by Him but by others and us as well.

> *For You formed my inward parts; You wove me in my mother's womb. I will give thanks to You, for I am fearfully and wonderfully made; Wonderful are Your works, And my soul knows it very well. Psalm 139:13-14*

Therefore, the Spirit which was given to each of us the day we believed shows up every day to prune us, so that we can maintain this beauty God sees in us. All we need do on our end is to let the Spirit do His work, as He clips and cuts away at old sinful habits that should not be a part of our lives anymore. He does this first by helping us see what He sees, then encourages us to ask for His forgiveness when we have fallen short.

In the midst of this pruning process, the Spirit is always moving us to pray on a regular basis so that we can keep up with the various old sins that creep back into our lives. And finally, He urges us to read and meditate on the Scriptures as often as we can, so the cleansing beauty God gave us at salvation can never be replaced by the ugliness of old sins.

If we let things go in our Christian lives by letting things happen as they happen, as my wife and I did with those old overgrown bushes and unkempt trees, then we can lose sight of the cleansed life God gave us at salvation. We can also lose touch with the cleansed life He intends for us to experience daily while on earth.

June
Week 4

Pruned

The Lord will continually guide you and satisfy your desire in scorched places. He will give strength to your bones, and you will be like a watered garden and spring of water whose waters do not fail. Isaiah 58:11

A few years ago, we had a gardener come to trim our bushes and trees because my wife and I were getting ready to sell our home and move. Our realtor recommended we do this to have better curb appeal for selling our home.

We were gone most of day when the gardener started trimming the shrubbery and cutting away dead branches from several of our trees. When we returned home after dark, we didn't notice anything different until the next morning. As we awoke and looked out of our bedroom window, we couldn't believe the change that had taken place. Where old and untrimmed bushes and dead branches hanging down from trees existed, there were now beautiful flowers, plants, and healthy limbs in view. All had been covered up and hidden before the gardener did his work.

Not only for your good but the good of everyone else around you. *(Romans 8:28)*

Scripture References

Malachi 1:6 *A son honors his Father…*
Romans 8:28 We know that God causes all things to work together for good to those who love God, to those who are called according to *His* purpose.

When he got up to speak, Ted said at first he had no intention of reading any Psalm, because his heart was bitter about his dad that day. Then after a few minutes of sitting underneath a huge Sequoia tree, looking up at the falls, curiosity got the best of him, and he started searching out the Psalm that matched his birthday. After he found it, he read it again and again with growing emotion and intensity. After he finished reading it one last time before making his way back to our meeting, Ted told us that tears began to well up within his heart and roll down his cheeks, for as far as he was concerned, God had spoken to him that morning about his father.

Of course, as Ted spoke, we all wanted to know the Psalm he had found. After holding back for a minute or so, he told us it was Psalm 2:7, which read, *"I will surely tell you of the decree of the Lord, for He said to me, "You are my Son, today I have begotten You."* When Ted read these words, he felt God telling him, "You are my son, Ted, and I am your father, and I will never abandon or stop loving you, no matter what." As we all listened to Ted talk some more, we could see a growing calm come over his face and a new spirit of joy within. This calm and joy lasted throughout the weekend, and long after returning home from Yosemite. Whether this was the correct application of that Psalm really didn't seem to matter, for Ted's anger and bitterness about his father was gone.

In a week or so after Yosemite, Father's Day came, but as far as Ted was concerned, the Father's Day he had always hoped for happened in Yosemite. Only his own children's celebration of him on Father's Day years later compared, for Ted ended up becoming not only a loving husband but a very attentive father to his children. He was always there for them, as God was there for him that day at Yosemite. *(Malachi 1:6)*

Last Thought

Sometimes in life, God moves you to an alternative, particularly when His initial plan (Plan A) for you is not going to work. This change is not just because of something you have done, but often what another has done, as was the case with Ted. The best response is to accept God's new plan and move on with it. By responding this way with a loving attitude, God knows He can then trust you to the highest degree in this life. And it may very well be that an alternative in life may surpass that first plan for which you had hoped for so long. For as the Scripture teaches, "All things," even the changes you must endure and adjust to, "work together for good."

when he was in junior high. Even though Ted had given his life to Christ, he still struggled mightily with what his dad had done. In the meantime, God sent others to Ted to help fill that role of his Father, but this just wasn't working for him. He simply didn't want God's plan B for his life; he wanted plan A, which was his dad back. However, that was not possible, so Ted languished in his despair and became more and more angry and disappointed with God. Fortunately for Ted, as with all of us, God was very patient, understanding, and loving with him as he worked through his hurt.

During this trip to Yosemite on a late spring weekend before Father's Day, God spoke to Ted in an incredible way that completely changed his heart about his dad, and God. The way God did this surprised me, but it was the vintage God I knew who always knows how to get through to someone who is struggling.

On this trip I took about one hundred and fifty high school students to Yosemite to build unity and better relationships between them. Large youth group ministries can be very infectious in winning other young people to Christ but tend to lose intimacy and affection for one another in the process. So, I had to work on this with our youth group all the time.

In preparation for the Saturday morning devotion, I gathered the kids together for a time of worship and singing in a meadow beneath Yosemite falls. After we finished, I asked each to find a separate place in the meadow for a quiet devotion. Before they took off, though, I asked them to read one of the Psalms and be prepared to share what they had learned when they returned. I also suggested they pick a Psalm nearest to their birthdays. I do not know why I decided to do this; it was a last-minute inspiration brought on by the Spirit, I believe.

As I explained how to find their birthday Psalm, I gave them an example. If February 7th was their birthday, then pick Psalm 2, because February was the second month of the year. Since their birthday was on the 7th day of that month, choose verse seven to read. If this formula did not work exactly, then adjust and find a Psalm nearest to their birthday.

After about forty-five minutes, each of the kids began making their way back to our meeting place. Their sharing during this time was special; it was very personal, sincere, and lasted about two hours. Yet during this time, no one seemed anxious to get it over, which said a lot about these high school students. Out of all the comments made, Ted spoke the loudest to everyone that day.

June
Week 3

Father's Day

For I know the plans that I have for you, declares the Lord, plans for welfare and not for calamity to give you a future and a hope. Jeremiah 29:11

A few years ago, my wife and I spent a weekend in Yosemite where we celebrated a wedding anniversary. Over the years we visited this beautiful national park many times, hiking up various trails, including ones to Vernal and Nevada Falls. This time around, though, we decided to bike around the park. As we pedaled passed old sites like Camp Curry, Mirror Lake, and Yosemite Falls, an old memory surfaced of a previous trip to Yosemite. Recapturing this memory, I reminded Myrna of a boy on that trip who was a part of our youth group at church. Since Father's Day was only a few weeks away, I thought this boy's story might be a good basis for a Father's Day message. She agreed, and so I wrote the following article with that young boy in mind.

Ted was 15 years old and a part of the church youth group I pastored. Most of the kids came from well-adjusted homes where their fathers were great examples and good portraits of God the Father. But not Ted. His Father had been awful and abandoned him along with the rest of the family

toward God, as He lights your way with a new understanding. And while enjoying the blaze of an answered prayer, begin to recognize how different you are now from where you were when you first began asking. Lastly, help others learn how to strike and rest as they strive, hope, and wait for the Lord to ignite their fires.

Scriptures References

Psalm 61:1-4 *1 Hear my cry, O God; Give heed to my prayer. 2 From the end of the earth I call to You when my heart is faint; Lead me to the rock that is higher than I. 3 For You have been a refuge for me, A tower of strength against the enemy. 4 Let me dwell in Your tent forever; Let me take refuge in the shelter of Your wings.*

Matthew 7:7-8 *7 Ask, and it will be given to you; seek, and you will find; knock, and it will be opened to you. 8 For everyone who asks receives, and he who seeks finds, and to him who knocks it will be opened.*

Psalms 27:14 *Wait for the Lord; be strong, and let your heart take courage; wait for the Lord!*

freezing out in the cold and desperately want some immediate warmth, hot food, or light.

In a parallel way, striking the flint is what the Christian life can be like at times, especially when seeking God's will on a particular issue or direction. Like the continual striking of flint, we sometimes pray over and over again about things that bother us, hoping God will respond and answer according to our wishes.

The repeated striking of the flint with no responding fire is like seeking God's answer to an issue but with seemingly no response, at least not the kind of response for which we are looking. Too often in these instances, we give way to confusion, worry, and even hopelessness, as we get colder and colder in our circumstances. Then night comes, and we are as cold as ever, so we moan, complain, and grumble to God, saying, "Where are you? Have you not heard our pleas? Do you not care? Come on, Lord, how often do we have to strike?"

Amidst our frustration, a hiker comes along and says, "Take a break from striking and just rest in the Lord for a while." This sounds good, and we decide to do just that. Climbing into our sleeping bag, so to speak, we get some warmth, but still no fire, no answer to our prayers. Then we get up and strike again and again with our prayers, seeking and knocking, yet still no fire. In our resting in the Lord, we once again grow impatient, and strike again and again with more prayers, becoming exhausted and more frustrated. We can hardly move; we are so tired.

Finally, God sends another hiker who has been where we are right now. This person tells us how to strike the flint and rest at the same time. "When striking," he says, "Do it with as much energy as you can muster, but after striking, rest a little longer before striking again. In your resting, recognize that God is probably delaying so that your faith and patience will grow to new levels." This may be far more important to God, then the answers you are seeking.

This hiker goes on, "Realize that what you may want will likely involve others as well. That will take perfect timing, which only God can accomplish. And remember God loves and has as much a will for you as He does for others around you."

Last Thought

One day when perhaps you least expect it the fire will ignite, and your prayers will be answered. At that moment, you will feel a new warmth

June
Week 2

Flint and the Fire

You will seek Me and find Me when you search for Me with all your heart, and you will be found by me,' declares the Lord. Jeremiah 29:13-14

Several years ago, I gave my son-in-law, Nic, a flint fire starter. He is very much an outdoorsman, so I thought he could use it one day on one of his camping trips. After all, what outdoorsman wants to start a fire in the wild with matches when he can do it with a flint fire starter? And besides, on a more practical note, if his matches got wet from the rain or by crossing a river, then how would he start a fire? Anyway, my son-in-law loved the gift, and it was right up his alley.

A flint by itself cannot produce a spark; it must be struck against another piece of steel. The friction created by doing this causes a small curl of steel to peel off and ignite. If you do this near some dry leaves or brush, then you'll get fire.

To better understand how steel ignites in this process, take a coat hanger, and bend it over and over again in one spot until it gets so hot you can hardly touch it. This is basically what goes on when you repeatedly strike flint against another piece of steel; it gets hotter and hotter with every strike. Unhappily, though, sometimes it takes a lot of striking to get a strong enough spark to work, which can be frustrating, especially if you are

God's foreknowledge
John 11:1, 11, 17, 32,33,35,41,43-44 *1 Now Lazarus of Bethany was sick, in the village of Mary and her sister Martha. 4 But when Jesus heard this, He said, 'This sickness is not to end in death, but for the glory of God, so that the Son of God may be glorified by it.' 17 So when Jesus came, He found that Lazareth had already been in the tomb four days 32 Therefore, when Mary came where Jesus was, she saw Him, and fell at His feet, saying, 'Lord, if You had been here, my brother would not have died.' 33 When Jesus saw her weeping and the Jews weeping, He was deeply moved, 35, and wept. 41 So they removed the stone at the entrance of the tomb. 43 and He cried out with a loud voice, 'Lazarus, come forth.' 44 and he came forth bound hand and foot with wrappings, then Jesus said, 'Unbind him, and let him go.'*

God's foreknowledge and sovereignty
Luke 22:31,32-34,56,60-62 *31 Simon, Simon, behold, Satan has demanded permission to sift you like wheat; 32 but I have prayed for you, that your faith may not fail; 33 But he said to Him, 'Lord, with You I am ready to go both to prison and to death!' 34 And He said, 'I say to you, Peter, the rooster will not crow today until you have denied three times that you know Me.' 56 And a servant-girl, seeing him as he sat in the firelight and looking intently at him, said, 'This man was with Him too.' 60 I do not know what you are talking about. 'Immediately, while he was still speaking, a rooster crowed. 61 The Lord turned and looked at Peter. And Peter remembered the word of the Lord, how He had told him, "Before a rooster crows today, you will deny Me three times.' 62 And he went out and wept bitterly.*

graduation, a reward that would erase her disappointment and bring great joy to her and her family.

Dominique's mother arrived and took her home. After sleeping all afternoon, she recovered enough to go to graduation. She and her entire family sat in the front row, watching the whole program go off without a hitch. At the end, I got up to announce the award, for the principal of the school asked me if I would do it this year. I did, and sure enough, all that pain, struggle, and hard times gave way to joy when Dominique's name was read.

Last Thoughts

There are many lessons to be grasped from this story; God's foreknowledge and sovereignty are just two of them. Just as I knew what was ahead for Dominque at the end of that graduation evening, so God foreknows what is ahead for us in each situation. Even though we may suffer for a while, as Dominique did in her circumstances, God will again turn all of our tears into joy at the end.

What of His sovereignty? I knew early on that Dominique was going to receive the reward she won; I made sure of this in our teacher meetings. God in His sovereignty also makes sure of what He intends for us during our lifetime. Yet in this, He allows us to make choices, to do this or that, and even give way to discouragement or doubt at times. But in the end, He can work together all that we do with what He plans for us. He can do this because He is sovereign, and He is God.

PS

By the way, I talked with Dominique a few years ago; she was married and had four children at the time. She is still trusting God, did so at eleven years old, and now as a young mother!

Scripture References

God's sympathy
Revelation 21:4 *He will wipe away every tear from your eyes, and death shall be no more, neither shall there be mourning, crying, or pain, for these will have died."*

around. Our efforts that night as a class were a success, and if there was a prize given for effort, we might have gotten it.

The morning after open house, all the projects had to be taken down, and classrooms put back in order. When I arrived early the next morning to do this before school, there was Dominque with her dad. She asked if her dad could see her project before I took it down. "Of course, Dominque, take your time." Holding onto him, she took him upstairs into the classroom. They were there for several minutes, and upon leaving, I heard him say, "Honey, I am so proud of you; you've made my recovery better."

Not too many weeks later, Dominique shared in class during our prayer time that her dad had recovered and that he was able to go back to work. The trial was over for Dominique, or was it?

At the end of the school year, which was not too far off, sixth-grade graduation ceremonies were on the horizon. As big as the open house was, 6th grade graduation was even more significant, for more than a thousand parents, grandparents, aunts, uncles, brothers, and sisters came. During graduation, all of the sixth-grade classes put on a program before receiving their diplomas. The program involved individual musical performances, student speeches, and a speaking choir of 150 students presenting a patriotic theme.

At the end of the evening, after the diplomas had been given out, a special award was traditionally given to the student who demonstrated the best academics and Christian character during the school year. The reward was free tuition for the following year. Of course, Dominique was going to receive this, but it was to be kept secret until the end.

When graduation day finally arrived, and the last rehearsals were being practiced, Dominique got extremely sick during the last rehearsal, so much so that she had to be replaced in the program by another girl. As she was escorted off stage to one of the auditorium seats, where she waited for her mom to come and pick her up, I made my way toward her. As I sat behind Dominique, I saw something I had not seen all year from her, tears, a multitude of them rolling down her face. For the entire year, Dominique had been a courageous and resilient girl, always depending upon her faith in God to make things better. But I guess this last incident broke her.

In her tears, she looked back at me as if to say, will this year ever end? I felt her pain and anguish and began to fight back my own tears. I wanted so much to tell her about the reward awaiting her at the end of

Without realizing it, though, competition between the classes developed over the years to see which class had the most impressive projects and dazzling rooms. I must admit, perhaps due to my past sports involvements, that I fell into this competitive battle. So instead of having my kids do desk projects, I got a brainstorm and went another direction.

At the time, my class was studying about Egypt, which was a part of our sixth-grade world history curriculum. During our study, we compared the afterlife tenets and thoughts of the Egyptians with early and present-day Christian beliefs. The distinctions between the two were significant in many ways, but it was the tombs of each that visibly expressed the differences. The tombs of the Egyptians, specifically those of the Pharaohs, were impressive and larger than life. In contrast, Christian tombs, notably Christ's tomb, were comparatively small, underground, and unimpressive. This is because a Christian's glory, as we all know, comes in heaven with God, not on earth with man.

Therefore, my student's open house projects involved building within the classroom several pairs of tombs, some representing the pharaohs and others of Jesus. Some tombs with a mummy and others empty, because of a resurrected Christ. There were captions and inscriptions put on the outside of the tombs that read, "Here lays Pharaoh, dead in his tomb, thought he was god, but was not." Another read, "This is where Christ was buried, but He is not here, because He has risen. He is God."

Within one of the groups working on a tomb was an eleven-year-old girl named Dominique, who was struggling. Her distress did not come from the class project, but difficult times at home. Her dad had a heart attack and could not work to support the family for a while. Bills were piling up, and everyone in the family helped in one way or another. But all young Dominique could do was pray for her dad and be the best possible student at school. As the days slowly progressed, Dominique's father seemed to make little progress.

At the beginning of this trial, for I knew what was going on, Dominique's faith was strong, but as time passed, her face began to show more and more strain. Yet even when things seemed to be at their worst, possibly losing her dad, she never quit praying nor missed an assignment.

As the class tomb projects were wrapping up, it did not look like Dominique's dad was going to be well enough to come to the open house and see what she and others in her group had done. Even so, her tomb was a huge draw, hundreds of parents came to see it, for the word had gotten

June
Week 1

(Open house project of Christ's tomb)

A Little Girl's Tears

We know that God causes all things to work together for good to those who love Him and are called according to His purpose. For those whom He foreknew, He also predestined to become conformed to the image of His Son, and these whom He predestined, He also called; and these whom He called, He also justified; and these whom He justified, He also glorified. Romans 8:28-30

The following personal story gives what I believe is a good portrait of God's sympathy, foreknowledge, and sovereignty at work in our lives. Plus in the midst of this, the Lord has given each of us a free will of our own. A will He can work together with His overall sovereignty.

It was a spring day in 1993 when I was a sixth-grade teacher at a Christian school. Most of my students were putting their final touches on their history projects. They were pretty excited about this because their projects, along with all the projects from other grades, would be displayed on their desks for the school's open house that evening. The school's open house was really something because several hundred parents came every year to see what their children and other classes had done. It was a big deal for our school, one of the biggest events of the year!

June

**A Little Girl's Tears
Flint and the Fire
Father's Day
Pruned**

might help. God used those words; He will use your words as well to help others who are hurting, especially those laced with the Scriptures.

Last Thought
Make every effort to always say something helpful to others in need, and never sell short what you say, for God can use any or all of your words to make a tremendous difference.

Scripture References
Proverbs 25:11 & Proverbs 16:24 *Like apples of gold in settings of silver are timely words spoken in the right circumstance. They are like a honeycomb, sweet to the soul and healing to the bones.*

as possible, two young women approached me; one was with her husband and the other with her children. They knew who I was and began to praise the home and all of its staff for what had been done for their husbands, who were children at Hollygrove. They were especially appreciative of the Christian faith their husbands found while at the home.

Hollygrove was not a Christian home; it was secular. However, it just happened to have a staff where most were Christians. Because of this, the hope of Christ was often shared with kids who had lost hope with their families. The bottom line was that many kids at Hollygrove found Christ during their years there.

While talking with these two gals, all of a sudden, a big 6'5" man grabbed me from behind and raised me up in the air. He was not mad at me, just excited to see me once again. The last time I saw him he was eleven years old.
He cried out!

> "It's Brian," Mr. McClain, "it's me."
> "Oh, my heavens," I said, "Not the little boy in cottage five."

Then he said something that took me back a little, for I did not always remember every experience I had while working at Hollygrove. Here is what I remember Brian saying although I am not sure all of the words are 100% accurate.

> "Thanks, Mr. McClain, for writing me that letter after you left the home; what you said really helped and encouraged me, for I had been struggling with God back then, wondering if He really loved me. When I got your letter out of the blue, I knew He did by what you said."

As Brian continued and told me about how his life went over the years, I was so proud of him, for he not only turned out to be a man who loved God but was a good provider and a great husband and father to his children as well. For what he missed while growing up, he made up for by always being there for his wife and children.

I don't remember all that I wrote to Brian at the time. It had been several years since I saw him. But when Bob, the manager of Hollygrove, called and told me about his struggles, I immediately wrote what I thought

May
Week 4

Timely Words

A man has joy in an apt answer, and how delightful is a timely word! Proverbs 15:23

Several years ago I attended a reunion at Hollygrove where I worked during my college days. It was a home for orphans and kids who were wards of the court. The home was under the auspices of the Los Angeles Orphan's Home Society. It encompassed a two-story building with several cottages and was right in the middle of Hollywood. The whole complex was surrounded by trees and bushes so that hardly anyone knew where it was located.

This is where, many years before, a child named Marilyn Monroe lived when her family was in turmoil. I know this to be true because I ran across her file one day while at Hollygrove. Her name then was Norma Jean Baker, a very pretty name. I don't know why she changed it later on, perhaps, and I am just guessing, to separate herself from a very troubled childhood,

Walking into the lounge/cafeteria where the reunion was being held, I wondered if I would recognize any of the kids with whom I worked during my college days. Or would they even know me, for it had been 15 years.

As I looked around the room, which numbered about 50 or so, some faces looked familiar, but I couldn't recall their names unless I looked at their name tags. Then while moving through the room talking with as many

disappoint, because the love of God has been poured out within our hearts through the Holy Spirit who was given to us.
Daniel 2:46-47 *:46 Then King Nebuchadnezzar fell on his face and did homage to Daniel and gave orders to present to him an offering and fragrant incense. 47 The king answered Daniel and said, 'Surely your God is a God of gods and a Lord of kings and a revealer of mysteries since you have been able to reveal this mystery.*

However, if we go around the cliff from where these treasured pebbles lay to an area that shields other rocks from the constant force of the ocean, we will find an abundance of stones never admired or taken home.

Why is this? Why are they not collected? Why are these rocks so lowly esteemed? The simple reason is that they have escaped the constant grinding brought on by the ocean waves, which is the very instrument that would have made them smooth, beautiful, and collectible. Regrettably, for these stones, the cove that protected and made their cycle of existence peaceful and serene ended up making them look rather rough, angular, and jagged. They are rocks that no one seems to value or want to take home.

There is a great spiritual lesson here, especially when we undergo difficult times or circumstances that stretch us to the limits. These difficulties are like the waves that God allows us to experience in this life, not to hurt us, but to make us more beautiful. Because each wave of trouble that comes our way is an opportunity to trust in Him for resolve and do what is right to others and even ourselves. If we look at the life of Daniel in the Old Testament, we will see a man that was honored and respected by every king under which he served. He is still known today as one of the Bible's most significant and wisest leaders.

What made Danial so great and beautiful in God's eyes as well as others? It was the trials he had to go through, trials that ground against his spirit, demanding every inch of his faith. These trials began when he was young and continued until old age. He was threatened by King Nebuchadnezzar when he was only 15 years of age and thrown into the lion's den when he was 80. Due to each of these difficult circumstances and much more in-between, he developed into a man like those pebbles on the beach in Pescadero, California, beautiful, valuable, and very collectible.

Last Thought

The next time you encounter a difficult trial, or a set of tough circumstances that never seem to let up, realize that God may be making you more and more beautiful as you trust Him through every hit of a wave.

Scripture References

Romans 5:3-5 *3 And not only this, but we also exult in our tribulations, knowing that tribulation brings about perseverance; 4 and perseverance, proven character; and proven character, hope; 5 and hope does not*

May
Week 3

Pebble Beach

Consider it all joy, my brethren, when you encounter various trials, knowing that the testing of your faith produces endurance. And let endurance have its perfect result, so that you may be perfect and complete, lacking in nothing. James 2:2-4

Pescadero, California, is the site of one of the most striking coastal landscapes in the world. Many know of this pristine area because of the famous Pebble Beach Golf Course nearby, where well-known celebrities and pros often play. The long line of white surf on the beach comes up with a roar and crashes against every stone onshore. The rocks are tossed continuously back and forth, day after day, without a break.

What is the outcome of such an impact? Tourists come from all over the world to see and gather these newly formed and beautiful pebbles to take home as souvenirs. Some of these reformed stones, depending on who gathers them, are displayed in glass cabinets, or put on mantels, desks, and bookshelves.

abandoned or abused. When God creates a child, He will complete the job of parenting, whether it is done through another family member, friend, or even someone outside of the family.

God does take care of children left behind, whether it be with those who have lost a parent to cancer like Laura or have lost a parent due to other circumstances. And sometimes it takes longer than what is hoped for, but in the end, God delivers; He always has and always will.

I will ask the Father, and He will give you a Helper, the Holy Spirit, and He will be with you forever. John 14: 16

I am confident of this very thing, that He who began a good work in you, will perfect it until the day of Christ Jesus. Philippians 1:6

Last Thought

What enabled Laura to move into heaven? Laura entered not because she was a good mother; she certainly was that. And not because she remained upbeat and faithful to her family during those last months, she did that also. But because of one major decision made earlier in life, confessing her sins and accepting Jesus as Lord and Savior. That is why she was able to do as she did in those last days, and why she is in heaven today.

God speed and celebrate this Mother's Day with love and appreciation. Bad times come and go, but the good always seems to remain, especially when it is manifested in Godly mothers, grandmothers, or anyone else who loves children.

Scripture References

(Verses allowing Laura into heaven)

I John 1:9 *If we confess our sins, He is faithful and righteous to forgive us our sins and to cleanse us from all unrighteousness.*
Rom 10:9-10 *9.that if you confess with your mouth Jesus as Lord, and believe in your heart that God raised Him from the dead, you will be saved;.10. for with the heart a person believes, resulting in righteousness, and with the mouth he confesses, resulting in salvation.*

> *But we do not want you to be uninformed, brethren, about those who have died, so that you will not grieve as do the rest who have no hope. For if we believe that Jesus died and rose again, even so, God will bring with Him those who have died in Jesus. I Thessalonians 4:13-14*

> *He said to him, 'Truly I say to you, today you shall be with Me in Paradise.' Luke 23:43*

Why did God not heal her?

Since the Lord decided not to extend Laura's life for which we had prayed and hoped, what heavenly responsibility or plan overrode our request? In other words, what is Laura doing in heaven that was more vital to God than keeping her on earth? We don't know, and really won't until we get to heaven and ask God, face to face, about this. Until then, we must submit to God's greater insight and oversight of Laura when making this decision. With as much faith as we can muster, we must accept His sovereign reasoning in every decision He makes. After all, He turned down Jesus' request at Gethsemane, "Please remove this cup from me, yet not My will, but Thine be done." Had God not said, "No," then our sins would not have been taken care of on the cross, and none of us would have ever been saved.

> *For now, we see in a mirror dimly, but then face to face; now I know in part, but then I will know fully just as I also have been fully known. I Corinthians 13:12*

> *For I know the plans that I have for you, declares the Lord, plans for welfare and not for calamity to give you a future and a hope." Jeremiah 29:11*

What help is there for those left behind?

When Jesus left His disciples to join the Father in heaven, He promised to leave them with the great "Helper," the Holy Spirit. God has never left any of His loved ones on earth to fend for themselves, and this includes children who lose parents, as well as those who have been

Afterward, Laura seemed to improve, but then the cancer came raging back, which put her in the hospital. Her pain grew unbearable, which moved some of us to begin to pray, "Please, Lord, take her quickly." God did just that; He took Laura to heaven only a few weeks later, after school had ended.

The times we all had with Laura were unforgettable. I remember how funny and brave she was in different situations. Linda, one of her close friends, who drove her back and forth to doctor's appointments, shared that one-time Laura poured ice down her back following one of those visits. When Linda exclaimed, "Why would you do such a thing after such a serious appointment?" Laura said, "So you won't ever forget this moment."

On another occasion, when Laura visited me at my office, I took a chance and cracked a joke about her cancer. Her response was as expected; she couldn't stop laughing. I told her the entire state of Idaho would never suffer an energy crisis as long as she hung around. All Idaho had to do was plug into her for its power needs, because of all the radiation stored in her.

Regarding her strength and bravery, I remember a conversation I had with Laura about Michelle, another mother at our school who succumbed to cancer in the middle of the year. It was at Michelle's funeral, which Laura was attending that I saw her and said, "I'm so surprised to see you are here." Laura quickly responded, "I simply wanted to see how Michelle's children respond to their mother's funeral, and what it would be like from this end to be memorialized by loved ones and friends." As you can see, Laura was not short of courage.

Due to Laura's well-chronicled last year with us, some biblical assurances help answer some of the tough questions surrounding her difficult passing.

Where was Laura after she died?

She went immediately in the presence of God when Laura breathed her last, God instantly swept her away into heaven at that very moment. What a change she must have experienced when this happened, one moment agonizing in pain and unbearable discomfort, and the next liberated from all of it and in the arms of God. She currently resides with Him, along with other family members and friends who put their trust in Jesus and have died.

May
Week 2

A Mother to Remember

Strength and dignity are her clothing, and she smiles at the future. Her children rise up and bless her; Her husband praises her. Proverbs 31:25, 28

This Mother's Day devotional is dedicated to Laura, one of the most wonderful mothers I had the pleasure of knowing. Happy Mother's Day, Laura, as you continue to carry out God's will and work in heaven.

Several years ago, when I was a Christian school administrator in Idaho, I had the privilege of getting to know one of my faithful school moms, Laura, who passed away during my time there. Despite her battle with cancer during the school year in which she died, Laura always cared deeply for her children, and hoped and prayed for their best after she was gone.

The events surrounding her the year she died were a mixture of hope and discouragement, with lots of ups and downs. One moment it seemed like Laura might recover from her cancer, and the next as if she only had a few days to live. During these times, many of her fellow mothers at school rallied to support Laura and her family. They regularly prayed for her, spoke words of encouragement, and brought food to her family when she was too weak to fix meals herself. They even drove her children back and forth to school each day when Laura couldn't drive anymore.

In the late spring as her condition worsened, many of these moms gathered in my office one day after school to pray for Laura, that God would heal her. We all laid hands on her and prayed and prayed and prayed. While we were doing this, another mom took care of her kids outside until we had finished. It was a precious time which none of us ever forgot.

more thrashing about, I decided to take his advice, and sure enough, I made it to shore safe and secure.

Is this not true of our own lives many times and in many ways, particularly when we experience situations where we don't know what to do or where to go next? Sad to say, we usually panic and try to swim out of things by our own means. Instead, we should have prayed, listened to Him through others who love us, and then waited for Him to float us ashore by His own resolve, which often is a path we had not even considered.

Last Thought

Do we really think the Lord who loved and gave His life for us, would actually let you drown in your circumstances? Hardly!

So "relax" and let God float you out of your different dilemmas. He will not only give you the right instructions at the right time but will remain close by to save you in case you panic, just like my grandfather did with me.

Scriptures References

Exodus 33:14 *The Lord's presence shall go with you always, and He will give you rest.*

Matthew 11:28 *Come to Me, all who are weary and heavy-laden, and I will give you rest.*

John 14:27 *Peace I leave with you; My peace I give to you; not as the world gives. So, do not let your heart be troubled, nor let it be fearful.*

May
Week 1

(The Dead Sea)

Floating with God's Will

Don't be anxious for anything, but through prayer, let your requests be known to God, and the peace He gives will guard your heart, mind, and thoughts. Philippians 4:6-7

During my last trip to Israel, both my wife, Myrna, and I swam in the Dead Sea, or should I say floated in this salt laden body of water. In addition to being earth's lowest elevation of land, it is filled with so much salt (34.2%) that it is impossible to drown in it. To give a perspective of how salty this is, the Dead Sea is nine and half times saltier than the ocean.

It was kind of fun for Myrna and me to watch others try to swim in the Dead Sea. No matter how hard they tried, all they could do was walk on its bottom or float on its top. And God help them if they got water in their eyes, for it would sting like crazy.

This experience reminded me of the time when my grandparents took me as a child to the Great Salt Lake in Utah. It, too, was filled with salt (27%). My grandfather, whom I greatly trusted, said, "Just relax and don't try and swim; otherwise, you may get salt in your eyes, and it will burn." But did I listen? Of course not! As I got too deep, my swimming toward shore only worked against me. Again and again I went under only to pop up without any progress. My grandfather was close by, but instead of grabbing me, said, "Relax, Kent, and eventually, you'll just float in." So, after a little

May

Floating with God's Will
A Mother to Remember
Pebble Beach
Timely Words

others went on to do great things for the kingdom. They even gave up their own lives in the end, preaching the Gospel.

Last Thought

No matter what you have or haven't done for Christ during your lifetime, remember this story, for His forgiveness is just as much available for you as it was for Peter and the other disciples that morning. And as Jesus said to them, I love you and tend my lambs, so He says to you, "I love you without measure, go, and win others to the kingdom."

Scripture References

To inspire, strengthen, and even lift your spirits read these passages during Easter, *Matthew 28, Mark 16, Luke 24, John 20, John 21, Acts 1:1-11, I Corinthians 15:5-7, and Matthew 16.*

on the other hand, was a much deeper love, the kind that would cause you to do everything possible for another, even at the cost of your own life. This is the love Jesus had for the disciples and the rest of mankind when He gave up His life on the cross.

When Jesus asked Peter, "Do you love me?" He used *agape* love when asking this question. In response, Peter must have thought for a minute or two before answering, because he responded with *phileo* love. In other words, "Yes, Lord, I love you like a friend." This might have surprised some of the disciples listening because Peter seemed to always be the one who answered confidently and boldly, sometimes for good, and sometimes not. Jesus did not rebuke him for his answer, but simply said, "Tend my lambs."

Then a few minutes passed, and after eating a few more bites of fish and bread, Jesus asks him again, "Simon, son of John, "Do you love me?" Still, Jesus uses *agape* love in His question. Peter begins to struggle within, and answers back, "I love you like a friend." Jesus once again does not rebuke him, but says, "Shepherd my sheep."

Finally, for a third time, Jesus asks, "Do you love me like a friend, using *phileo* this time around. Peter really struggles now and begins to grieve, but in his struggle, he says, "You know I love you like a friend." Jesus says one last time, "Then tend my sheep."

Jesus knew Peter was troubled, so what was Jesus doing with him during this time, and what was His message to him? I believe Jesus was repairing Peter, because in each of Jesus' answers, "Tend my lambs, shepherd my sheep, and tend my sheep," none of Peter's responsibilities were removed. Jesus was basically saying to Peter, "You are still the rock I declared you to be, and upon what you teach about Me and the kingdom, I will build my church. I told you I would make you a fisher of men at the beginning, and a fisher of men you will continue to be. Regarding your past failures, and even your inability today to love me as I love you, you are forgiven. In time you will love Me and others as I have loved you. Count on it!"

As breakfast ended, the other disciples knew that Jesus was not just talking to Peter that morning, but to them as well. Each knew that they had their moments of faith in their own hearts, but failures, too, particularly when they hid during his trials and torture. Yet, like Peter, these failures would not be held against them. As history proves, these disciples and the

The disciples were to meet Jesus at the end of this time on a mountain in Galilee, probably Mt. Carmel. From there, they would take a four-day walk to Jerusalem, where He would ascend to heaven in their presence.

Before the disciples got to the mountain to make this last trek with Him, Peter and six other disciples took off to go fishing on the Sea of Galilee. This is where Peter had made his living before meeting Jesus. John and James, who also made their living as fishermen, were among the six on this fishing trip.

When Peter and the others cast out their nets during that early dawn, they heard Jesus' voice onshore. He was beckoning them to come and join Him. They knew it was Jesus because they had heard His voice many times before. As they were making their way to shore where Jesus had built a fire, Peter could not wait and jumped into the water, clothes and all, to get there as soon as he could.

As they were all eating breakfast together, Jesus asked Peter some probing, yet very healing questions. As Jesus did this, you have to wonder what Peter was thinking about himself concerning his relationship with the Lord. On the one hand, he could bring up to himself some great memories and experiences. After all, he had given up his fishing profession to follow Jesus and even walked on water with Him; that is until he panicked and began to drown. He was also the first to identify Jesus as the Messiah when others stayed silent. And when the soldiers came to take Jesus away to trial, he took out his sword and began to fight. On the other hand, Peter also knew that he had denied Jesus three times during His time of need and had run and hidden with the other disciples while Jesus was being tortured and crucified. Ugh!

Perhaps during this fishing trip, which turned out to be the last for him, Peter was thinking about all of these things, particularly his failures. Isn't that true of most of us? We tend to dwell more on our failures than our victories. Maybe that is why Peter was out fishing again, saying to himself, "Well, back to fishing, at least I can do this, for I am not qualified to be the kind of disciple Jesus needs or wants."

As they all gathered on the beach and began to cook and eat their fish and bread, Jesus asked Peter in front of all, "Do you love Me?"

A few Greek words are used in the New Testament for love, one is *agape*, and the other is *phileo*. This latter love speaks only of friendship, the kind you could have with many who share your common interests. *Agape*,

April
Week 4

(Sea of Galilee today)

Breakfast with Jesus

Come and have some breakfast. John 21:12

    A few years ago, my wife, Myrna, and I sat on the Sea of Galilee's shore, not far from Capernaum. This was a little sea town where Jesus asked Peter to be one of His disciples at the very beginning of His ministry. As Myrna and I had our devotions, we could feel the presence of the Lord when the sun came up. We also knew we were not far from where Jesus had a special breakfast with Peter and the other disciples not long before He ascended to heaven. Perhaps Myrna and I were right on the spot where they had breakfast together, who knows.

    The breakfast took place about 33 days after Jesus' resurrection. It was a special breakfast because Jesus was going to tell Peter something he needed to know that would help him the rest of his life. Six other disciples were present during this discussion, so what He said helped them too.

    After the resurrection, Peter only met personally with Jesus a few times. During the days that followed this incredible miracle, Jesus spent most of His time with others who had been faithful to Him, possibly up to 500 of them, as I Corinthians 15 indicates. Who were included in the 500? I am not entirely sure, but they were likely those who had responded to His many teachings, miracles, and healings.

expectation that God would restore their lives and nation. But at the height of their hope, Jesus was crucified. All was lost! All was lost! All was lost!

After Jesus' body was torn down from the cross, all returned to their homes, likely heads down, broken, and downtrodden. Then all of a sudden, for some, perhaps those who had held onto their faith, loved ones who had recently died began showing up in the streets of Jerusalem and even at their doorsteps. With tears joyously rolling down their cheeks, how many ways did they say, "How can this be? How can this be?" But it was because when God is in charge, anything is possible.

At the height of their despair, God sent two great miracles, one of the risen Saints, and the other of Jesus Himself. The Saints brought more evidence of Jesus, and Jesus brought victory over death and sin, and the promise of eternal life to all who believe.

All was restored, all was restored, and all was restored! Is He not still restoring you in different ways today? I think so.

Scripture Reference

I Corinthians 15:55-58 55 Oh death, where is your victory? Oh, death, where is your sting? 56 The sting of death is sin, and the power of sin is the law, 57 but thanks be to God, who gives us the victory through our Lord Jesus Christ. 58 Therefore, my beloved brethren, be steadfast, immovable, always abounding in the work of the Lord, knowing that your toil is not in vain in the Lord.

Therefore, be always of good courage, and know that while we are at home in this body of ours, we are absent from the Lord, for we walk by faith, not by sight. So, be of good courage, for I personally prefer to be absent from my body and at home with the Lord. II Corinthians 5:6 -8

We do not want you to be uninformed, brethren, about those who are asleep, so you will not grieve as do the rest who have no hope. For if we believe that Jesus died and rose again, even so, God will bring with Him those who have fallen asleep in Jesus. II Thessalonians 4:13-14

What did the risen Saints do before entering Jerusalem?

There is no way of actually knowing what these believers (Saints) did after their old bodies were raised and resurrected and when they first appeared in Jerusalem. They were to be there, though, right after Jesus's resurrection, giving more evidence of His victory over sin and death. Anyone who saw them and Christ that day had to realize that He was truly the Son of God, and right about everything He had ever said.

How long did they live before returning to heaven?

There is no direct Scriptural reference regarding how long they stayed on earth after their role was completed in Jerusalem. Perhaps they were taken back to heaven when Christ ascended. Or maybe, God left them to remain on earth for a while to live out an extended life, as was the case with Lazarus in John 11. Whether it is one situation or the other, I surmise there were a lot fewer tears the second time around when they departed again to heaven.

Last Thoughts

As you celebrate Easter, no matter the difficulties you may be going through, God is still making miracles. Two thousand years ago, the Jewish people had lost everything; the Roman occupation had wiped them out, and many were living from one meal to the next. Then Christ came, and things began to change. For the first time in years, they had hope, a renewed

Jesus' resurrection? How long did they live before returning to heaven? These are all challenging questions, but I will do my best to answer them according to my knowledge of the times and the Bible.

Who were these Saints, and what was their purpose?

A few Bible commentators purport that these Saints were some of the earlier Patriarchs: men like Moses and Elijah. After all, these two showed up at the Mount of Transfiguration; why not again to accomplish God's purpose? But I do not believe so, for no one in Jerusalem would have recognized them. There were no previous portraits or pictures to draw from to identify them.

In respect to God's purpose in raising these Saints from the dead, I construe they were believers in Christ who had recently died. They were men, women, and even children who would have been recognizable by all when they walked through Jerusalem after Jesus' resurrection. This works well into God's purpose, which was to give Jerusalem further evidence that Jesus had indeed risen from the dead, just as those who stood before them.

Where were the Saints before their bodies were raised from the dead?

The Scriptures are pretty clear about where believers and the faithful go when they die, whether in Old Testament times, Jesus' day, or today. All are immediately put in the presence of God. In our culture, we use the term *pass on* for death to soften the blow. In Jesus' time, they used the term *fallen asleep*. But no matter the term, when believers die, they go to be with God, just as Moses and Elijah proved when they appeared to Jesus, James, John, and Peter at the Mount of Transfiguration.

> *Later, Jesus took Peter and James and John up on a high mountain by themselves. And while there, He was transfigured before them; and His face shone like the sun, and His garments became as white as light. Then behold, Moses and Elijah appeared talking with Him. Peter said 'Lord, it is good for us to be here; if You wish, I will make three tabernacles, one for You, and one for Moses, and one for Elijah.' Matthew 17:1-4*

Tehachapi earthquake near Bakersfield. This 1952 earthquake shook our house in Pasadena (117 miles away) at 5 am. I was only six years old at the time, but I remember my parents being knocked out of their beds. It turned out to be a 7.7 earthquake on the Richter scale.

Although several other quakes hit California over the next several years, one of the worst was the Northridge quake in 1994, when my own little family was caught off guard early one morning. This quake killed seventy-two people, injured 9,000, crushed several freeways and buildings, and caused at least fifteen billion dollars worth of damage.

In our house, which was close to the epicenter, everything was shattered into pieces or broken. We slept outside in our van for the rest of the week until the aftershocks subsided. It was scary!

As frightening as earthquakes can be, the one that hit Jerusalem 2000 years ago during Jesus' crucifixion must have been very alarming, for they did not have the structures to handle such a destructive event. Yet even though this quake caught everyone by surprise, this was nothing compared to what was about to happen, and I am not just talking about Jesus' resurrection.

Matthew is the only one of the Gospel writers to record this astonishing event because he may have been the only one to see it firsthand. Regardless, it is in the Scripture and plays a significant part around the events of Jesus' death and resurrection. As we read the following verses, take note that the first verse about the veil of the Temple was in each of the other Gospels, which gives context to what Matthew recorded.

> *And behold, the veil of the temple was torn in two from top to bottom; and the earth shook, and the rocks were split. The tombs were opened, and many bodies of the saints who had fallen asleep were raised and came out of their tombs. After His resurrection, they entered the holy city and appeared to many. Now the centurion, and those who were with him keeping guard over Jesus, when they saw the earthquake and the things that were happening, became very frightened and said, 'Truly this was the Son of God!' Matthew 27:51-54*

Who were these Saints who came out of the tombs? What was God's purpose in raising them from the dead? Where were they before their bodies were raised from the dead? What did they do before entering Jerusalem after

April
Week 3

(Gethsemane church overlooking Jerusalem)

All Was Lost

Behold, I am the Lord, the God of all flesh; is anything too difficult for Me? Jeremiah 32:27

    This Easter article is one of the more intriguing ones I have ever written; it is based on a passage of Scripture that describes a very unusual event during Jesus' crucifixion and resurrection. Very few pastors or Bible teachers, I have found, attempt to teach, or explain Matthew 27:51-54 during Easter. Yet, this passage is deserving of not only mention but inclusion during this hallowed week, for it dramatically highlights the incredible victory Jesus had over death.
    Earthquakes were quite frequent in Israel in Jesus' day; there were many of them with varying magnitudes, much like Southern California where I grew up. So, when two earthquakes hit Jerusalem during His crucifixion and resurrection, this most likely did not take the Jews by surprise. The only ones who might have been caught off guard by such seismic activity were the Roman soldiers who were new to the region. But regardless of whether Jew, Roman, or otherwise, earthquakes did cause fear and got everyone's attention.
    I know this to be true because my family has been through several earthquakes that hit California over the last few years. One of those was the

Scripture Reference

Luke 8:1-2 *1 Soon afterward, He began going around from one city and village to another, proclaiming and preaching the kingdom of God. The twelve were with Him, two and also some women who had been healed of evil spirits and sicknesses: Mary who was called Magdalene, from whom seven demons had gone out, three and Joanna the wife of Chuza, Herod's steward, and Susanna, and many others who were contributing to their support out of their private means.*

Easter, and it comes from Peter and John's observation of Jesus' facecloth, which was folded and put by itself *(John 20:7)*. Why was such a detail mentioned by these two disciples? Perhaps there is yet another message to be gained at the tomb.

There was a tradition in the Hebrew culture where a folded cloth had particular meaning. It had to do with the master of a household, or father, and the one serving dinner. As the custom went, which all Jewish children knew, the one serving the meal was to set the table according to the father's direction. When the meal began, nothing was to be removed from the table until he was finished. When the father was done, he would rise from the table, wipe his fingers, mouth, and clean his beard with a facecloth. He would then wad it up and toss it onto the table. When this happened, dinner was over, and the one serving the meal was free to clear the table. Therefore, in Jesus' day, a wadded facecloth meant, "I'm done." However, if the father got up from the table and folded the cloth and laid it beside his plate, then the one serving could not clear the table because the folded towel meant, "I'm not finished, and I'm coming back!"

Maybe just maybe what was meant in the tomb that day, when the facecloth was neatly wrapped and put by itself, was that Jesus was not finished but coming back. Perhaps! I think so! Nevertheless, Jesus is not finished with us or the rest of humankind yet and will be coming back, as many other Scriptures affirm.

> *If I go and prepare a place for you, I will come again, and receive you unto myself; that where I am, you may be also John 14:3*

> *For the Lord Himself will descend from heaven with a shout, with the voice of the archangel and with the trumpet of God, and the dead in Christ will rise first. Then we who are alive and remain will be caught up together with them in the clouds to meet the Lord in the air, and so we shall always be with the Lord. Therefore comfort one another with these words. I Thessalonians 4:16-18*

Last Thought

If it is Easter when reading this, have a great one, and please do all you can to be prepared for His return, for the facecloth that is still folded may not be for long.

from John's Gospel. They have been rephrased but not at the expense or integrity of what was written.

> *Now on the first day of the week Mary Magdalene came early to the tomb, while it was still dark, and saw the stone rolled away. She quickly ran and came to Peter and John and said to them, 'They have taken away the Lord out of the tomb, and we do not know where they have laid Him.' Immediately, Peter and John ran to the tomb, and when they reached it, John stooped in first and saw the linen wrappings lying there, but did not go in. Then Peter entered the tomb; and also saw the linen wrappings but noted the facecloth which had been on Jesus head was not lying with the linen wrappings. Instead it was folded up and put in a place by itself. John subsequently entered the tomb and began to understand what Jesus meant about rising from the dead. Afterwards both disciples left and returned home. Mary who was standing nearby, weeping, eventually made her way to the tomb and stooped in to look. When she did, there were two angels, one sitting at where his head had been, and the other at His feet. Noticing that Mary was crying, the angels asked as to why she was weeping? Mary exclaimed, 'Because they have taken away my Lord and I do not know where they have laid Him.' Then she turned around and saw another standing behind her but did not know it was Jesus. He spoke, 'Woman why are you weeping? Who are you looking for?' Mary supposing him to be the gardener, said, 'Do you know where they have laid Him, for I will take Him away?' Jesus responded again, 'Mary,' She lifted her eyes and cried out, 'Teacher,' and immediately began to cling to Him. Jesus said, 'You cannot cling to Me Mary, for I have not yet ascended to the Father; but go to My brethren and say to them, I ascend to My Father and your Father, and My God and your God.' Mary, excitedly did as He asked, announcing to the disciples, 'I have seen the Lord,' and that He had said these things to her. John 20:1-18*

Not much more needs to be said or added to this account, for it speaks for itself. Although there is one additional thought to consider this

April
Week 2

(Possible tomb site of Jesus' burial)

Jesus' Facecloth

Peter came and entered the tomb and saw the linen wrappings lying there, and the face-cloth which had been on His head, not lying with the linen wrappings, but rolled up in a place by itself. John 20:6-7

There are so many beautiful accounts in the Scripture of Jesus' resurrection. But the one that has always had my heart over the years at Easter is Mary's response to Jesus' reappearance at the tomb. This was not the Mary to whom the Lord ministered by raising her brother Lazarus from the grave a few days earlier. Neither was this Mary the mother of Jesus, who birthed and raised Him. It was also not the other Mary at the grave, which was the mother of James and John. It was Mary Magdalene for whom Jesus cast out seven demons early in His ministry. When Jesus met this Mary, she was being tormented, beleaguered, and made to suffer by seven demons. Jesus saw her plight and stepped in and cast them out. From then on, Mary Magdalene put her trust in Jesus and followed Him for the rest of her life. By the way, there is no Scriptural evidence Mary Magdalene was ever a prostitute, but only a woman who had lost control of her life to seven wretched and self-serving demons. *(Luke 8:1-2)*

This account of Mary's meeting with Jesus after his death and resurrection is recorded in all four Gospels. Here are several verses taken

*crucified, died, and **was buried; he descended to hell**. The third day he rose again from the dead. He ascended to heaven and is seated at the right hand of God the Father almighty. From there he will come to judge the living and the dead. I believe in the Holy Spirit, the holy catholic* church, the communion of saints, the forgiveness of sins, the resurrection of the body, and the life everlasting. Amen.*

from the Lord; 7 for we walk by faith, not by sight 8 we are of good courage, I say, and prefer rather be absent from the body and to be at home with the Lord. 9 Therefore we also have as our ambition, whether at home or absent, to be pleasing to Him.

Luke 24:1-6 *1 But on the first day of the week, at early dawn, they came to the tomb bringing the spices which they had prepared. 2 And they found the stone rolled away from the tomb, 3 but when they entered, they did not find the body of the Lord Jesus. 4 While they were perplexed about this, behold, two men suddenly stood near them in dazzling clothing; 5 and as the women were terrified and bowed their faces to the ground, the men said to them, 'Why do you seek the living One among the dead? 6 He is not here, but He has risen.'*

Ephesians 4:7-9 *7 But to each one of us grace was given according to the measure of Christ's gift. 8 Therefore it says, "When He ascended on high, He led captive a host of captives, and He gave gifts to men." 9 (Now this expression, "He ascended," what does it mean except that He also had descended into the lower parts of the earth? He who descended is Himself also He who ascended far above all the heavens so that He might fill all things).*

I Peter 3:18-19 *18 For Christ also died for sins once for all, the just for the unjust, so that He might bring us to God, having been put to death in the flesh, but made alive in the spirit; 19 in which also He went and made proclamation to the spirits now in prison, 20 who once were disobedient, when the patience of God kept waiting in the days of Noah, during the construction of the ark, in which a few, that is, eight persons, were brought safely through the water.*

Matthew 12:38-40 *38 Then some of the scribes and Pharisees said to Him, 'Teacher, we want to see a sign from You.' 39 But He answered and said to them, 'An evil and adulterous generation craves for a sign, and yet no sign will be given to it but the sign of Jonah the prophet; 40 for just as Jonah was three days and three nights in the belly of the sea monster, so will the Son of Man be three days and three nights in the heart of the earth.'*

Apostle's Creed

I believe in God, the Father almighty, creator of heaven and earth. I believe in Jesus Christ, his only Son, our Lord, who was conceived by the Holy Spirit and born of the virgin Mary. He suffered under Pontius Pilate, was

understand and see who Jesus was and what they missed by not repenting and believing as they should.

The Scripture in Romans 14:11 does tell us that every knee shall bow, and every tongue will confess that Jesus Christ is Lord. I guess that means everyone, even those who have died and are lost forever. The point is that Jesus was working on *Silent Saturday*, for *Good Friday* was over, and *Resurrection Sunday* was yet to come.

Last Thought

In a parallel way, God works behind the scenes for you, too, even when you think He is not. You just can't see all that He is doing, as was the case with the disciples and others who followed Him. But it all made sense when Jesus came bursting out of the tomb, and all will make sense to you when your *Silent Saturday* is over.

So, if you are in that waiting time, perhaps between a trial that has happened and a victory yet to come, realize God is hard at work for you. And if anything, during this time, do whatever is in front of you to do. If that includes a lot of praying, then pray a lot.

Scripture References

John 3:16 *For God so loved the world that He gave His only begotten Son, that whoever believes in Him shall not perish, but have eternal life.*

Mark 1:14-15 *14 Now after John had been taken into custody, Jesus came into Galilee, preaching the Gospel of God, 15 and saying, 'The time is fulfilled, and the kingdom of God is at hand; repent and believe in the gospel.'*

II Corinthians 4:7-12 *7 But we have this treasure in earthen vessels so that the surpassing greatness of the power will be of God and not from ourselves; 8 we are afflicted in every way, but not crushed; perplexed, but not despairing; 9 persecuted, but not forsaken; struck down, but not destroyed; 10 always carrying about in the body the dying of Jesus, so that the life of Jesus also may be manifested in our body. 11 For we who live are always being delivered over to death for Jesus' sake, so that the life of Jesus also may be manifested in our mortal flesh. 12 So death works in us, but life in you.*

II Corinthians 5:2, 6-9 *2 For indeed in this house we groan, longing to be clothed with our dwelling from heaven, 6 Therefore, being always of good courage, and knowing that while we are at home in the body we are absent*

Before we look into that Saturday over 2,000 years ago, I would like to revisit and remark on *Good Friday* and *Resurrection Sunday*, the great bookends to *Silent Saturday*.

Good Friday reminds us of many remarkable things; the most important is that Jesus died for our sins. He laid all of them on the cross so we could have a forever relationship with Him. All we need do is repent of our sins and believe in Him as Lord and Savior *(John 3:16, Mark 1:14-15)*. Without this supreme sacrifice of Jesus, we would all be lost, separated from God and His loving grace forever. Perhaps this is why *Good Friday* is called *Good Friday*, miserable and punishing for Him but good for us.

A secondary message of *Good Friday*, a very encouraging one indeed, is that when the worst has happened, the best is yet to come. Even though the *Good Fridays* in our lives may be tough and even unbearable at times, God promises that these times will pass and come to an end. God also promises that He will bring peace to every circumstance, whether realized here on earth or in heaven to come *(II Corinthians 4:7-12, II Corinthians 5:2, 6, 7-9)*.

On *Resurrection Sunday* churches around the world pack out their worship centers and meeting places every year to honor Christ for His victory over sin and death. A victory which also proved Him to truly be the Son of God. This day like no other brings an incredible sense of peace, joy, and hope to all who have put their trust in Him. *(Luke 24:1-6)*

Silent Saturday, as quiet as it seemed during that first Easter, did not mean Jesus was not at work on that day. Nor is He when we experience *Silent Saturdays* in our spiritual lives, those long times between a trial and a victory.

According to the Scriptures, even though Jesus' body stayed in that tomb until *Resurrection Sunday* morning, His spirit did not. Shortly after He had been wrapped in linen clothes, sprinkled with the traditional burial myrrh, and shut behind a massive stone door, Jesus' spirit left His body. Where did He go? What did He do during this time?

He visited those who had rejected God's plan for salvation during the course of their lives while on earth. While with them, on that *Silent Saturday*, in hell, where they were relegated to, He explained the Gospel, as well as who He was, the Son of God *(Ephesians 4:7-9, I Peter 3: 18-19, and Matthew 12:38-40, Apostles Creed)*.

Why did He do this for they were already lost? We don't know for sure, but perhaps even those who were lost forever deserve a right to finally

April
Week 1

Silent Saturday

Where can I go from Your Spirit? Or where can I flee from Your presence? If I ascend to heaven, You are there; If I make my bed in Sheol, behold, You are there. Psalm 139:7-8

Too often, when we remember the events of Easter Week, we tend to make a leap from *Good Friday* to *Easter Sunday*, straight from crucifixion to the resurrection. We skip right over what I call *Silent Saturday*. I don't know why this is; perhaps it is because there is more biblical material supporting *Good Friday* and *Resurrection Sunday*. Nevertheless, there was a Saturday in-between these two renowned Easter days, and it appeared to be a quiet and seemingly uneventful day.

Similarly, as Christians, we have *Good Fridays* and *Resurrection Sundays* throughout our lives. We have times when we encounter conflict, pain, hurt, and rejection. We also have victorious days, when our prayers are answered, and everything works out as we had hoped. And then we have Saturdays too, which are quiet days where we sometimes wonder if God is doing anything in our lives.

April

Silent Saturday
Jesus' Facecloth
All Was Lost
Breakfast with Jesus

Last Thought

God is always watching over you, and He knows your circumstance. He will never leave your side, for you are incredibly greater than a sparrow to Him.

Scripture References

I Peter 5:7 *Cast all your anxiety on Him because He cares for you.*

John 14:27 *Peace I leave with you; My peace I give to you; not as the world gives do I give to you. Do not let your heart be troubled, nor let it be fearful.*

John 14:1-3 1 *Do not let your heart be troubled; believe in God, also believe in Me. 2 In My Father's house are many dwelling places; if it were not so, I would have told you; for I go to prepare a place for you. 3 If I go and prepare a place for you, I will come again and receive you to Myself, that where I am, there you may also be.*

Yet, 2020 with its unrelenting pandemic, violent demonstrations in our cities, political hatreds and battles between political leaders, high levels of unemployment and evictions, record wildfires, numerous hurricanes, and floods surpassed 1968 in respect to the anxiety and apprehension we felt as individuals and as a nation during this year.

Here is some encouragement when anxiety filled years like 1968 and 2020 come along again, as they probably will, for we may be closer to the world's final days and Christ's return than we think. There was a hymn my wife and I used to sing when we were first married, a song that settled our hearts during rough times.

The song is *His Eye is On the Sparrow* and was written by Civilla Martin back in 1904. She wrote it after visiting a friend who was bedridden and struggling in a bad way. She asked her friend if she was discouraged by what she was going through. To Civilla's surprise, her friend wasn't, for she knew that the same God who keeps tabs on even the sparrows would certainly keep watch over her. When Civilla got home, she wrote the song *His Eye Is on the Sparrow*.

Here are the words that will hopefully bring you the peace you need, especially during a challenging year.

> Why should I feel discouraged, why should the shadows come,
> why should my heart be lonely, and long for heav'n and home,
> when Jesus is my portion? My constant Friend is He:
> His eye is on the sparrow, and I know He watches me;
>
> Let not your heart be troubled, His tender word I hear, and resting on His goodness, I lose my doubts and fears; though by the path He leadeth, but one step I may see;
> His eye is on the sparrow, and I know He watches me.
>
> Whenever I am tempted, whenever clouds arise, when songs give place to sighing, when hope within me dies, I draw the closer to Him, from care He sets me free;
> His eye is on the sparrow, and I know He watches me;
>
> Refrain
> I sing because I'm happy, I sing because I'm free, for His eye is on the sparrow, and I know He watches me.

March
Week 4

His Eye Is on the Sparrow

Are not two sparrows sold for a cent? And yet not one of them will fall to the ground apart from your Father. But the very hairs of your head are all numbered. So do not fear; you are more valuable than many sparrows. Matthew 10:29-31

When reading this article, 2020 will have come and gone, and who knows what kind of year each of us will be experiencing right now. Hopefully less anxious than 2020, which may go down as one of the most tumultuous, discouraging, and difficult years our country has ever gone through.

Although I would say 1968 held this dubious honor for many years, when there were riots in many large cities over the Vietnam war and college violence on campuses, initiated by groups like the SDS (Students for Democratic Society). There were a couple of terrible assassinations too during this year, that of Dr. Martin Luther King and Robert F. Kennedy.

I grew up in the same community as Sirhan Sirhan, who killed Kennedy. I believe he visited my church a few times; we should have reached out to him in a better way.

There was also a significant racial divide in the country, which sparked factions like the Black Panthers. Years later, through a random circumstance, I had dinner with Eldridge Cleaver, one of its leaders. During our conversation, he shared how Christ had come into and changed his life.

Scripture References

Isaiah 41:10 *Do not fear, for I am with you; do not be dismayed, for I am your God. I will strengthen you and help you; I will uphold you with my righteous right hand.*

Romans 15:1 *Now we who are strong ought to bear the weaknesses of those without strength and not just please ourselves.*

Exodus 17:12 *But Moses' hands were heavy. Then they took a stone and put it under him, and he sat on it; and Aaron and Hur supported his hands, one on one side and one on the other. Thus, his hands were steady until the sunset.*

principle is that the closer we get to achieving any or all of these, the more difficult the time can become. When climbing to the top of Half Dome, the steepest and most difficult came toward the hike's end. The spiritual application being to hang in there and wait for the Lord to send help or provide it Himself if we cannot seem to make it by the faith we have at the moment.

Another application is that life will have many ups and downs, count on it, therefore find some Christian friends or family members with which to hike it. They will help during the lows, just as my kids and son-in-law did with me all along the way to Half Dome.

One more application is that when all seems impossible or lost, don't be surprised if God sends something entirely out of the blue to encourage us, just as He sent Sonny to me on the steep switchbacks of the trail. And don't be offended if the Lord sends someone to give each of us the last shove to finish off what we have begun. Just as my daughter did to me with one last push to the top of Half Dome. Remember, these final pushes, from whoever they may come, are done in love, even though it may not seem so at the time.

Last Thoughts

When I got back home from this trip, I saw my doctor, and he diagnosed that my great tiredness on the hike came from an irregular heartbeat condition called AFIB. As I found out later, AFIB runs in my family and usually doesn't show up until later in life. It cannot really be "cured", just controlled by different medications. However, it is dangerous if not treated and can lead to a heart attack.

It is one thing to have an AFIB attack while walking up a steep stairway near home or having too much caffeine or suffering a good deal of stress in a situation, but quite another on a 16-mile hike to Half Dome and back. I probably should have died on this hike, but I didn't because God had other plans for me, as He will for you during your lifetime.

For I know, the plans that I have for you declares the Lord, plans for welfare and not for calamity to give you a future and a hope. Jeremiah 29:11

Yosemite, most of Sonny's youth group tried to climb to Half Dome, but only a few made it to its crest.

As Brodie, Shannon, Nic, and I got closer to the top, we all became tired in differing degrees, but me in particular. I was older, not a twenty-year-old, and definitely more tired than I should have been. Nevertheless, my kids encouraged me to keep going even though the walk up got steeper and steeper as we got closer to the summit.

On the last leg of our journey, the switchback trails which preceded climbing up a cable to Half Dome were much more challenging to traverse than I had remembered. When only half-way up these switchbacks, it seemed as though I could not take another step. I told Brodie, Nic, and Shannon to go on ahead that I would catch up with them later. After convincing them a little more with this idea, Brodie and Nic took off, but Shannon stayed behind with me. Isn't that what daughters do?

As I walked slower and slower with labored breathing, I told her again about my first trip up to Half Dome, which I calculated to be about 36 years ago to the month. Talking about this experience helped divert my mind and thoughts from the overwhelming tiredness I was experiencing.

But as I happen to look up, I thought I saw Sonny coming down the trail. "Surely, this couldn't be, could it?" But it was Sonny, and as I yelled out his name, he stopped, ran, and gave me a big hug. Immediately I introduced him to Shannon. For several minutes we ate, drank, and had a great time talking and recalling old times and memories. Then as he parted, Sonny yelled back, "Keep going, you only have a couple more switchbacks to go." Revived and forgetting how tired I had been, I trudged on toward the top. Not even the cables which lay ahead to scale the last 100 feet of the mountain thwarted me from finishing this hike.

When I was making my last few yanks on the cable, both Brodie and Nic saw me and yelled, "You've got it now, dad, you've got it now!" Those words were very encouraging, to say the least, but not as encouraging as the big push my daughter gave me on my *gluteus maximus*. I made it with her final assistance, and boy, was it ever beautiful standing up there, looking out over the entire Yosemite Valley.

Although very hard for me, the hike was well worth it because of the great fellowship I had with Brodie, Nic, and Shannon, the surprise meet-up with Sonny, and, of course, the victory of making it to the end.

There are some good parallels in this story to how God works with us to achieve a particular goal, hope, or answer to prayer. The overriding

March
Week 3

(Cable path to Half Dome)

Steeper Near the Top

I will lift my eyes to the mountains; from where shall my help come? My help comes from the Lord, who made heaven and earth. He will not allow your foot to slip and is the shade on your right hand. Psalm 121:1-3,5

Several years ago, when I was hiking up to Half Dome in Yosemite National Park, I almost did not make it to the top. It was my fourth trip to Half Dome; the first was when I was a 20-year-old college student. If not familiar with Half Dome, it is one of Yosemite's most well-known and striking sights. The summit's climb includes passing two beautiful waterfalls, but from the bottom of the valley floor to its summit is about 8,000 feet up and a 16-mile round trip.

On this particular trip, I was with my son, daughter, son-in-law, Brodie, Shannon, and Nic. All three were in their young adult years and exceptionally fit and ready for this trek.

During the earlier parts of this hike we were all very upbeat and excited. We walked, talked, drank water, and ate granola bars. While on the way up, I shared with them my first experience to Half Dome when I climbed it with my church youth pastor, Sonny. During that trip to

you haven't already, and then meditate on, and claim the following words of Christ, for He loves, accepts, and thinks of you like no other.

You are an everlasting love to me. (Jeremiah 31:3)
You are my child. (I John 3:1, 2)
You are the salt of the earth. (Matthew 5:13)
You are the light of the world. (Matthew 5:14)
You are a part me, a channel of My life. (John 15: 5)
You are chosen to bear fruit for Me. (John 15:16)
You are united with Me. (I Corinthians. 6:15)
You are a new creation. (Colossians 1:2)
You are a member of My church. (I Corinthians. 12:27)
You are joint heirs; everything that is mine is yours. (Rom 8:16-17)
You are My temple, a dwelling place where I dwell. (I Cor. 3:16, 6:19)
You are chosen of God, holy and dearly loved. (Colossians 3:12)
You are a son of light and not darkness. (I Thessalonians 5:5)
You are being built up in Me as a spiritual house. (I Peter 2:5)
You are a member of the chosen race, a royal priesthood. (I Peter 2:9)

Scripture References

I Timothy 2:4 *For God desires all men to be saved and to come to the knowledge of the truth.*

John 11:25-26 *25 Jesus said to her, 'I am the resurrection and the life; he who believes in Me will live even if he dies, 26 and everyone who lives and believes in Me will never die. Do you believe this?'*

March
Week 2

Esteem

You are my friend. John 15:15

The building of self-esteem is possibly one of the most accepted and honored ways to promote good mental health amongst us all in America and the world today. Public schools, parents, and even well-meaning churches crusade for varying ways to build self-esteem.

Yet the focus on self-esteem often comes up short because it is built on the comments, discernments, and feelings of others. And as we well know, others sometimes, if not often, let us down when we least expect it. But God never does; as the Scripture states. He holds so many great thoughts for us each day that they cannot be counted. Now, what friend in the world does this, even the best of all our friends?

> *How precious are Your thoughts to me, O God! How vast is the sum of them!*
> *If I counted them, they would outnumber the sand of the sea. Psalm 139:17-18*

Last Thought

How can you move from self-esteem, which depends on other's words and thoughts, to more of a God esteem? Accept Christ as Savior, if

enough to accommodate two vehicles, tickets were being given by the police to stop this practice. It worked; the next day none of us were taking the emergency lane to turn right.

During this incident, I misconstrued what this guy was doing for me. Instead of trying to irritate me, he was trying to save me from a ticket. After making the turn, I then realized the purpose of his wave. I only wished I could have waved back, but he was long gone.

When I got home and told my wife about this, she immediately said, "Isn't this a picture of how it is in our lives with other issues, especially those with spiritual outcomes?" I thought for a long while on what Myrna said and began to recall in my past where God sent people into my life, to stop me from doing certain things I would regret. At the time, I thought some of these people were being too critical, or judgmental. Perhaps they were being too harsh in what they said or in how they said it to me, but the bottom line is the advice they gave did come from the Lord, as I later found out.

Last Thought

When you get clobbered by someone on an issue in your life, instead of raging within or attaching back in return, take a moment and see if what they said is coming from the Lord. Until you know for sure, sit in your car, relax, and wait for the light to turn green to reveal what is truly ahead.

And if you have opportunity, wave so to speak, to the person who brought a timely word or suggestion to you from the Lord, even if they didn't do it perfectly.

Scripture References

Proverbs 15:31 *He who listens to life-giving reproofs will dwell among the wise.*

James 1:19 *This you know, my beloved brethren, be quick to hear, slow to speak and slow to anger.*

March
Week 1

Emergency Lane

How delightful is a timely word! Let the righteous smite me in kindness and timely reproofs, for It is like soothing oil upon my head. May I never refuse it. Proverbs 15:23, Psalm 141:5

Early one evening while driving home I got backed up in traffic on a well-traveled four lane road. All I had to do to get out of this mess was to turn right at the next light and I was within a few blocks of being home. While waiting behind the long line of cars in front of me, I contemplated what to do and decided to take the emergency lane to the right as so many other folks were beginning to do. After all, there were no emergencies taking place, and the lane was empty!

It was illegal to drive in this lane, but I never saw any emergency vehicles ever use it, not one time. In point of fact, the commuters who traveled this road everyday complained to the City of Bakersfield for making the emergency lane so wide which eliminated another lane being put in place to alleviate traffic. Nonetheless, I, like so many others that late afternoon, entered the emergency lane to turn right to save some time getting home. As I traveled down the lane, a guy ahead pulled out in his car to block me. I was a bit miffed when he did this because I was sure he wanted to force me to wait at the light like everyone else.

As I waited, fuming a little more within, the light turned green and all of us moved forward. As we did this guy moved back into his lane and waved at me. I thought what is it with this guy waving at me? But what he could see ahead, which I could not, was the police ticketing everyone taking the emergency lane to turn right that day. Even though the lane was wide

March

Emergency Lane
Esteem
Steeper Near the Top
Eye on the Sparrow

Weeping may last for the night, but a shout of joy comes in the morning. Psalm 30:5

Scripture References
(Other passages to guide us in Red Sea times)

Isaiah 41:10 *Do not fear, for I am with you; do not anxiously look about you, for I am your God. I will strengthen you, surely, I will help you, and surely, I will uphold you with My righteous right hand.*
Deuteronomy 31:8 *The Lord is the one who goes ahead of you; He will be with you. He will not fail you or forsake you. Do not fear or be dismayed.*
Philippians 4:6 *Be anxious for nothing, but in everything by prayer and supplication with thanksgiving let your requests be made known to God.*

Do we not worry some, get a bit anxious, or quite stressed, even though we have seen God save us from past situations? Be honest, how would you have really responded at the Red Sea?

After the Red Sea miracle, Israel went through 40 more years of tests. At the end of the time, most of the adults of this generation died before entering the promised land. However, their children who were fairly battle tested and faith-ready, walked into it as God had asked them to do.

Unfortunately, according to the Bible, the Israelites did not always do what God wanted them to do in the centuries to come. At different times they were very disobedient to His will, and embarrassingly so. But because of God's unconditional love for them, they are exactly where He wants them to be today, in Israel, their ancestral home. Ready when the time comes to help God bring about an end to this world, so that a new one can be formed, one without sin or evil.

Last Thoughts

What can you take from this Red Sea story? First of all, what is the use of worrying, especially when God is in control of a situation in your life? Just as worrying did not help those Israelites who agonized all night at the Red Sea, it won't help you either in the *Red Sea* circumstances of your life. Worry as you have learned, will not make you any stronger, nor help you better see God's escape path when it becomes visible. Prayer and faith will, but not worry. Therefore, if you feel you are at the end of a so-called rope with a *Red Sea* trial before you, then tie a knot of prayer at the end of it and hang on with faith until God finishes parting the waters.

Further, if you are in a night portion of a long-lasting trial, and can't seem to see God's way out, then don't forget He is much closer to you than you think, always working on your behalf. As the Israelites did, perk up your ears and listen to the work going on.

How do you best listen? Read other accounts in the Scripture where God has done mighty works in impossible situations. The accounts of Shadrack, Meshack, and Abednego in the fiery furnace *(Daniel 3)*, the events surrounding Jesus' resurrection, or the circumstances leading to Paul's conversion, are just a few. And don't forget when morning comes, and it will, God's answer will be there for you, just as it was for the Israelites when they woke up to see the massive Red Sea parted with a dry bottom.

It was a great teachable moment for Israel, that God could and would protect them even in the most precarious of circumstances. However, what really happened according to the Bible, is that the pillar of fire which delayed Pharaoh's attack continued all through the night. And then some time at the beginning of that night, Moses stretched out his hand over the sea, causing something to happen to the waters, which the Israelites could not clearly see because of the darkness, but could hear.

As the night dragged on with only a distant pillar of fire giving them any light at all, the Israelites must have wondered what was going to happen to them. Some might have confidently prayed, believing God would rescue them, while most probably worried to the nth degree. When the sun rose early the next morning, the Red Sea had been miraculously parted. Before them lay a path of escape, which was dry and very walkable.

This is a little different than how DeMille portrayed this event, which disregarded the night in which the Israelites could only hear but not see what God was doing.

> *The angel of God, who had been going before the camp of Israel, moved and went behind them; and the pillar of cloud moved from before them and stood behind them. So, it came between the camp of Egypt and the camp of Israel; and there was the cloud along with the darkness, yet it gave light at night. Thus, the one did not come near the other all night. Then Moses stretched out his hand over the sea; and the Lord swept the sea back by a strong east wind* **all night and turned the sea into dry land**, *so the waters were divided. The sons of Israel went through the midst of the sea on the dry land, and the waters were like a wall to them on their right hand and on their left. Exodus 14:19-22*

Had we been there, how would each of us have done in this *Red Sea* circumstance? Would we have confidently prayed or been quite worried, nervous, and stressed? Confidently prayed is the best answer, of course, after all we would have just experienced firsthand God's miracles of the ten plagues and pillar of fire. With this under our belts, we would have certainly trusted Him at the Red Sea. But then, we must be honest and ask ourselves, how have we done so far with the *Red Sea* challenges God has put before us? You know, those challenges where all is apparently lost, and seemingly only disaster is awaiting us.

February
Week 4

(After crossing the Red sea)

Red Seas in Life

Behold, I am the Lord, the God of all flesh; is anything too difficult for Me? Jeremiah 32:27

In 1956, the movie *The 10 Commandments* won best picture at the Academy Awards. It was produced and directed by Cecil B. DeMille who made over 70 films during the course of his illustrious career. This great producer and director, one of Hollywood's most renown, died three years after *The 10 Commandments* was made.

DeMille did a great job showcasing the Bible back in 1956, though, there was one scene in which he fell a little short. Had he done this particular scene the way the Scripture described it, then his *10 Commandments* film would have been even better and more impactful.

The scene came toward the end of the movie at the Red Sea when the Israelites were penned up against the water by the Egyptians. Pharaoh's army was being delayed from attacking the defenseless Israelites by an incredible pillar of fire coming down from a cloud, which protected the people from impending slaughter. At this point the Red Sea was parted by the power of God, which allowed all of Israel, children, parent, and grandparent alike, to escape. Then when they were all safe on the other side of the sea, the fiery pillar was lifted and Pharaoh's army was allowed to rush forward with their attack, at which time God closed the sea and all of them were drowned.

Footnotes

1. Franklin Graham, Quote *by Abraham Lincoln* (Washington D.C., Inaugural Invocation of President George W. Bush, January 20th, 2001).
2. Jack Keismer, *Trivia Book: If at First You Don't Succeed* (Saddle River, New Jersey, Red-Letter Press, Inc., 1986), page 35.
3. William J. Johnson, *Abraham Lincoln the Christian* (Amsterdam, The Netherlands: Fredonia Books, 2004), page 191.
4. Lincoln Memorial Album, O.H. Oldroyd, 1883, page 366 & William J. Johnson, Abraham Lincoln the Christian (Amsterdam, The Netherlands: Fredonia Books, 2004), page172.
5. William J. Johnson, *Abraham Lincoln the Christian* (Amsterdam, The Netherlands: Fredonia Books, 2004), pages171-172.
6. William J. Johnson, *Abraham Lincoln the Christian* (Amsterdam, The Netherlands: Fredonia Books, 2004), page 182.
7. William J. Johnson, *Abraham Lincoln the Christian* (Amsterdam, The Netherlands: Fredonia Books, 2004), page 107.

He was termed by many of the press on both sides of the conflict as America's worst President. Along with all of these events, his beloved son Willie died. Yet in Lincoln's hours of agony, he dedicated his life to Christ, and openly confessed his love for Him.

After his commitment to God, the war began to gradually change; Lee lost a huge battle at Gettysburg for the South, and eventually surrendered at Appomattox. As the war drew to a close, Lincoln went from being reported as the worst President to being the best. Sad to say, this was very typical of the media back then, as it is today.

All of this did not matter to Lincoln for his newfound relationship with Christ was his anchor. On the way to Ford's theatre, the last day of his life, he talked of going to Jerusalem to walk where Jesus walked. [6] And that evening he did just that.

Last Thought

When the celebration of President's Day comes, remember the commitment Lincoln made to God, along with other American Presidents who also made Christ their Savior and Lord. I leave you with some of Lincoln's words, delivered on March 30th, 1863, when proclaiming a national day of fasting for our nation.

> *"Whereas, it is the duty of nations as well as of men to own their dependence upon the over-ruling power of God; to confess their sins and transgressions in humble sorrow, yet with; assured hope that genuine repentance will lead to mercy and pardon; and to recognize the sublime truth, announced in the Holy Scriptures and proven by all history, that those nations only are blessed who God is the Lord."* [7]

Scripture References

Romans 10:9-11 *9 If you confess with your mouth Jesus as Lord, and believe in your heart that God raised Him from the dead, you will be saved; 10 for with the heart a person believes, resulting in righteousness, and with the mouth he confesses, resulting in salvation.*

Before Lincoln became President, he was not highly successful in much of what he tried, whether in business or politics.

In 1832, at age twenty-two he failed in business. During the same year he ran for the legislature and was defeated. In 1833, he failed in business again. In 1836, he suffered a nervous breakdown. In 1838, he lost in an effort to become Speaker of the House in the Illinois State Legislature. Five years later, he ran for Congress, but lost. In 1846, he ran for Congress and won, and then lost his re-election bid in 1848. He ran for the U.S. Senate in 1854 and lost. He ran for the Vice-Presidential nomination in 1856 and lost. Once more he ran for a Senate seat in 1858 and lost. And then in 1860, after all of his endurance, Lincoln amazingly became the sixteenth President of the United States.[2]

Like Lincoln's early business and political careers, his relationship with God started rather poorly too, even hardly existent at times. Drifting best describes his early years as a boy and young man when it came to God and the Bible. Questioning describes Lincoln's spiritual thoughts in his early twenties, and religious indifference in his late twenties and thirties. During Lincoln's forties he put forth some serious doubts about God. However, when he became President and the Civil War began, Lincoln gradually had a change of heart. For the first time in his life he started showing evidence of a real faith in God and Christ. And then in his last years, as the Civil War wound down, Lincoln's belief in God and Christ soared to new heights.[3]

> *"When I left Springfield, I asked the people to pray for me. I was not a Christian. When I buried my son, the severest trial of my life, I was not a Christian. But when I went to Gettysburg and saw the graves of thousands of our solders. I then and there consecrated myself to Christ. Yes, I do love Jesus."* [4]

For decades, though, historians refused to believe Abraham Lincoln ever embraced Christianity. They felt he only used Christian words and phrases to advance his political causes. Perhaps this was due to his earlier questioning, indifference, and expressed doubts about God and the Bible. But Lincoln, in the second year of his Presidency, made a noticeably clear profession of faith. During this critical year, the second year of the Civil War, Lincoln suffered greatly. His Union Army suffered one loss after the other. The mounting criticism he received for these losses was unbearable.

February
Week 3

Lincoln the Christian
President's Day Message

"We have been the recipients of the choicest bounties of heaven. We have been preserved these many years in peace and prosperity. We have grown in numbers, wealth and power as no other nation has ever grown. But we have forgotten God. It behooves us then to humble ourselves before the offended powers, to confess our national sins and to pray for clemency and forgiveness."[1]
Abraham Lincoln
1809-1865

In February each year, we as a nation have often celebrated two holidays commemorating the birthdays of George Washington and Abraham Lincoln. That has somewhat changed in the last several years, as Washington and Lincoln's birthdays has been replaced by Presidents Day. Only a few states still take a holiday specifically in honor of Lincoln, but regardless he remains one of our greatest Presidents because he kept our nation together at a very critical time and did away with the awful institution of slavery.

270 A.D. when the Romans were heavily persecuting Christians for their beliefs and faith.

One account of Dr. Valentine occurred after he befriended a jailer during his imprisonment. When Dr. Valentine learned that this man's daughter was blind, he did all he could for her as a physician. Yet, she could not see. Then he prayed for her with great earnestness and fervor. Amazingly, soon after, this young girl's sight returned. Needless to say, this was a very loving thing Dr. Valentine did, especially since he was in jail being persecuted.

There are many other stories about this loving man, but what made him stand out was that he consistently did loving deeds for others.

Eventually, the good doctor was beheaded because of his loyalty to Christ and other Christians. After the day of his execution, February 14, his fellow Christians began to honor him for his life and the love he gave so willingly to others.

Last Thought

Today, on February 14, you probably won't think of Dr. Valentine as you celebrate Valentine's Day. Perhaps you should. But if you don't, at least celebrate this day by loving others as he did. Teach your loved ones and friends to do the same.

Scripture References

(I leave you with some Scriptures written by Paul on love, who also loved others as Valentine did.)

I Corinthians 13:4-8 *4 Love is patient, kind, and is not jealous. 5 It does not act unbecomingly and is not provoked. It does not consider when wronged. 7 Love bears all things, believes all things, hopes all things, and endures all things for others. 8 Love never fails.*

Romans 12:10 *Be devoted to one another in brotherly love; give preference to one another in honor.*

February
Week 2

Valentine's Day

The greatest of all is love. I Corinthians 13:13

February 14 is Valentine's Day, which is celebrated all across America, especially in schools. When I was a sixth-grade teacher, my room mothers always made Valentine's day an incredibly special time for my class. At the end of the school day, these mothers asked me to take my kids out for a little recess time so that they could fix up the room. I gladly did, for the kids were pretty excited, and, of course, they always loved recess.

During this time, my room mothers decorated the room, made special desserts, and put on each child's desk candy hearts. The hearts had written on them loving sayings like: "Be my valentine," "You are a cutie pie," and "Love you," to name a few.

Then the mothers put on each desk valentine cards my students brought to school to give to other classmates. While placing these cards out, if one of my students received fewer valentines than others, then my room mothers added some of their own to make things look equal. After all, they determined, every child needs to be loved and appreciated just as much as another.

Valentine's day was always a time of joy, celebration, encouragement, and love for our class. I hope it will be the same for all of us when we celebrate it.

But did you know how Valentine's Day first got started? There are a few stories, but one tradition that holds up more than others is about a doctor/priest named Valentine who lived in the first century. This was about

of people who knew the couple. There were even some dignitaries and high-ranking officials who came.

On the morning of the wedding, the young man got dressed in his tuxedo as any young groom would do. Except in his case, his eyes were still covered with bandages. His father drove him to the church, but before the official ceremony started, his doctor showed up and wanted to see him in one of the side rooms of the church. He felt it was time to determine if his operation had worked, and so why not now before the wedding ceremony was to begin.

As this was going on, the young bride arrived at church with her father and began to ready herself for the walk down the aisle. She was extremely excited and a little nervous as any bride would be. When the ceremony started, the girl's father escorted her and then joined her hand to her young groom. Bandages were still over his eyes, but before the vows were taken, to her surprise, the young man removed his bandages. He looked into her eyes and saw her for the very first time, for the operation had been successful. He immediately exclaimed with great joy, "Beautiful, how beautiful you are; you are everything and more than all of my dreams."

Last Thought

This story was obviously dramatic, with a wonderful ending and resolve. The same will be for you when you see Christ, face to face in heaven for the first time. And you may likewise say, "Beautiful, how beautiful you are, oh Lord, how beautiful." But until then, finish your work here on earth, so that when you see Christ, He will be proud of you for being so faithful, as this woman was to the young man she loved so much.

Scripture References

Psalm 27:4 *One thing I have asked from the Lord, that I may dwell in His house all the days of my life, to behold the beauty of Him.*

Isaiah 33:17 *Your eyes will see the Lord in His beauty.*

Rev 22:3 *There will no longer be any curse, and the throne of God and the Lamb will be in it, and His bond-servants will serve Him, and see His face.*

February
Week 1

How Beautiful You Are!

For now, we see in a mirror dimly, but then one day face to face with Jesus; now we know in part, but then we will know fully just as we also have been fully known by Him. I Corinthians 13:12

    A remarkable incident occurred at a wedding several years ago. A young man who was well known and popular in his community was about to marry a beautiful young girl he had never seen before. This was because he had been blind since ten years of age when he had an unfortunate and regrettable accident. However, this tragedy did not dissuade him from pushing forward with his life, which included attending college. While there, struggling through his studies, he met a young girl who fell in love with him. His blindness did not bother her whatsoever, for she saw his heart, which was all she cared about. He, too, fell in love with this young girl, not knowing what she even looked like. He heard what others said about her but could only dream about how beautiful she might be. Happily, the wedding was planned.
    Before the marriage day was to take place, this young man decided to submit himself to a new course of medical procedures for his eyes, the result of which would not be known for a few weeks, perhaps not even until the day of his wedding.
    That day finally arrived, and still, the bandages remained over his eyes. Many well-wishers piled into the church; the worship center was full

February

**How Beautiful You Are
Valentine's Day
President's Day
Red Seas in Life**

let endurance have its perfect result, so that you may be perfect and complete, lacking in nothing.

II Corinthians 4: 16-18 *16 Therefore we do not lose heart, but though our outer man is decaying, yet our inner man is being renewed day by day. 17 For momentary, light affliction is producing for us an eternal weight of glory far beyond all comparison, 18 while we look not at the things which are seen, but at the things which are not seen; for the things which are seen are temporal, but the things which are not seen are eternal.*

Paul's conversion was like a first coating of nacre, a spiritual nacre that is, with which God covered him.

This would not be the last coating Paul would need or receive from God; there would be many other irritants and resulting pearls that would embody his life before making his final exit to heaven.

Paul's irritants and grains of sand could be extremely uncomfortable, perplexing, and even harsh at times. For example, it was difficult for Paul to be intentionally isolated from other Christians during his first years as a believer. Then when he did enter into ministry, he was beaten several times by non-Christians, and even stoned and left for dead on one occasion. Add to this being shipwrecked, imprisoned, bitten by a viper, and heavily criticized by others about his different views on grace and law.

Yet, at the end of Paul's life he not only had many pearls to his name because of the way God coated him with His love, acceptance, and wisdom, but one big pearl representing his perseverance and proven character.

> *And not only this, but we also exult in our tribulations, knowing that tribulation brings about perseverance; and perseverance, proven character; and proven character, hope; and hope does not disappoint, because the love of God has been poured out within our hearts through the Holy Spirit who was given to us. Romans 5:3-5 (Paul's own words to Roman believers)*

Last Thought

The same can also be true of you if you have received Christ. God allows irritants to come into your life as well, and coats you with additional levels of His love, acceptance, and wisdom. Therefore, do not be too quick to pray irritants (trials) away when they come, instead let God do His coating work. For like Paul and all other maturing Christians, you are being made into a beautiful pearl in His kingdom here on earth and heaven to come.

Scripture References

Jeremiah 30:17 *For I will restore you to health and I will heal you of your wounds, declares the Lord. Jeremiah 30:17*

James 2: 2-4 *2 Consider it all joy, my brethren, when you encounter various trials, 3 knowing that the testing of your faith produces endurance. 4 And*

into an oyster's shell. When it does it grates against the sides of the shell so much, that it produces a wound.

To alleviate the wound, the oyster secretes a substance called nacre, which coats the irritant. The more coats applied over time, the better for the oyster. Eventually this coating of the irritant produces a beautiful pearl, or even a few pearls at one time. In essence then, a pearl is nothing more than the result of a wound, which can be very painful at first, but not so when the coatings are complete.

In our lives we have also experienced many wounds of one kind or another. I believe the wounds which injure us the most are cuts made to our hearts, where our spirit, emotions, and feelings reside. Wounds made here are the hardest to heal, because they usually encompass negative circumstances like the loss of job, home, friends, or death of someone close to us. They can also occur when someone says something despairingly to or about us. The bottom line is we do get wounded and hurt in this life, like the oyster with a grain of sand rubbing its insides.

Yet when grains of sand enter our lives, ones that injure our hearts, we have a God who knows how to deal with them. And His work is not just to expel these irritants, but to coat us with new measures of His love, acceptance, and wisdom during these times. His coating not only reshapes and refines our character but will make each of us a beautiful pearl of a person in His sight. A pearl, so to speak, He would be pleased to put on His tie if he should ever wear one.

> *How precious also are Your thoughts to me, oh God! How vast is the sum of them! If I should count them, they would outnumber the sand. Psalm 139:17-18*

The story of Paul is an example of God making a pearl from a wound. Before Paul believed in Christ, he was a self-righteous Pharisee, persecuting Christians for their faith. But then God saw fit to wound him by throwing a piece of grating sand into his life. As Acts 9 recounts, Paul was blinded by Jesus one day on the way to Damascus. He was going there to persecute more Christians. During his blindness, Christ spoke out from heaven to Paul, confronting him about all the persecutions he was carrying out against Him. Stunned by this surprise encounter with Christ, Paul responded and repented and accepted Him as his lord and savior. In a way,

January
Week 4

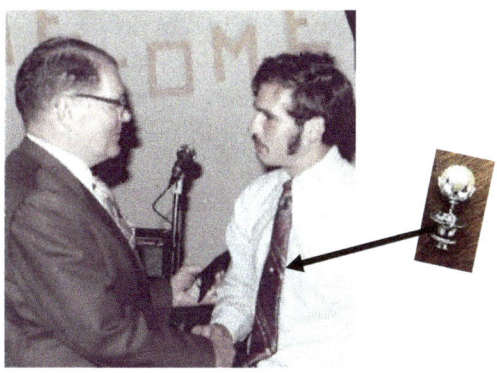

The Making of a Pearl

Upon finding a pearl of great value, he went and sold all that he had and bought it. Matthew 13:46

Often when I dress up and want to look particularly nice on a special occasion, I retrieve from my small collection of jewelry a tie tack that was given to me years ago by a very generous pastor, friend, and mentor, Reverend Brown. He was older than me and was significantly more well-off than I during the time I knew him.

The pin was a beautiful pearl that usually upstaged most of the ties with which I chose to wear it. It was not only rather large for a piece of jewelry, but flawless and very striking. I often got comments on the pin, and many questioned whether it was a real pearl or not. It was real, and awfully expensive. Had Reverend Brown not given it to me because of the great relationship we developed while working together at church, I could have never afforded it myself.

While studying the origin and nature of a pearl for a sermon one day, I found that compared to most other gems that are found in the earth, the pearl is rather unique. It comes as a result of a wound. Yes, that is right, a wound, like one you might have suffered when getting hurt.

You see, pearls come from oysters, which we may have eaten at one time or another, and unless an oyster suffers a wound there can never be a pearl. This wound can only happen when an irritant or grain of sand gets

do to us. Even the cuts, chops, and slashes we may receive from others during our lives will be healed and repaired by God, who daily sends through our core a steady stream of His unconditional love, acceptance, and help. We may look a little worse for wear at times, or even feel a bit damaged because of what others have done to us, but we are alive, very much appreciated by Him, and will remain so until He calls us home to heaven. Then, and only then, will our old tree (body) get exchanged for a new one that is flawless and impervious to anymore damage or pain.

> *For our dying bodies must be transformed into bodies that will never die; our mortal bodies will be transformed into immortal bodies. I Corinthians 15:53 (New Living Translation)*

Last Thought

For the sake of remembering, the next time you see a palm tree, think of your core which has a steady stream of Christ and the Spirit running through it from bottom to top always replenishing and repairing you when damaged by others.

Scriptures References

Jeremiah 17:8 *For you will be like a tree planted by the water, that extends your roots by a stream. And you will not fear when the heat comes; but your leaves will be green, and you will not be anxious in a year of drought nor cease to yield fruit.*

Psalm 139:17-18 *17 How precious also are Your thoughts to me, O God! 18 How vast is the sum of them! If I should count them, they would outnumber the sand. When I awake, I am still with You.*

Hebrews 13:5-6 *5 For the Lord said, "I will never desert you, nor will I ever forsake you," so that we confidently say, 6 "The Lord is my helper, I will not be afraid. What will man do to me?"*

January
Week 3

A Palm Tree's Core

The faithful will flourish like the palm tree and grow like a cedar in Lebanon. Psalm 92:12

When I read *Psalm 92:12* the other day, I wondered what *"to flourish like a palm tree"* really meant? After studying about palm trees, this verse really began to make sense to me. To no surprise, this tall tree, which is quite simple, beautiful, and recognizable by most of us, thrives best in the tropical and semi-tropical regions of the world. Because of the hot climates in which the palm must live and survive, its growth and development is vastly different than other trees. If it was not, then it would never live to be 100 years old, as palm trees do.

One huge difference between a palm tree and other trees is how it collects moisture (sap) from its roots. The moisture it needs is not drawn up between the bark and wood to feed its branches, produce, and leaves, as is the case with other trees. Rather, the moisture it needs travels up through the core of its trunk. Therefore, the tree cannot be permanently harmed or destroyed by injuring any part of its outer frame. The palm can only be truly harmed or destroyed by cutting it down, and nothing less. It may look a little uglier when its branches are chopped off, bark slashed, or wounded in other ways, but it will not die. Its life is maintained by what is at its core, its heart, so to speak.

Thus, it is with those of us who have put our trust in Christ, for like the palm tree we cannot be permanently harmed or destroyed by what others

make sure to keep asking until He answers. He will, after all God loves you, and wants you to be a part of His kingdom here and in the heavenly life to come.

> *Ask, and it will be given to you; seek, and you will find; knock, and it will be opened to you. For everyone who asks receives, and he who seeks finds, and to him who knocks it will be opened. Or what man is there among you who, when his son asks for a loaf, will give him a stone? Or if he asks for a fish, he will not give him a snake, will he? If you know how to give good gifts to your children, how much more will your Father who is in heaven give what is good to those who ask Him! Matthew 7:7-11*

Then after praying, start reading the Scripture, for it will tell you a lot about God and His plan and purpose for you. One of best books to read in the Scriptures is the Gospel of John. It only has 21 short chapters and contains some incredible verses to think about and claim for yourself.

Here are three verses that you have probably heard many times over from others, yet they capture the whole book of John, especially in respect to God's plan and purpose for you after your life is over.

> *For God so loved the world, that He gave His only begotten Son, that if you believe in Him will not perish, but have eternal life. God did not send the Son into the world to judge it, but that the world might be saved through Him. Therefore, if you believe in Him you are not judged, but if you don't then you will be judged, because you did not believe in Christ, God's Son. John 3:16-18*
> **God speed and see you in heaven if not before!**

Scripture References

John 12:5 *Your days are determined, and the number of months are in His hands.*

Psalm 39:4 *Lord, make me to know my end and what is the extent of my days. Let me see how momentary I am.*

saddened when this happened, for we were to meet the next week for coffee and fellowship.

And then there was a young boy in the school of which I was an administrator, a boy who loved God deeply, yet was killed one weekend in a head on car crash by a drunk driver. All of us at the school were shocked and devastated, as was the family as you can imagine.

The point in all of these shortened or premature deaths is that the Scriptures tell us that we each only have so many days here on earth. His decision to take us doesn't depend on who we are, famous or not, our age, young or old, or even how good or bad we've been. When God created each of us in our mother's womb, He also attached a time to depart from this earth (to die).

> *The Lord formed my inward parts, and has woven me in my mother's womb. I will give thanks to You, oh Lord, for I am fearfully and wonderfully made, for my soul knows this very well. My frame was not hidden from You when I was made in secret. Your eyes saw my unformed substance; and in Your book were written all the days ordained for me to live, when as yet there was not one of them. Psalms 139:13-16*

Last Thoughts

Considering all of these early departures, an important question to ask is not when will be your time to leave this earth, for it surely will come like everyone else, but what do you need to do in preparation for that moment?

More specifically, what do you need to do with the God who made you in the first place? For He is the One who had a purpose and plan in mind when He created you.

If the answer is that you know God's purpose and plan for your life, then continue to accomplish it with as much gusto as possible until your last breath. Because as life has shown, your last breath can come at any time in a variety of ways as it did for John Denver, Steve Patterson, Eldridge Cleaver, the young mother, and young boy.

If after contemplating about the time you think you have left you realize you don't really know God all that well, nor His purpose or plan for your life, then don't waste any more time. Begin first by praying that God will reveal Himself to you. Use whatever words that come to mind, but

Steve was part of the Bruins' string of seven consecutive NCAA titles. He went on to play in the NBA for five years, became head coach at Arizona State University, was Commissioner of the Continental Basketball Association, and chairman of the organizing committee for Super Bowl XXX.

Along with all of these accomplishments, Steve also started a ministry on the UCLA campus called the Jesus Christ Light and Power House. This is where I met and developed a friendship with him, which fostered many discussions between us on how to answer certain questions about Christianity that his fellow players brought up. Steve was born in 1948 and died of lung cancer in 2004; he was only 56 years old.

Another renowned person I met by happenstance was Eldridge Cleaver who was one of the leaders of the Black Panthers during his early years. The Black Panthers was a revolutionary political organization which became rather vocal, radical, and notorious in the 1960's. Although they did some good things, like the sponsoring of the Free Breakfast for Children's programs in Oakland, they were also very militaristic and violent.

I was introduced to Eldredge one Sunday evening after going over to a church elder's home for dinner. When I arrived, Cleaver was already sitting at the table and was there because he was our guest speaker that night at church.

Right before that church meeting, Roy, the elder I mentioned, invited him to join us for dinner. I immediately recognized Cleaver for he had been in the news quite often. What I did not know was that he had an encounter with God and had walked away from the Black Panthers.

We had a great conversation during dinner; he was very transparent about the changes that had taken place in his life since his newfound relationship with God. He was going to share those changes that evening at church. How he matured in his faith after meeting him, I am not sure, but at least that evening Cleaver seemed very much at peace with God. Eldridge Cleaver was born in 1935 and died of prostate cancer in 1998; he was only 62 years of age.

There were others I met and knew in my life who died earlier than expected and in a variety of ways. A young mother, for instance, who had a wonderful husband and four children died of breast cancer. It was an incredibly sad day for all who knew her.

A college friend and schoolmate of mine, without any symptoms whatsoever, died of a stroke. I was taken back, surprised, and greatly

January
Week 2

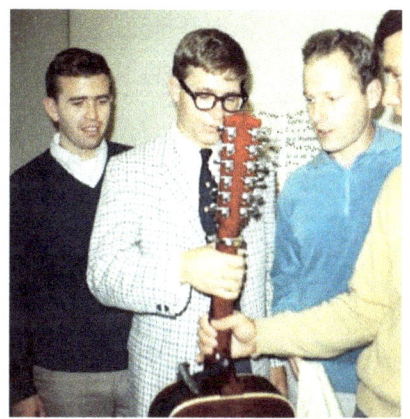

(John Denver with guitar at my brother's home)
(My brother, in the dark sweater, starting in show business himself)

Coming and Going

There is an appointed time for everything, and a time for every event under heaven; a time for birth and a time to die. Ecclesiastes 3:1-2

In the book of Ecclesiastes, King Solomon of Israel writes that there is a time for everything under heaven, including a time to be born and a time to die. As life has proven over and over, the time to die can come at any moment, by any means, to anyone, even to the most known or celebrated among us.

I have met and talked with a few of these well-known individuals over the years who died before their time. I chatted with the singer-songwriter John Denver when he was breaking into the entertainment business. He often came over to my brother's house who was also in that business. His name back then was Henry John Deutschendorf Jr. My brother called him Dutch for short as I remember, and even named his dog after him. John was born in 1943 but died in a plane crash in 1997; he was only 53 years old.

Steve Patterson was someone else I knew very well. He was UCLA's starting center during the seasons between the Lew Alcindor (Kareem Abdul Jabbar) and Bill Walton eras.

Last Thought

Don't let any opportunity go by, in fact, ask yourself who you can show gratitude and appreciation to this week, or even today. It may encourage them more than you think. It may also draw them closer to you which would be good, but even better than that, closer to the Lord, and that would be great.

Scripture Reference

Proverbs 16:24 *Pleasant words are a honeycomb, sweet to the soul and healing to the bones.*

```
54/248.
                                              Magdalen College,
                                                    Oxford.
                                              28th.April 1954.
    Dear Mrs.Young,
             Many thanks for your most kind and encouraging letter of
    the 9th. All stories begin for me simply with mental pictures which turn
    up I don't know where. The writing consists merely in connecting them.
    Yes: I think the dead do affect us. But, on your life, keep clear of "mediums
    With all good wishes,
                                              yours sincerely,
                                              C. S. Lewis
```

(One of the thousands written by CS Lewis)

I thank my God in all my remembrance of you, always in every prayer of mine for you all making my prayer with joy, because of your partnership in the gospel from the first day until now. Philippians 1:3-5

Perhaps though, it was just a part of Lewis' character to give as much gratitude to others as possible. But regardless of his inspiration or motivation, finding this out about him certainly inspired me to do the same with others who have complemented me in one fashion or another. And not just to say a simple, "Thank you," but to write or say as much as I can in return

Finally, let me share another example of someone with whom I knew and spent time, who, like Lewis, also showed great gratitude toward others. He was a pastor of an exceptionally large church, over 10,000 in its hay day.

Of course, it would have been impossible for him, Guy Davidson, to remember and know something about everyone who attended his church, but he did! Somehow, due to a lot of prayer and note-taking, Guy knew everyone at his church, all 10,000 of them. Seems impossible doesn't it, yet I know this to be true by the testimony of so many who knew him, including myself.

I met him just once and had a very brief conversation with Guy about my family. Months later I ran across him in a coffee shop by chance. Seeing me there, he immediately came over and said, "Hi Kent, how are you doing with your family life ministry, how is your daughter Shannon doing in high school, and how is your wife Myrna doing in her teaching?" I couldn't believe he even remembered my name, much less something about my daughter and wife, but that was Guy. Not just some big-time pastor too busy for everyone in his congregation, but someone who highly regarded everyone he met, enough so to take the time and effort to remember their names and something about them.

What should we take from men like C.S. Lewis, Paul, and Guy Davidson who showed uncommon gratitude toward others? Take time to respond to those who have taken their time to say or do something nice to us. A trait all churches need more of if they are going to experience the joy and unity God has planned for them.

can imagine, Lewis was a very productive, effective, and a busy person during the course of his short life; he only lived to be 64.

Lewis had many wonderful attributes, like being generous, kind, faithful, and incredibly perceptive of the Scriptures, but his most hidden attribute might have been gratitude. Not just the gratitude he showed to God for giving him salvation, but the gratitude he exhibited to others throughout his life.

According to those who knew him, Lewis quite often responded back to those who wrote to him. His handwritten responses were not just a quick, "Thank you," attached with an autograph either, but a personal note that could encompass a page or two.

I saw one of his original responses when at a friend's home several years ago. While visiting one afternoon I noticed on the living room wall a framed letter written by Lewis. It was written to someone who had complimented him on something he had done. How my friend and wife got this letter they do not remember, but valued it enough to display to all who came to their home.

How was it possible for Lewis to respond to those who wrote to him, for there may have been several hundred if not thousands?

According to the accounts I read, Lewis made responding to others one of his main priorities, along with speaking, teaching, and writing. With the assistance of his brother, with whom he collaborated on every letter, a response was given.

The question then begs why Lewis made this such a priority. His reputation, popularity, and notoriety had already been established and was certainly in no need of bolstering. A possible answer may have been that since God was always faithful to answer him during the course of his life, then why shouldn't he do the same with others.

Or maybe he decided to answer back because he read the accounts of another writer he admired, Paul the great Apostle. In many of Paul's writings, which were primarily letters written to other believers, gratitude and appreciation continually spilled out toward them, no matter what issue was being addressed.

> *It is right for me to feel this way about you all, because I hold you in my heart, for you are all partakers with me of grace. Philippians 1:7*

January
Week 1

(C.S. Lewis)

A Word of Gratitude

Encourage and build one another up! I Thessalonians 5:11

Many of us have seen the movies, *The Lion, The Witch and The Wardrobe, Prince Caspian, and The Voyage of the Dawn Treader.* In these stories were some unforgettable characters like Lucy, Edmund, Susie, Peter, and, of course, Aslan the lion who represented God.

Several years ago, Myrna and I bought a huge stuffed lion for our grandkids to play with and called him Aslan. They used to climb all over Aslan and spoke to him as if he was a real lion. And when we went to the zoo, the first lion they saw became Aslan to them.

Each of these movies was based on one of C.S. Lewis' most popular writings, *The Chronicles of Narnia.* Lewis was not only a profound British writer, intellect, and professor, he was also a great Christian apologist and radio speaker. C.S. Lewis was also considered by many of his generation as one of the most influential Christian leaders of the 20th Century. Even today, Lewis' books are still widely read; outside his Narnia Chronicles, *Mere Christianity* and *The Screwtape Letters* are two of his most popular. As you

January

**A Word of Gratitude
Coming and Going
A Palm Tree's Core
The Making of a Pearl**

Scripture references

II Timothy 3:16-17 *16 All Scripture is inspired by God and profitable for teaching, for reproof, for correction, for training in righteousness; 17 so that the man of God may be adequate, equipped for every good work.*

II Timothy 2:15 *Be diligent to present yourself approved to God as a workman who does not need to be ashamed, accurately handling the word of truth.*

John 14:26 But the Helper, the Holy Spirit, whom the Father will send in My name, He will teach you all things, and bring to your remembrance all that I said to you.

binoculars. I wanted the binoculars for several reasons, but the most important was for the football games we attended.

Because of the cheap seats I usually bought, my wife and I could not always see up close everything going on during the game. Add to this, the one TV replay screen, in the stadium, which was located right behind us. Hence, for us to see it, we had to look behind with strained necks. Nonetheless, the binoculars went home with my grandson, and so did the hope for a better view of the next game, which was the last of the season.

Between then and the game, thankfully, a friend of mine came by and said I could borrow his binoculars because he wasn't going to the game. And boy, what a difference it made at that game, for both my wife and I could see coaches and players up close. We even saw the expressions on their faces when a play worked or didn't work. We were also able to see up close the yardage needed for first downs, and who was coming in and out of the game on different plays. The bottom line is, we saw the game more clearly than ever before.

In a parallel way, as each of us prepare for this coming new year, God has given us a pair of binoculars, too, spiritual binoculars. These will help us see up close what His will is with each decision and circumstance we will face in the months to come. These spiritual field glasses of ours will greatly magnify what we need to see before making a tough decision, or when dealing with a difficult circumstance that needs to be overcome.

What are these divine binoculars? They are the Scriptures, which are God's own personal word on just about everything we will encounter in the months to come. The Scriptures are significant and vital to our lives, because they not only give us a history of what other believers have experienced in past centuries, they provide us with wisdom and direction on how to handle our own set of circumstances. If that is not enough, God sent His Holy Spirit to help us interpret and apply the great truths of the Scriptures to our own set of circumstances. He has also promised to empower us when you need empowering.

Last Thought

Before you settle into this new year with all of your wishes, desires, and hopes, please make a special time for the Scriptures each day, for they will be your binoculars to magnify what God wants you to see each day.

December
Week 4

Binoculars

You are my lamp, O Lord, and You illumine my darkness. II Samuel 2:29

As December comes to an end, and Christmas memories begin to fade, there is yet a new year ahead. Perhaps it will be a year that could realize new dreams, disciplines, and even answers to prayer.

There was a gift my grandson received at Christmas a few years ago that might visualize for you a way to gain some of the desires and hopes you have for the coming year. It was a pair of binoculars. Now I must admit, I actually bought these binoculars for myself and not Luke, but he ended up with them.

We have a family gift game we play every year at Christmas. I buy all the gifts for the game and wrap them. When the game starts, each family member gets to go to the pile of gifts placed in front of the Christmas tree and choose one. Everyone is assured of a gift, and often they get just what they wanted, but not always. This happens due to a lot of trading and bargaining that goes on during the game. The goal is for everyone to have fun and end up with just the right gift for themselves.

Since I was selecting all the gifts for the game, I thought for sure my grandson, Luke, would want this one particular gift, but instead, he took the

Silent night! Holy night!
Son of God, love's pure light.
Radiant beams from thy holy face,
With the dawn of redeeming grace,
Jesus Lord at Thy birth,
Jesus Lord at Thy birth.

Mohr replied, "Please, provide the music to go along with it. Only you can write it, and then we can surprise the congregation at Christmas with this new song."

Franz shook his head and said that the church organ was broken, so it would be difficult to develop a melody without it. Mohr then glanced about the room and saw a guitar tucked away in the corner. Picking it up, he said, "Let this be your instrument at our Christmas service."

With guitar in hand, Franz sat down and began to work out a melody. As he played on, a softly flowing tune came to him. He began to score it, and when finished, a graceful movement and spirit seemed to blend with the words. From there on, a beautiful and unforgettable harmony was born.

Franz then came to Mohr's study and played the notes he had created. They both began to sing *Silent Night* for the first time; it was perfect. And so, *Silent Night* was composed and arranged and has been sung ever since by millions upon millions of Christians.

Last Thought

From a simple and unpredictable beginning, a great carol was written, can God not do the same with your life if you humbly follow Him? I think so, but as you wait on God, be as still and quiet as that night was when Jesus was born.

Scripture Reference
Psalm 46:10 *Be still and know that I am God.*

Silent Night, Holy Night

Silent night! Holy night!
Shepherds quake at the sight!
Glories stream from heaven afar,
Heavenly hosts sing Alleluia.
Christ, the Savior is born,
Christ, the Savior is born.

professional singer. However, no real opportunity ever presented itself, so this moved him to dedicate his life to the priesthood.

To the delight of his parents, his church was within traveling distance from his childhood home in Salzburg, so they were able to regularly hear him preach and sing in his services.

A couple of days previous to one of his Christmas services, Mohr sat in his study preparing for the sermon and music to follow when he heard a knock on the door. It was one of his parishioners from the hill country, a woodchopper. He came asking Mohr to come and minister to a sick family member.

Mohr immediately got up from his desk, put on a heavy coat and hiking boots. He threw a wrap around his neck, picked up his walking stick for the long hike ahead, and said, "Let's go." For apart from being a very musically talented pastor, Mohr was also one that was willing to serve others at a moment's notice.

Throughout his steady and toiling climb, Mohr became more and more impressed with the silence of the night. As he looked up, there was a brilliant array of stars, so quiet, still, and peaceful.

Soon the window light in a woodchopper's cottage came into sight, and in a few minutes both entered into its warmth, for it was a frigid night. He prayed over and blessed the one who was sick and then ended by saying, "Jesus the Savior has come," for the celebration of His birth was only two days away.

After returning, Mohr sat down in his study once again, but before reading through his notes he gazed through his windows across at the mountain he had just climbed. Filled with a sense of inspiration, Mohr wondered if the night Jesus was born was just as beautiful and peaceful. From those thoughts, Mohr began to write the words to the carol, *Silent Night*.

The next morning, Mohr rushed to see Franz Gruber, a friend, church member, and fellow musician. When he read the first draft of his song to his Franz, his face immediately brightened.

> *Franz said to Mohr, "This is the Christmas song I have said so many times had yet to be written, and you have found it."*

December
Week 3

(Our family singing Silent Night on Christmas Eve)

Silent Night, Holy Night

When the fullness of the time came, God sent forth His Son, born of a woman. And you will find this baby wrapped in swaddling clothes lying in a manger. Galatians 4:4; Luke 2:12

As my wife and I look back at past Christmases, we remember when our little family used to sing Silent Night on Christmas Eve in church. My son, Brodie, was only 10, and daughter Shannon was 6, but each knew the song very well and could carry a tune. Nonetheless, the congregation had no choice but to listen to our rendition of this great Christmas carol for I was the senior pastor.

Those were special days for our family; we were so young and loved every moment surrounding Christmas. We chose Silent Night over other carols because of its pure harmony, beautiful words, clear message, and rich history, which I shared more with my kids when they got older.

Josef Mohr, who wrote the lyrics to Silent Night was a very humble and uncomplicated man born in Salzburg, Austria, on December 11, 1792. Father Mohr, as he was referred to, was an Austrian priest who had a lovely tenor voice. Before becoming a priest, it was always his dream to become a

Matthew 2:9-12 *9 After hearing the king, they went their way; and the star, which they had seen in the East, went on before them until it came and stood over the place where the Child was. 10 When they saw the star, they rejoiced exceedingly with great joy. 11 After coming into the house, they saw the Child with Mary, His mother; and they fell to the ground and worshiped Him. Then, opening their treasures, they presented to Him gifts of gold, frankincense, and myrrh. 12 And having been warned by God in a dream not to return to Herod, the magi left for their own country by another way.*

Footnotes

Edersheim, Alfred, *The Life and Times of Jesus the Messiah, Volume I*, (Longmans, Green and Company, London, 1910) Pages 212-215.

The Wise Men and others were perhaps influenced by believers from the far past, like Daniel, Shadrach, Meshack, Abednego, and others. They, as many others like them, spent years in these Eastern kingdoms, sharing who God was and what He was like. Over time, and through several different kingdoms like the Babylonians and Medo-Persians, the testimony of these believers must have taken root and spread. Somehow and in some way, a belief in the real God landed on the Wise Men, enough for them to take off for Bethlehem on a two-year trek following a moving star.

The third reason for God sending the Wise Men, was for them to later become witnesses to the East about Jesus. When they returned, many who were awaiting their return would want to know what they saw and experienced. The first words off their lips might have been, "Jesus, the Savior of the world was born." And so, through the Wise Men, as was the case with Daniel and others before them, knowledge of God and salvation continued to spread in that part of the world.

Perhaps without realizing it, the light of the star they followed for so many months now became Christ's light within them that emerged every time they shared the story of His birth and its purpose. Should we not also let Christ's light emerge from us as well, especially during the Christmas season, when many lose their way and are looking for help, rescue, or even a Savior. Therefore, be a light, be a star of Bethlehem to others at Christmas.

> *You are the light of the world, a city set on a hill cannot be hidden; nor does anyone light a lamp and put it under a basket, but on a lampstand, and it gives light to all who are in the house. Matthew 5:14-15*

Last Thought

If you are with your family this Christmas, take your children or other family members outside on Christmas Eve for a time of reflection. As you look into the sky together, pretend one of the stars is the star of Bethlehem. Recount the story of the Wise Men and the star as best you can. Afterward, tell your family that each of them is like the star of Bethlehem, that is a bright light to shine and show others the way to Jesus, their Savior.

Scripture References

Matthew 2: 2 *Where is He who has been born King of the Jews? For we saw His star in the East and have come to worship Him.*

Proof of their belief was evidenced when they showed up and immediately fell down and worshipped baby Jesus. Only God at work in them could produce such a response.

In addition to their belief, what of the star that directed them to Bethlehem? Was it possible for such a star to move continuously as it did, and for two years?

Historically speaking, and without much argument, the star of Bethlehem did exist around the time of Jesus' birth. According to astronomy records, a remarkable conjunction of planets (Jupiter and Saturn in the constellation Pisces), which only occurs every eight hundred years, took place two years previous to the birth of Christ.

Several Christian scholars determine that this star cluster was perhaps the first sign that initiated the Wise Men's sojourn to Bethlehem. It was an extraordinarily brilliant spectacle in the night sky; everyone in the East would have taken note of it. In the following year, another planet (Mars) joined this constellation. As a result, these three planets (Jupiter, Saturn, Mars) joined together appearing as an astonishing effervescent star.

This conjunction of stars took place over Jerusalem right before the birth of Jesus. The final movement of the star from Jerusalem to Bethlehem, the night of Jesus' birth, was according to the Chinese astronomers of that day, like a purpose-driven meteor.[1]

Although I love the way these historical star clusters came together to collaborate Matthew's account concerning the Bethlehem star, it does not really matter. For as far as I am concerned, a God-created phenomenon like driving a star to a specific destination also works for me, as did all the other miracles in the Bible.

Regardless of either instance, God's purpose for the Wise Men was the same, to bring them to Bethlehem, the birthplace of Jesus, the Savior of the world. It is likely God brought them there for three reasons: the first being to provide financial help to Joseph and Mary who were poor and had to move quickly to Egypt before Herod found and killed Jesus. The three gifts had significant symbolic meaning and should always be highlighted when this story is told, but mostly they provided the means for Joseph and Mary to get up and go.

The second reason for the Wise Men's coming was likely in response to their personal relationship with God. How was this possible since polytheistic and varying pagan religions dominated the East?

December
Week 2

Bethlehem Star

Where is He who has been born King of the Jews? For we saw His star in the East and have come to worship Him. Matthew 2:2

Every Christmas we recount many stories and Scriptures surrounding the birth of Jesus, the Savior of the world. The story of the Wise Men (*Magi, Kings*) taking gifts to the Christ child is one of those. It is a beautiful story for many reasons. One facet of the story that is often overlooked is how they got to Bethlehem from so far away. The path they took was not only remarkable and unusual but close to being miraculous.

According to Matthew's gospel, great Wise Men (Magi) from the East came bearing three gifts to Joseph, Mary, and Jesus after His birth. It is not truely known how many Wise Men there were, but since there were three gifts, it has always been assumed there were just three. The number does not matter, but what does is how they got to Bethlehem when they did from such a great distance.

In respect to some historical records below, their journey to Bethlehem probably began about two years before their arrival. What started their trek was a belief in a coming Messiah, and a very bright and moving star. How they attained this belief is not known, but God has His ways of getting through to those called according to His purpose.*(Romans 8:28)*

it be a teammate or one from another team, then so be it. And sad to say, the taunting that also goes on between players today has become too commonplace and a terrible example to young people trying to learn how to treat others amid their own competitions.

During this Christmas, while in the middle of all your pursuits, love and put others first, even above your own needs and wants. Should this mean accepting many third-place trophies along the way to win others to the kingdom, then do it. What a wonderful Christmas gift to God this would be, who already gave you the best Christmas gift of all, His Son, who took care of your sins on the cross.

Scriptures References

Romans 15:1 *We who are strong ought to bear the weaknesses of those without strength and not just please ourselves.*

1 Corinthians 10:24 *Let no one seek his own good, but that of his neighbor.*

Matthew 7:12 *In everything, therefore, treat people the same way you want them to treat you.*

disaster. I did not find out until I got home that evening from my church meeting that my son, who was still up, was rather uptight about something.

>I asked, "Are you okay, Brodie? How did practice go?"
>"Not good, dad, Sam quit the team."
>"What?" I replied. "Why?"
>"Your assistant coach kind of ran him off; in fact, Sam's dad came and picked him up in the middle of practice."

As I found out later from the reports of other parents and kids, my assistant coach made practice difficult for Sam, hoping he would quit. If he left, then we would not have to play him in the championship game.

I was angry, to say the least, and tried to get ahold of Sam's dad to make things right, but he wouldn't talk with me. A couple of days before the game, Brodie and I talked again about what to do. Brodie said he would go over to Sam's house and talk him into coming back. And that is exactly what Brodie did; he went over to Sam's house and talked him into coming back. I asked Brodie what he said to Sam and his dad. Brodie told them he would not play unless Sam came back. That seemed to get through to Sam and his father, so Sam rejoined the team.

As the games went on during this championship weekend, we got to the semi-finals, and I would like to say we won, but we didn't. We just barely lost in the last two minutes of this game. And the team we lost to went on to win it all. The loss put us in contention for the consolation game, and we won that easily. At the award ceremony, we got the third-place trophy.

In the years to come, Brodie and Sam became good friends, and his parents even attended my church from time to time. Tom, our tall center, later became a star in high school and went on to play in college.

As Brodie and I finished wrapping our gifts and talking about this third-place trophy experience, Brodie said, "Dad, that's why this trophy was so special, through the sacrifice made I won a friend, and that was more important than a championship." He was right; for sure, he was right.

Last Thoughts

I know in sports today, especially in professional sports winning is the goal. Regrettably, I have heard on TV from too many professional athletes that victory is everything. If others get hurt in the process, whether

the best players and keep their teams together. Any new teams, like ours, had to scramble for players, mostly taking new players who had never played before or players from other teams who had not done so well, only playing the minimum required minutes in games.

Regardless, I put together a team with my son on it. If I had an advantage, I knew pretty much from my own playing days how to help kids practice, play in games, and even reach their potential. After seeing my team after the first few meetings, I extended upcoming practices and scheduled a few extra besides. We had a lot of work to get done to get ready for our first games. Yet, through all the hard work the kids put in, they seemed to enjoy their time and never complained. Neither did their parents, who saw marked improvement in their sons.

Each practice, I had a rule for the whole team; twenty-five lay-ins had to be made in a row before any scrimmaging was to be done, which all the boys always loved. In some of those earlier practices, we spent most of the time just doing this drill because one of our players, Tom, the tallest player in the league, could not make a lay-in. I think the reason I was able to pick up Tom for my team was because of this. Nevertheless, Tom had to make his lay-ins for the team to move forward. But the team was supportive of Tom no matter how many times he missed. And then he started making them, bringing about an ovation of relief from all of his teammates.

When the games started, we lost the first couple, but the kids never gave up and worked harder in practice. Then we began to win one game after the next, with Tom starting to make his shots, which no one could block because he was so tall. Teams who had not wanted him were now worried about him. Other players on our team also started to play well, and we made it to the playoffs.

During the playoffs, there was a rule that if a kid showed up to practice, he had to play at least one quarter in the next game. We had one player, Sam, our next-door neighbor, who tried hard in practice and every game but still had difficulties playing basketball. It was probably just not his sport because he did well in other sports. Anyway, we made it to the finals, which were to be played the next weekend.

I could not coach practice that week because I had an elder meeting at church that night. And it is always good to make it to an elder's meeting when you are the pastor of the church, which I was. My assistant coach, who also had a son on the team, took over, which ended up being quite a

December
Week 1

Third Place Trophy

With humility of mind, regard one another as more important than yourselves; do not merely look out for your own personal interests, but also for the interests of others. Philippians 2:3-4

One Christmas while wrapping gifts with my son, we started reminiscing over some of his past sporting experiences. He was in college now, playing volleyball for Washington State University, but had not forgotten earlier days when he played competitive basketball, soccer, and football. As we talked, I asked him which of his teams meant the most to him. To my surprise, it was not any of the championship teams on which he had been, but rather a team that ended up with a third-place trophy. After thinking about it, I agreed. This particular team was the most special because of what we both learned through that experience.

This little basketball team for which I was the coach was made up of a bunch of fifth and sixth graders. It was part of a city league in Colorado that had a great reputation for being competitive at every age level. Kids who played year after year in this league ended up being excellent players on their junior high and high school basketball teams, and even some went on to play in college.

It was a little precarious and a bit unfair how teams got their players though, for certain teams who ended up winning each year were able to get

December

**Third Place
Bethlehem Star
Silent Night, Holy Night
Binoculars**

whereas both Houses of Congress have, by their joint committee, requested me to recommend to the people of the United States a day of public Thanksgiving and prayer, to be observed by acknowledging with grateful hearts the many and signal favors (signs) of Almighty God, especially to establish a form of government for their safety and happiness. Now, therefore, I do recommend and assign Thursday, the 26th day of November to be devoted by the people of these states to be the service of that great and glorious Being (God), who is the Benefit Author (Creator) of all the good that was, that is, or will be." [6]

Footnotes

1. William J. Johnson, *George Washington the Christian* (New York, Forgotten Books/ Abingdon Press, 1919), pages 26-28.
2. William J. Johnson, *George Washington the Christian* (New York, Forgotten Books/ Abingdon Press, 1919), pages 29-31
3. David Barton, *The Bulletproof George Washington* (Aledo, Texas: Wall Builder Press, 1990), pages 45. *(The content of this quote was not changed, but it was revised in the context for a clearer reading)*
4. David Barton, *The Bulletproof George Washington* (Aledo, Texas: Wall Builder Press, 1990), pages 33-40
5. David Barton, *The Bulletproof George Washington* (Aledo, Texas: Wall Builder Press, 1990), pages 49-51.
6. William J. Johnson, *George Washington the Christian* (New York, Forgotten Books/ Abingdon Press, 1919), pages 172- 173.

chief finally tracked Washington down 15 years later to let him know what he felt about him and the power of His God.[4]

> *"I am chief and ruler over my tribes. My influence extends to the waters of the great lakes and the far Blue Mountains. I have traveled a long and weary path that I may see the young warrior of that great battle. It was on the day when the white man's blood mixed with the streams of our forest that I first beheld this chief, George Washington. I called my young men and said, mark yon tall and daring warrior. He is not of the red-coat tribe, he has Indians wisdom, and his warriors fight as we do; himself is alone exposed. Quick let you be certain, and he dies. Our rifles were leveled, rifles which knew not how to miss, was all in vain, a power mightier far than we, shielded you. Seeing you were under the special guardianship of the Great Spirit, we immediately ceased to fire at you. I am old and soon shall be gathered to the great council fire of my fathers in the land of shades, but ere I go, there is something that bids me speak in the voice of prophecy. Listen! The Great Spirit protects that man (pointing at Washington), and guides his destinies; he will become the chief of nations, and a people yet unborn will hail him as the founder of a mighty empire. I am come to pay homage to the man who is the particular favorite of Heaven, and who can never die in battle."* [5]

Washington began fighting for his country six years later, and most of what the chief said ended up being true.

Last Thought

As you celebrate Thanksgiving do all you can to honor, respect, and give thanks to God as Washington did throughout his life. You can begin this by reading Washington's Thanksgiving proclamation before the dinner prayer. The proclamation was put together and declared on October 3, 1789, when George was 57 years old and President of our country.

> *"Whereas, it is the duty of all nations to acknowledge the sovereignty of almighty God, to obey His will, to be grateful for His benefits, and humbly to implore His protection and favor; and,*

confidence in a personal, all-knowing, and all-powerful God. This conflict took place during the French and Indian War 20 years before the American Revolution. At this time, American colonists were still a part of the British Empire and engaged with the French and Indians for control of North America. George was a commander under British General George Braddock, who at the time was one of the premier generals in the British army. During this particular fight, though, Braddock made some critical errors in judgment, and because of these miscalculations, the battle was soundly lost.

To stop a possible massacre, Washington was put in charge of the British retreat. Due to his bravery and wisdom on the battlefield that day, Washington helped save many soldiers' lives. Of the 86 officers on horseback, only Washington escaped unharmed with his life. He was the tallest of all the other officers and should have been the most natural target to hit. Two horses were shot from underneath him, and four bullet holes were found in his coat after the fight. Yet he was never hurt or wounded.

What was so defining about Washington in this horrific battle when it was publicized that he had died, was his view of God's sovereignty, which he felt kept him safe and protected. Upon returning to Fort Cumberland, his headquarters, Washington, wrote the following message to his brother.

> *"As I have heard, since I arrived at Fort Cumberland, a circumstantial account of my death and dying speech. I take this opportunity of contradicting such and assure you all is well. I give all credit to God's providence for this. He has protected me beyond all human probability or expectation; for I had four bullets through my coat, and two horses were shot from underneath me, yet I escaped unhurt, although death was leveling my companions on every side of me"* [3]

During the battle of Monongahela, General Braddock was killed, along with 714 other British soldiers. 85 out of 86 officers were also killed or wounded, and 70 out of George Washington's 100-man company perished. The French and Indians lost 30 soldiers and three officers. It was considered one of the worst defeats in British history.

When George arrived home unharmed, all were impressed, including those who fought against him. The enemy chief who controlled the battle from his end kept track of George for many years afterward. The

I walked from one end of Mount Vernon to the next, I was quite impressed with the words Washington left behind for all to read, words about God, the Bible, and Jesus Christ. It inspired me to study further and learn more about this man who was supposed to be a Deist. Below are some prayers George Washington prayed when he was a young man. Following them is an account of an incredible battle Washington fought when he was only 23 years old. Both his prayers and this battle give an excellent feel for the kind of genuine faith he had in God.

As you read excerpts from two of his many daily prayers, take note of his humility and confidence in God, for such paved the way for him in so many instances, not only in the battles he fought for our nation, but in the decisions he made for us as President. As many historians would assert, Washington was one of, if not, the greatest President in American history.

Washington's Monday morning prayers

> *"Thou gave Thy Son to die for me, and hast has assured me of salvation, upon my repentance and sincerity to conform my life to His holy precepts and example. O God, pardon me for Christ's sake, instruct me in the particulars of my duty, and suffer me not to be tempted above what Thou givest me the strength to bear. Bless my friends and grant me the grace to forgive my enemies as heartily as I desire forgiveness of Thee, my heavenly Father."* [1]

Washington's Tuesday Prayers

> *"O blessed Father let thy Son's blood wash me from all impurities, and cleanse me from the stains of sin that are upon me. Give me the grace to lay hold upon His merits; that they may be my conciliation and atonement unto thee that I may know my sins are forgiven, by His death and resurrection."* [2]

This does not sound like a Deist to me, but quite the opposite.

The Battle of Monongahela (1755)

The Battle of Monongahela near Pittsburgh demanded a great deal from a young George Washington, especially concerning his prayerful

November
Week 4

The Thanksgiving President

"Thou gave Thy Son to die for me, and hast has given me assurance of salvation, upon my repentance and sincerity to conform my life to His holy precepts and example."

George Washington

Thanksgiving is one of America's most sacred holidays and began over 200 years ago. George Washington, one of our greatest leaders and presidents, inaugurated this holiday. He did because he felt, as a nation, we needed to give God continual gratitude for all He had done to help us gain our freedom and independence.

Washington certainly gave God His due in his own life. By his statements, he felt God, directly and indirectly, helped him with every battle he fought, the decisions he made, the Constitutional amendments he helped pass, and the political position he achieved.

It is incredible that with all George Washington said in the course of his life, some historians paint George Washington as a Deist. A Deist, for the most part, is one who only accepts God based on nature and reason. This belief accepts the morality of Christianity but does not recognize Christ, God's Son, as divine. Nor does this belief accept the Bible as God's revelation. Hence, a Deist would never claim a personal relationship with Christ, nor ever pray to Him for salvation or any other reason.

Unfortunately, this is the view taught today by many public schools about George Washington. I was duped into thinking this myself when I attended public school. It was not until I visited Mount Vernon (Washington's home and burial place) with my daughter, many years later, that I realized how this view of Washington was misleading and untrue. As

had later on with their two other daughters, as they established the American Colony in Jerusalem together.

Perhaps you need to do the same, not to dwell so much on past tragedies or disappointments, but to look at what is before you now and ahead in the future. For it could be that the rest of your life may end up being the best of your life, that is if you trust God with it.

Scripture References

Psalm 121 1-3, 5-8*: I will lift my eyes to the mountains, from where shall my help come? 2 My help comes from the Lord, who made heaven and earth. 3 He will not allow your foot to slip; He who keeps you will not slumber. 5 The Lord is your keeper, the shade on your right hand. 6 The sun will not smite you by day, nor the moon by night. 7 He will guard your going out and your coming in from this time forth and forever.*

Matthew 6:34 *Do not worry about tomorrow; for tomorrow will care for itself. Each day has enough trouble of its own.*

Hebrews 13:5-6 *5 God said, 'I will never desert nor forsake you,' 6 so that we can confidently say, 'The Lord is my helper, I will not be afraid. What can man do to me?'*

Biography

1. Rachael Phillips, *Well with My Soul*, (Barbour Publications, Uhrichsville, Ohio), 2003.
2. Bertha Spafford Vester, *Our Jerusalem*, (Doubleday and Company, Garden City, New York), 1950.
3. Thomas Corts, *Seeking Solace, The Life and Legacy of Horatio G Spafford*, (Samford University Press, Birmingham, Alabama), 2014.

like the return of Israel as a nation, the rebuilding of the temple, the rule of a world leader (Anti-Christ), and Armageddon type battles, to name a few.

So, in 1881, they packed their bags and took off for Jerusalem with a few others from their Overcomer's ministry. Perhaps more than anything else, Horatio and Anna most likely wanted to start anew somewhere else, for things in Chicago had grown exceedingly difficult for them. Of course, the second coming of Christ did not happen, but instead of returning to America, they settled in Jerusalem and began a new ministry.

During their ministry in Jerusalem, which lasted beyond their lives, the entire Spafford family made a lasting impression for the Gospel on Jews, Muslims, other Christians, Turks, the British, and those from other countries as well. They invited all to their ministry, regardless of religious, political, or cultural background. They called their ministry the American Colony, which established soup kitchens, hospitals, and orphanages for the poor and suffering.

Their two daughters, Bertha and Grace, carried on this ministry with their mother Anna, after Horatio died. In 1948, after 70 years of incredible ministry, the American colony closed down. To know how many they helped or reached for the Gospel is not known, just too many to count.

Today, the American Colony is a hotel and meeting center. The Israeli government has used it on different occasions to conduct international business. For instance, the 1993 Oslo Peace Accord between the Palestinians and Israelis was held at this site. But I believe it will always be best remembered for what the Spaffords did there.

What do we learn from Horatio and Anna in this latter stage of their life and ministry? The willingness to let God lead them to another part of the world if asked.

Of course, by leaving, it probably helped them get over the constant memory of losing their four girls and boy. But by going, their two other girls Bertha and Grace came into focus as they did their Jerusalem ministry together with them. Today, they are all together having a great time with one another in heaven.

Last Thought

Because I found Horatio's gravesite in Jerusalem a few years ago, I now know how he got there and what he did after the loss of his first four daughters. When I sing *It Is Well with My Soul* at church, I don't think so much of that tragic shipwreck, but of the times he and his wife must have

evangelistic team. DL Moody was the Billy Graham of that century. In his role, Bliss was in charge of the music at the crusades, much like Cliff Barrow's role with Billy Graham. He wrote other songs and melodies as well, which are still sung in churches today. *Hallelujah, What a Savior* and *My Redeemer* are two of many.

But like Horatio, his family suffered greatly when he and his wife were killed in a train accident on the way to joining Moody for a crusade. Because the train fell into a raging river, their bodies were never found. Fortunately, their children were left behind with a sister on this trip. It seems as though heartache and tragedy follow this song to some degree, which brings out its words and message all the more.

As the Spaffords continued their lives following the tragedy at sea, Anna gave birth to three more children, Horatio Jr., Bertha, and Grace. Sadly, Horatio Jr. died at three years of age of scarlet fever, and so once again, heartache struck. Still, both Horatio and Anna did not give up but forged forward to serve God in any way they could.

Included in Horatio's various ministries were Bible studies in prisons, visits to hospitals, and giving much of his income to evangelistic and benevolent causes. Horatio even downgraded his law practice for real estate investment because it allowed him more time to do ministry.

During these years, Horatio and Anna also formed a new ministry called the Overcomers. It was a church born out of frustration with their old church. Due to the hassles, disagreements, and comments made by some in that old church, leaving seemed to be the best option for the Spaffords.

Some crushing comments from the old church members included suggesting another church family adopt newly born Bertha so that she would survive. Another suggested that the loss of the Spafford children was due to some sin Horatio and Anna had committed. How other people were actually on board with comments like these is not known, but it was enough for the Spaffords to leave and start the Overcomers church. Many joined them after they left.

Not many years after establishing this ministry, Horatio and Anna felt they had received a vision from the Lord to go to Jerusalem. They sensed He was about to return as He had promised in the Scriptures and wanted to be there for His second coming. Had they read more thoroughly books like Daniel and Revelation they would have realized there were too many prophetic signs that had not come to fruition for this to happen. Signs

November
Week 3

(Anna Spafford with daughters Bertha and Grace)

The American Colony

Be strong and courageous! Do not tremble or be dismayed, for the Lord your God is with you wherever you go. Joshua 1:9

    A few years ago, when on a study tour to Israel, I ran across Horacio Spafford's gravestone. After listening to and singing his famous hymn, *It Is Well With My Soul*, too many times to count, I was surprised to see he was buried in Jerusalem. After all, he and his family were from Chicago, quite a distance from the Holy Land.
    If you have not read my first article on Horatio and how this hymn came about, then I suggest reading it first. It deals with the heart-wrenching circumstances surrounding the writing of that incredible song. This article deals with what happened afterward to Horatio and his family, as well as who composed the tune that went with *It Is Well With My Soul*.
    Phillip Bliss is the one who arranged the melody to *It Is Well With My Soul* and was not without heartbreak as well. Bliss was 38 years old when he wrote the melody and was a key part of the DL Moody's

1. Rachael Phillips, *Well with My Soul*, (Barbour Publications, Uhrichsville, Ohio), 2003.
2. Bertha Spafford Vester, *Our Jerusalem*, (Doubleday and Company, Garden City, New York), 1950.
3. Thomas Corts, *Seeking Solace, The Life and Legacy of Horatio G Spafford*, (Samford University Press, Birmingham, Alabama), 2014.

What do we learn from this account with the Spaffords, and even the youth pastor in my dad's church who lost his three children? First, it does not matter how mature we are in our faith, tragedies and trials come to us all in varying ways. With the Spaffords, their tragedy with the four young girls was crushing but deepened their faith. It also changed the focus of their ministry in the years to come. Had this tragedy not occurred, what they ended up doing would have never been done, at least not by them anyway.

So, when Paul writes in Romans 8:28 that all things work together for good, even the awful things, then the Spafford's tragedy is included, because what they ended up doing was particularly good.

Last Thoughts

In the end, both Horatio and Anna were eventually reunited with Annie, Maggie, Bessie, and Tanetta in heaven, along with their other children and loved ones who came later. Did this take the sting out of their tragedy? Perhaps not, especially at the beginning. What did take the pain out of it was seeing those girls rushing to them with arms wide open as they showed up in heaven—what a joyous reunion that must have been, what a *well-with-my-soul* feeling.

If you have anything close to an experience like this in your lifetime, then I implore you to rely on the Scriptures, prayer, and good Christian friends to help you through as Horatio and Anna did. And if you are ever in a position to help another going through a tragedy or severe trial, then be sensitive, be a great listener, and be as comforting as you can be, just as the Lord would if He were in your place.

Scripture References

Matthew 11:28-29 *28 Come to Me, all who are weary and heavy-laden, and I will give you rest. 29 For I am gentle and humble in heart and will provide peace to your souls.*

I Peter 5:7 *Cast all your anxiety on the Lord because He cares for you.*

II Corinthians 1:3-4 *3 Blessed be the God and Father of our Lord Jesus Christ, the Father of mercies and God of all comfort, 4 who comforts us in all our affliction so that we will be able to comfort those who are in any affliction with the comfort with which we have been comforted by God.*

Bibliography

And Lord haste the day when the faith shall be sight,
The clouds be rolled back as a scroll.
The trump shall resound, and the Lord shall descend—
Even so, it is well with my soul.

For me, be it, Christ, be it Christ hence to live.
If Jordan above me shall roll,
No pang shall be mine, for in death as in life,
Thou wilt whisper Thy peace to my soul.

Horatio later writes to a friend that his dear lambs were safe in the folded arms of God and before long, they would all be together again. In the meantime, "Thanks to God, we have an opportunity to serve and praise Him for His love and mercy."

After returning home, Horatio and Anna were greeted by the large portraits of the girls in their living room. Both were silent and in tears, envisioning the girls. As they walked upstairs to the girl's rooms, the beds were neatly made and toys in place, just as they were when they left. Horatio and Anna then walked down the stairs to unlock the back door, when before them lay four pairs of rubber boots, and four pairs of ice skates on the screened porch.

Heart-wrenching, so heart-wrenching! Then while looking into the backyard, Horatio broke the silence and said, "There's the post office," a big hollow elm tree from which the girls made a make-believe mailing station. Horatio stuck his hand into the trunk, to see if there was anything in it. "Here's a letter," he exclaimed, pulling out a crumpled, damp piece of paper. He opened it with trembling fingers and read the letter. It was short, and from Maggie, their second daughter. "Goodbye, dear Lake View home, I will never see you again." She never did but got a much better one in heaven with her sisters.

Horatio and Anna would go on to have other children and do many good works for the Lord, including leaving us with one of the most revered and sung hymns in Christian history. Further trials and tragedies, though, would continue to accompany them as they fulfilled the rest of God's plan for their lives. In a second article on the Spaffords, what they did and how they ended up in Jerusalem of all places will be explored, along with a brief look at Phillip Bliss, the man who put together the familiar tune that accompanies, *It Is Well With My Soul.*

Meanwhile, Horatio was at home getting ready to make his voyage in a few days. During the tragedy, he thought of the delayed Thanksgiving they would all have together once they were reunited. In those days, there was no way to communicate immediately what happened; only the transatlantic cable could telegraph such news when a port was eventually reached.

As witnessed by those who survived, the Spafford girls fought with all of their hearts to stay alive, but their small little bodies were unable to withstand the relentless force of the sea. During their struggle, the oldest Annie shouted out with her faith, "Don't be afraid, the sea is His, and He made it." And then she held onto Tanetta, the two-year-old, with all her might, until both were swept away. Maggie, the seven-year-old, cried out, " Mama, God will take care of us!"

Anna was, of course, heartbroken, seeing her daughters drown before her eyes. What made it even worse was that it took several days before she could contact Horatio about what had happened. Once in port the news spread quickly about the shipwreck and the many lives lost, but all she could cable Horacio was, "Saved alone."

Horatio immediately booked passage on a ship to comfort Anna and bring her back home. While on his voyage there, the captain of his ship knew about where the disaster had taken place. He, in as sensitive of a way as possible, called Horatio to his private cabin and told him their ship was about to pass over the general area where Horatio's daughters had probably drowned.

Upon this news, Horatio went out to look for a while, and then took out a piece of paper and began writing down the words to his song, *It Is Well With my Soul*. The following are just three verses of that great hymn, which gave Horatio a measure of much-needed peace in his life. He had no idea that in the future, his daughter Bertha, not born yet, would sing this song as a ministry to many young soldiers in Jerusalem during their last hours of life.

When peace, like a river, attended my way,
When sorrows like sea-billow roll, whatever my lot,
Thou has taught me to say,
It is well; it is well with my soul.

from this tragedy, and had other children, but I do not think they were ever the same again. I know because I talked with him years later when I was older and in college

In a similar sense, Horatio Spafford, who wrote the lyrics to *It Is Well With My Soul*, lost all four of his children in a shipping disaster. It changed his life as well as his wife's, who survived the shipwreck.

Here is a little background and what led Horatio to write the words to this incredible hymn. The shipwreck took place in 1873 when both steamships and sailing vessels were used to cross the oceans. Steamships were more modern, faster, luxurious, and maneuverable.

Horatio and his wife Anna were wonderful parents and dedicated Christians who helped the cause of Christ in many ways. Horatio was a young lawyer who spent much of his time helping his church and DL Moody, the Billy Graham of his day. Anna did the same and oversaw the women's ministry in this great evangelist's ministry.

They had four young daughters who were the love of their lives. When the shipwreck happened, Annie was nine, Maggie seven, Bessie five, and little Tanetta was just two years old.

Anna and the kids were on their way to France, where the family was to spend a year traveling and getting a taste of the schools in Europe. Horatio was going with them, but at the last minute, postponed his travel due to a delayed real estate deal. After it was completed, he would catch another ship and join them.

Maggie, the second daughter, did not want to go on the trip and made it known, but Anna counseled her that all would be well. Later, it would be discovered that Maggie left a note at home expressing her prophetic feelings about leaving.

On their voyage, in November of 1873, they traveled on one of the best and most modern steamships of the day, the Ville du Havre. However, one evening in a very calm sea, where visibility was perfect, they were struck at 2 am by the Loch Earn, an iron sailing vessel. No one knows why this happened, but if there were any last maneuvering to be done, it would be up to Ville du Havre, because it had the capability to change course quickly. The Ville du Havre did not change course and was struck and sunk within 12 minutes. Even though 87 survived, 226 men, women, and children perished, including the four little girls. Anna somehow survived being rescued by the ship that struck the Ville du Havre.

November
Week 2

Annie Age 11   Maggie Age 9   Bessie Age 7   Tanetta Age 2

The Four Spafford Sisters

The Shipwreck

The righteous cry, and the Lord hears and delivers them out of all their troubles. The Lord is near to the brokenhearted and saves those who are crushed in spirit. Many are the afflictions of the righteous, but the Lord delivers them from all of them. Psalms 34:17-19

This is the first of two articles on how one of the most beloved hymns of all time, *It Is Well With My Soul*, originated. Horatio Spafford wrote the lyrics to this song but there are a couple of different versions of his life. After reading a few books about him and his family, I landed on an affirming account of their lives together in the ministry.

There is quite a story behind the making of this hymn, with too many spiritual lessons and applications to pack into just one article.

I knew someone who suffered the loss of their children like Horatio Spafford. That person was Don, my dad's youth pastor. He had three children who were young. Tragically, while traveling in the back of a pickup, they were all killed in a horrible accident. I remember attending the funeral of these three children, and what stood out for me, even to this day, was the three white hearses lined up outside the church to take them away to their place of burial. Don and his wife eventually recovered to a degree

Whether God's preparation for us is at sea or on land, one thing is clear throughout the Scripture, we are all made to be launched and sail the ocean. That means entering this world with a visible Christ on each of our decks, so others can see and consider Him for their lives.

On a final note, don't ever forget God is the one who made us who we are. In His eyes we are what He wanted; He has no regrets. So, let us not throw away any part of ourselves by sinful disobedience, or by listening to the mistaken opinions of others. If we have sinned, then let us make it right with God and others as soon as possible, so that we can return and see ourselves as God sees us, with no regrets. And never forget that God will always love us no matter what, good, bad, or in-between, for His love is unconditional.

Remember, and I mean always remember, that He has given each of us certain purposes in this life to fulfill. Some purposes may have come and gone, while others will come in the future. And if God has purposes for each of us, then we need to have purposes for ourselves as well.

Last Thoughts

Realize that when you received Christ as Lord, it was like having the perfect captain come aboard who knows exactly how to run your ship and get it where it needs to go. Therefore, let Him do all of the steering, especially when the storms and hurricanes of this life hit.

When you asked Christ into your heart, and made Him your captain so to speak, you received a full measure of the Spirit, who is like a repair ship traveling with you day and night. His purpose is to fix everything that goes wrong in your life. All you need do is call out to Him for help. And when you do, like the motto of the USS Jason (*Ready, Willing, and Able*), you will be immediately equipped to accomplish all that God has for you today and tomorrow when it arrives.

Scriptural References

John 14:26 *But the Helper, the Holy Spirit, whom the Father will send in My name, He will teach you all things, and bring to your remembrance all that I said to you.*

Romans 8:11 *But if the Spirit of Him who raised Jesus from the dead dwells in you, He who raised Christ Jesus from the dead will also give life to your mortal bodies through His Spirit who dwells in you.*

in its own right, and all work together to keep our nation safe, as well as other nations safe who seek our help.

Comparatively, each of us have also been uniquely constructed, but our construction is not entirely from our biological father and mother, but from the hands of God, who had us in mind long before He put our parents on earth.

> *You had set me apart before I was born and called me by Your grace. You formed my inward parts and wove me in my mother's womb. I will give thanks to You, for I am fearfully and wonderfully made. Galatians 1: 5; Psalm 139:13*

Each of us is well thought out and designed by God who gives us various personalities, capabilities, skills, and purposes. And though it seems like we look or even act like others, we are uniquely different, for God broke the mold after each one of us was made.

In respect to this, my dad's ship, the USS Jason, was a repair ship; its purpose was to fix, rebuild, and restore other Navy ships that had broken down at sea. After the Jason was launched in 1943 and put into action, it developed a distinctive history totally unto itself, logging over 50 years of service for our country. How many ships the Jason saved is not known, perhaps hundreds. But the point is, just as there was only one USS Jason in this world, there is only one of us in God's kingdom. Each of us are one of a kind to God and incredibly special to Him.

Like the USS Jason, we were made by God to fulfill a purpose, and for some several purposes. Whatever that purpose is or purposes are, each of us is just as important to Him as another.

God's preparation for us may vary, just like that of the USS Jason, which probably took a little more time to equip because cranes, hoists, and winches had to be put in place. The Jason had big guns too, but not near as many as other naval ships. Similarly, some of us will experience longer periods of building time, depending on what kind of ship God is making out of us.

God's place of preparation and development may also be different for each of us, some do better with this while at sea, others need more time in the shipyard. This all depends upon what the Lord knows about us at the moment, and what He knows about our future ahead.

November
Week 1

(1945-The USS Jason repairing an aircraft carrier after a Kamikaze attack)

Ready, Willing, and Able
A Veterans Day Message

The Spirit of God has made me, and the breath of the Almighty gives me life. For I know the plans that I have for you, declares the Lord, plans for your welfare and not calamity to give you a future and a hope. Job 33:4 Jeremiah 29:11

I remember when I was a boy my dad, who was a naval chaplain, took my brother and me aboard his ship. He escorted us all over it, showing us everything about his vessel. At the end of our tour, we sat down with my dad at the captain's table for dinner. It was very formal, so we sat up straight, used good table manners, and were on our best behavior.

As many of us know, Navy ships have been vital to our nation's safety and security. But it takes a long time to build one of these vessels. Today, for instance, an aircraft carrier can take up to four years to construct. However, in World War II, when there was a great need to get as many ships into battle as soon as possible, it only took about a year to complete each one of them.

Back then, as is the case today, there were many kinds of Navy ships with different designs, sizes, capabilities, and purposes. Each is important

November

**Ready, Willing, and Able
The Shipwreck
The American Colony
Thanksgiving President**

Scripture References

III John 1:11 *Beloved, do not imitate evil but imitate good. Whoever does good is from God; whoever does evil has not seen God.*

Ephesians 5:11 *Take no part in the unfruitful works of darkness but instead expose them.*

I Thessalonians 5:21 *But scrutinize everything; hold fast to that which is good; abstain from every form of evil.*

Footnotes

Margaret Galitzin, *What's Good and Evil about Halloween* (Internet: Traditions in Action Incorporated, October 25th, 2007).

and President's Day honors great men like Washington and Lincoln who led our nation through difficult times. Martin Luther King Day gives honor to a man who fought for equality for all men, regardless of race, and Memorial and Veterans Days praise those who fought and died for our country.

Now, what does Halloween commemorate? It observes the celebration of evil things that are frightening, all for the sake of getting a bag of candy. Not wise, I would say, and very disheartening to God, I would suspect.

Hence, for this coming Halloween or the next when it rolls around again, there are a few alternatives to consider. One is not better than another, each works in its own way according to the circumstances.

The first alternative is to participate in Halloween fully and not take it seriously.

A second is to participate but make every effort to inform others about the history of Halloween and how it pales in comparison to other more important holidays.

A third is to downplay Halloween and make every move to substitute Halloween with another celebration. For instance, designating October 31st as a harvest festival, rather than a Halloween celebration. Instead of dressing up like figures of evil and death, dress up as men and women of great character. Florence Nightingale, George Washington, astronaut, military captain, or first responders are examples. Perhaps over time, with an effort like this, Halloween can evolve into something better than what it is today.

A fourth is to forego Halloween altogether, bypassing the costume, trick or treating, parties, and all the other traditions that go with it.

Last Thought

A last possibility you might consider is to make a ministry out of Halloween night by passing out tracks about Christ, attached to the candy.

A woman who wrote to me a few years ago said she and her family did this very thing. She didn't know if anyone responded to the tracts, but it did help her children become braver about their faith. Christian tracts with Halloween in mind can be found on the internet. Or better yet, if you have time, make up your own.

beginning of winter, a time of coldness and death. They built a bonfire and burned animals, crops, and even human sacrifices to honor their god of death.

During the 1800s, large numbers of immigrants from this area of the world brought with them this evil oriented celebration.

In America, this celebration was renamed Halloween. And the practice of trick or treating (a Celtic custom) became the most noted custom of Halloween. Many people in the United States do not know this history but perceive Halloween as a harmless activity in which children may participate.

Have most of us ever wondered how trick or treating ever came about with the Celts? Part of this Celtic ritual was a belief that dead souls would return to their original homes. The people were terrified of these evil spirits, and they would place sweet goodies on their doorstep to appease them. Their belief was if the evil spirits liked the treat, they would leave them alone, but if they didn't, they would "trick them by casting evil spells." A little like the spells that were cast in the Harry Potter films. Our custom of trick or treating evolved from this tradition.

Further, Halloween was not a party time for the Celtic people. They feared the evil spirits roaming the earth on October 31st, and so they stayed home. If someone were forced to leave the house, he or she would disguise themselves as a demon to fool the evil spirits.

Other Halloween traditions, such as the fear of a black cat, are also not without a root of evil. The Celtics believed that humans were punished for their evil deeds by changing them into black cats. Therefore, it was entirely proper to sacrifice a black cat in a ritualistic bonfire on October 31st.

Even something that seems as innocent as a Jack-o-lantern had a dark beginning. This tradition comes from a legend about Jack, who was turned away from heaven because of his wickedness. He was also turned away from hell because he had played tricks on the devil. Therefore, he was sentenced to spend the rest of his days roaming the earth as a demonic spirit, haunting anyone who crossed his path. The legend says he carved a face in a turnip and put a candle in it to guide him at night to his next victim. We have now substituted a pumpkin for a Jack-o-lantern at Halloween.[1]

Finally, the most memorable day observances or holidays in America are rooted in something good, joyous, or significant. Christmas, for example, celebrates the birth of Christ and Easter His sacrifice and resurrection, Thanksgiving gives thanks to God for helping us as a nation,

October
Week 4

"Mask, Mask, Take It Off!"

Be wise in what is good and innocent in what is evil. Romans 16:19

"Mask, Mask," yelled my son when he saw a horrifying Halloween mask on my face! "Take it off. Take it off!" And I did immediately, not wanting to scare him any further. I was trying on the mask to see if I should wear it to a Halloween party to which I was invited. I ended up not wearing it because I was not into Halloween anymore, especially after reading about its history. But Brodie was only two years old at the time and could not discern if what he saw was real or not. When I put the mask down on the table, he started hitting it with one of his toys to make it go away.

Halloween, which occurs every October 31st, has increased tremendously in recognition and spending over the years. This fall holiday, which celebrates the terror and scariness surrounding the dead, is only second in consumer spending to Christmas. This seems hard to believe, but when you consider all of the candy, decorations, haunted parties, and costumes purchased, along with the horror movies watched at the theatres, second to Christmas sounds about right. Not Easter, Valentine's Day, Mother's Day, Father's Day, or July 4th compares to Halloween when it comes to popularity, acceptance, and money spent.

If we are unclear about the root of evil in Halloween, here is a short history. The origin of Halloween is the Celtic festival of Samhain. The Celtics lived in what is now Great Britain, Ireland, and Northern France. Their new year began on November 1st, and the festival that started the previous evening honored Samhain, the Celtic lord of death. It marked the

Last Thought

From a distance both the Sea of Galilee and the Dead Sea look majestic and healthy; I know as I have stood on different mountain tops looking at each one of them. It was only when I got closer to the two seas that I could see what each was really like, one alive and well, and the other completely dead. So, it is I suspect, with the people and even many leaders of this world who from a distance look appealing and thriving, but as you get closer, you realize only a few actually are. Before you put your trust in anyone, get to know them better, to see if they are like the Dead Sea or the Sea of Galilee.

Scripture References

I John 4: 1 *Beloved, do not believe every spirit, but test the spirits to see whether they are from God, because many false prophets have gone out into the world.*

Colossians 2:8 *See to it that no one takes you captive through philosophy and empty deception, according to the tradition of men, according to the elementary principles of the world, rather than according to Christ.*

Why the difference between these two seas, one being so alive and the other dead? When the Jordan River flows into the Sea of Galilee, it also flows out of it too, making its water fresh to drink, healthy for fish, and lush for thriving trees and vegetation.

On the other hand, when the Jordan River flows into the Dead Sea, it has nowhere else to go. Thus it becomes stagnant and incredibly salty. In fact, it is so salty that it is impossible to drown in it because the salt concentration always keeps your body upright. It also smells to high heaven and can burn your eyes if your face goes under its waters.

There are two applications that can be drawn from these three bodies of water. In both applications, the Jordan River is the same, a continuous flow of God's truth via the Scriptures, and the life and witness of Christ.

In the first application, the Sea of Galilee corresponds to those who take in God's flow of truth, beginning by accepting Jesus Christ, as Lord and Savior. After that many other truths flow in that deal with living an abundant and fulfilled life here on earth. And just as this great Galilean Sea prospers because it receives and gives out, so it is for those who take in God's truth and give that truth back out to others.

The Dead Sea, on the other hand, represents many who refuse God's flow of truth, the most significant being to ignore or reject what is said about Christ. Because of this, they grow increasingly stagnant in their beliefs and lifestyles. And like the Dead Sea without any outlet and full of salt, they end up deadening themselves, and everyone and everything else around them.

The second application is for Christians whose lives became new and alive at salvation, a "Sea of Galilee" kind of experience. Sadly though, many still hold onto "Dead Sea" parts of their old lives that linger on. The solution is pretty simple, respond to God's continuous flow of truth by asking for His forgiveness and help. If we need to, do this every day until those "Dead Sea" parts are gone or at least not dominating us anymore. Who knows, perhaps persistence and reliance on God will result in your Dead Sea parts becoming more like a Sea of Galilee, full of life, not death.

Jesus said, 'Everyone who drinks of this water in the well will thirst again, but whoever drinks of the water I give shall never thirst again; because the water I give becomes a well of spiritual water springing up within and leading to eternal life.' John 4:13-14

October
Week 3

Sea of Galilee   Dead Sea

One River, Two Seas

Jesus spoke many things in parables, 'Behold, the sower went out to sow, and some of His seeds fell beside the road. This kind of ground was like those who were too hardened to accept the truth of My Gospel. So, after a while, Satan came and removed these truths, as birds do when seeing seeds on the road.' Yet, Jesus also said His seeds of the Gospel fell on good soil as well, which are those who believe and receive His truth, some a hundredfold, some sixty, and some thirty. Matthew 13:3, 4, 8, 9

    A few years ago, my wife, Myrna, and I visited the Holy Land. It was a terrific trip, and we loved every minute of it. We would love to return someday if possible. Three of the sites that impacted us were the Jordan River, where Jesus was baptized, the Sea of Galilee, where He stilled a storm with one command, and the Dead Sea, where nothing lives.
    The Jordan, which is the main water source for Israel, is not excessively big or wide. It flows north to south from Mount Hermon, spilling into the Sea of Galilee first, and then ends at the Dead Sea 112 miles downstream. Myrna and I swam in both seas, one full of life and the other barren of life. Both were large, but the Dead Sea outsized the Sea of Galilee by quite a bit. From a distance, both seas looked beautiful, but up close only the Sea of Galilee proved to be so.

to thrive. For whatever reasons, I grew tired of where I was in some of those circumstances and wanted to venture out. As I look back, had the Lord let me out, I would have been greatly diminished or even harmed in my faith. But He did not, and because of that I grew in my walk with Him as planned.

My caution is to stay where we are until the Lord, Himself, has made it clear for us to move on or leave. And He will, but according to His own timing, when conditions are right, and when we are ready.

How do we know when this time comes? The Lord will push us out when the time arrives as He did with the disciples who were sent to all parts of the world to preach the Gospel after the Lord made His exit.

Last Thought

Eventually the butterfly enclosure we visited was closed and shut down for the summer. The season of life for those butterflies came to an end, but not before their time was up. Ultimately the Lord will also move you on to other things and places as well, but not before your time for what you are doing and experiencing is up. Therefore, enjoy what you have while you have it, and do not be so quick to rush out of what God has provided for you.

Scripture Reference

Ecclesiastes 3:1 *There is an appointed time for everything. And there is a time for every event under heaven.*

October

Week 2

Butterflies

Not that I speak from want, for I have learned to be content in whatever circumstances I am. Philippian's 4:11

Last summer my wife and I took our two youngest grandchildren to the zoo to see the butterfly exhibit. Connor was about 3, and Elizabeth was eighteen months. In order to get into the exhibit, we had to be very careful not to let the butterflies escape. There were two sets of doors and a waiting area to go through to make sure none were released accidentally.

When we finally got in with all the butterflies, they were everywhere, flying from one part of the enclosure to the next. They were all incredibly beautiful and seemed content with each other and us as well. Aside from this there were plenty of leaves and foliage from which to feed, and the temperature inside was exactly right, not too cold or too warm.

The conditions were simply perfect for these butterflies to thrive; how could they want anything more?

Yet, at every instance there were a few who were always trying to escape, especially when the exit doors were opened. I remember when we tried to leave some even clung to our clothing and we had to shew them off.

Had they been successful in fleeing in this way, they would have died soon after escaping according to the staff. The conditions outside the enclosure would have been too harsh for them.

In a way these butterflies reminded me of times when I tried in the past to escape the set of circumstances God had provided for me in which

Last Thought

Paul's life ended two years after his imprisonment, but the greatest part of his ministry may have come through the second path he took after being arrested. Perhaps this will be the same for you. Don't be afraid to take the second path awaiting you if the first has come to an end. The rest of your life on this new path may end up being the best of your life.

Scripture References

Genesis 5:20 *As for you, you meant evil against me, but God meant it for good in order to bring about this present result, to preserve many people alive.*

Deuteronomy 31:8 *The Lord is the one who goes ahead of you; He will be with you. He will not fail you or forsake you. Do not fear or be dismayed.*

making this decision their economy soared as never before, because peanuts brought in much more profit then cotton ever did.

In response to Enterprise's renewed prosperity, a local businessman in the town suggested building a statute in the middle of the city as a tribute to how something disastrous could be a catalyst for change. The statute which remains today is a 13-foot-tall woman with arms stretched above her head victoriously holding an enlarged-scale boll weevil.

The boll weevil can be like the things that come into our lives that force us to stop what we are doing, and even end the path we are on. These may be losses of all kinds including financial, illness, broken relationships, job endings, accidents, or even the death of a loved one. To try and pursue putting things back as they once were may be like the farmers in Enterprise who at first resisted starting up a new crop of peanuts. But they had to, to exist. Similarly, we may have to walk away from the path we are on, so that God can open a whole new direction for us. The sooner we do this, with the Lord's help, of course, the better for us in our current moment, and every day after.

Paul, the great Apostle, certainly experienced such a dilemma in his own ministry, when after his 3rd missionary journey, he got tossed into jail for all his efforts. What a shock, what a change! He was sent to Rome to plead his case to Caesar, instead of continuing his work by starting new churches in the West. He made his case with Caesar for two years while in prison. During this time, he realized he had to abandon his old path to reach the West. Instead he decided to just focus on a new path, bringing as many Roman soldiers and others living in Rome to Christ as possible.

In addition to this Paul, wrote letters to many of the churches he had started. As this turned out, almost half of the New Testament has Paul's imprint on it. And because of all of the soldier conversations, much of the West was eventually reached for the Gospel, for many of these men were later stationed there.

And what of the letters Paul wrote to the churches? Christians still study them to this day all around the world for encouragement and explanation of God's truth. How many have received salvation through Paul's letters? The number is countless!

October
Week 1

(Statue of Boll Weevil)

Boll Weevil

We know that God causes all things to work together for good to those who love God, to those who are called according to His purpose. Roman 8:28

As I look back there were junctures in my life where the path I was following came to a screeching halt. No matter what I did, whether it was praying more, reading the Word, seeking other's advice, or intensifying my efforts to bring things about, nothing worked. In fact, what I deemed necessary and even hoped for, increasingly fell out of reach.

There is an illustration I ran across recently that perhaps gives a clarifying picture of these times when they come, as well as a possible answer or direction to take when they do.

Around the beginning of the 20th Century, there was a difficult dilemma the city of Enterprise, Alabama experienced. It was a juncture in its life as a city that would determine whether it would continue or cease to exist as a viable community. A deadly bug, the boll weevil, which feasted on cotton made its way up from Mexico to this town, as well as other southern areas dependent on this crop for their economic existence. Nothing could be done to stop the infestation, other than abandoning it for another crop not impacted by the weevil, which they did. Instead of putting any more efforts into cotton, they started planting peanuts in its place. After

October

**Boll Weevil
Butterflies
One River, Two Seas
"Mask, Mask, Take It Off!"**

Last Thoughts

Remember, when criticized or corrected by others, don't lick the knife of revenge, just take it and grow from it. And if that person has been unfair or ruthless in what they've said to you, just let the Lord take care of them. He will likely do it through another to bring them into account for what they've said or done.

Finally, learning to deal with criticism or correction in a God-honoring way will keep you from possibly bleeding to death spiritually.

Scripture References

I Thessalonians 5:15 *Make sure that nobody pays back wrong for wrong, but always strive to do what is good for each other and for everyone else.*

Galatians 6:1, *Brethren, if a man is overtaken in any trespass, you who are spiritual restore such a one in a spirit of gentleness, considering yourself lest you also be tempted.*

Matthew 18:15 *If your brother sins, go and show him his fault in private; if he listens to you, you have won your brother.*

Ephesians 4:29 *Let no unwholesome word proceed from your mouth, but only such a word as is good for edification according to the need of the moment, so that it will give grace to those who hear.*

Footnote
How to Kill a Wolf, Snopes.com (October 19, 2006)

would continue, causing him to bite into the blade, and eventually bleed to death.[1]

Had the wolf in this story been wise enough to just step back from the knife when tempted by its smell of blood, he would have survived. And so, it should be with us, for instead of taking revenge, being angry, or defensive when criticized or corrected, we need to backpedal a bit before saying or doing anything.

What are some back-pedaling steps? Here are just a few, for there are many.

A first step back from the blade of criticism or a poorly done correction is to stay quiet and just listen to the person offering the criticism or correction. In our silence we should pray that God will help control our feelings, which can range from surprise, despair, depression, to anger. Responding in anger with a counter criticism is like the wolf licking off the first layer of blood on the knife.

A second step back is to consider what is being said in the criticism or correction, for maybe there is a kernel of truth to what is indicated. If so, then God will show this to us. Sometimes He confirms this through our feelings, and at other times through others who love us. Not to consider what is said, is like licking off another layer of blood on the knife.

A third step is to thank the person for what they have said and tell them we will consider it. This shows real humility which the Lord always loves to see. Such an answer will not only help us recover from the criticism or correction more quickly, but it will also greatly help build a bridge with the person who shared his or her concerns. Not to do so, but walking away in anger and disgust, is like licking yet another layer of blood on the knife.

A fourth step is to apply what we have learned from criticism or correction to situations when we are in a position to help others with a timely word.

Make sure when in this position to say what needs to be said with feelings and words of genuine care and love. Use words that will bring the person to improved character, hope, and a closer relationship to Christ. Not to do so in this manner gets us nearer to that razor-sharp blade that can not only cut others to pieces, but us as well.

September
Week 4

The Wolf and the Blade

Do not say, 'I'll take revenge and do to them as they have done to me, but instead strive to do what is good for each other.' Proverbs 24:29, I Thessalonians 5:15

Today, more than ever, we can see what criticism can do to others, especially if done in the wrong way. Just look at our political arena, where one side is criticizing the other without reservation and with great malice. Whether these leaders realize it or not they are destroying the spirit of our nation, as well as themselves. However, this article is not about politics but about what we as Christians need to do when receiving untrue criticism or badly done correction.

There is an applicable story I want to share; whether it is true or legend I do not know. It is about a tribe of Eskimos that once put down dangerous wolves in an amazingly effective way. To begin, they sharpened the blade of a knife until it was razor sharp, and then dipped it in the blood of a seal they had recently killed. They put the knife outside until the blood froze on the blade. They repeated this process over and over until there were many coats of blood on the blade. Afterward the Eskimos planted the knife in the snow far from their igloos. The scent of the blood, even though frozen, could be easily picked up by a wolf in the area. It would then begin licking the blade, layer after layer, until only its sharp edges were left. The wolf

There are sometimes difficult circumstances in this life that can challenge our hope to the nth degree, as was the case with these men. Yet like each of them, we need to remain steady in our faith and prayers until God's rescue ship arrives. Meanwhile, we wait, do what we can to survive each day in our circumstance, and never give into despair.

Where are we in all of this? Are we sailing unhindered from one port to the next enjoying the beauty and peacefulness of our journey? On the other hand, are we at the beginning of a trial where our ship is damaged and even shipwrecked? Maybe we're in the middle of a crisis where we are freezing and losing hope. Or perhaps at the end of a trial when God's rescue ship is on the horizon.

Last Thought

No matter where you are, know this about God, He is really not like Shackleford in this illustration, for He has commissioned someone else to play that role with you. Or perhaps he has commissioned you to help rescue another. Where is the Lord then? He is always right beside you, accompanying you all the way until you are rescued from your set of circumstances.

So the next time you feel alone on your own Elephant island, and want to yell out in fear or frustration, "Where are you, Lord, where are you?" Remember, He's right next to you and is not deaf. He hasn't moved an inch from your side and hears every word you say. But if it makes you feel better, go ahead and yell, His ears can take it.

Scripture References

Psalm 41:10 *Do not fear, for I am with you; do not anxiously look about you, for I am your God. I will strengthen you; indeed, I will help you, surely, I will uphold you with My righteous right hand.*

Isaiah 43:1-3 *Do not fear when you pass through the waters, I will be with you; and through the rivers, they will not overflow you, for I am the Lord your God.*

Psalm 34:15, 17-19 *The eyes of the Lord are toward the righteous, and His ears are open to their cry. The Lord is near to the brokenhearted and saves those who are crushed in spirit.*

September
Week 3

(Elephant Island, Antarctica)

Never Deserted

The Lord said, 'I will never desert you, nor will I ever forsake you.'
Hebrews 13:5

    In January 1915, a British ship, the Endurance, was trapped and crushed in the ice off Antarctica's coast. In the summer months, temperatures can get as high as 48 degrees, and in the winter, which lasts about six months beginning in February, it can plunge to 128 degrees below zero.
    Aproximately 30 explorers, led by Ernest Shackleton, survived an unfortunate shipwreck and reached Elephant Island in three small lifeboats. It is called Elephant Island because it looks like an elephant lying down.
    Trapped on this uninhabited island and far from the standard shipping lanes, Shackleford took off with five of his men on one of the smaller lifeboats to get help. The help could only come from another island called South Georgia, almost 800 miles away. It seemed impossible that those left behind on Elephant Island could survive, but there was no hope for any of them if Shackleton didn't try.
    Meanwhile, the men left behind struggled and wondered what their final fate would be as the temperatures dropped. One month went by, then two, and then three, but no help appeared on the horizon. With their hopes fading at the end of the fourth month, a boat appeared in the distance. Sure enough, it was Shackleton who had made it to the South Georgia Island and returned with many others and supplies to rescue them.

Last Thought

If you are going through a tough time right now, or go through one in the future, ask yourself, "Did God ordain this for me to develop my spiritual wings, or did I cause my own trial because of my disobedience? In either case, there may be a lot of waiting to be done until God's will is accomplished in your life. And even though you may think He is taking too long, remember God is never too early or too late ending a trial. His timing is perfect, just as the mother eagle's was when dropping her youngster in midair. Like the illustration of the mother eagle, you will never perish, for the Lord is always there to save you if you cannot quite fly yet.

Scripture References

Jeremiah 29:11 *For I know the plans that I have for you declares the Lord, plans for welfare and not for calamity to give you a future and a hope.*
Deuteronomy 3:18 *The Lord himself will lead you and be with you. He will not fail you or abandon you, so do not lose courage or be afraid.*
Deuteronomy 31:8 *The Lord is the one who goes ahead of you; He will be with you. He will not fail you or forsake you. Do not fear or be dismayed.*

fly. If she had not done this, the eaglet would never have left the nest to become the majestic bird it was created to be.

As I pondered on this, I began to wonder if God was not doing something similar to me in a sense. Was my jobless situation like being cast out of the nest, to help me fly better with my faith and understanding of His love and plan for my life? Possible, very possible I thought as I ended my prayer that morning.

The next day, with this in mind, I read the story of Joseph in the Old Testament, and was struct about the part of his life when his brothers threw him into a pit and then sold him to a passing caravan. "Where are you, Lord, what did I do, and why?" he must have asked. But as he flapped his wings, one representing his need for a greater faith, and the other a deeper understanding of God's love, he flew.

And we know the outcome of the story of Joseph who became one of God's most important ambassadors to the Egyptians and his own people as well back in Israel.

As I ended my second devotion by the creek, watching a mother teach her youngster how to fly, and reading about Joseph, I realized what God was doing with me. After a few more weeks, sure enough, God opened the door, for I was ready. What was the job? A position as lead pastor of a church, my first of this type in the ministry. However, there would be other midair drops in my life by the Lord, just as there were for Joseph as he completed God's will. We should all reread the story of Joseph when we get a chance; it is in Genesis 41.

Not all trials we encounter are ordained by God to develop our faith and understanding of His love; some come about because of our own disobedience, selfishness, and return to sin. These God does not ordain but allows us to wade through until we can't stand it anymore. When we finally realize what we have done, and then seek His forgiveness and restoration, He gives it to us immediately. However, in the process, He may change the direction of our lives. In other words, God may change what we will do, because of what we have done. Nevertheless, whatever that may be, it is best for us, others, and His earthly kingdom. Heaven, though, is a different story for it is a whole new beginning for all of us as we will all find out.

September
Week 2

Midair Panic

Like a mother eagle that stirs up her nest and hovers over the young day and night, so too is the Lord with you. Deuteronomy 32:11, 12

Years ago, during the first years of my marriage to Myrna, I was in between jobs and knew a little about waiting on God, but definitely not enough to get me through the employment dilemma I found myself in, which had gone on for months.

As I poured through the Scriptures for insight and prayed every day for a job to open, I grew very discouraged. I wondered what possible purpose God had for not providing a job and home for my wife and me.

Fortunately, during this transition time, we were able to stay with her parents who lived on a beautiful 10-acre farm.

Then one morning while having a devotion by a creek on the south end of the property, I looked up and saw a nest of eagles at the top of one of the nearby trees. Along with the mother, it was filled with some young eaglets flapping their wings. As I noted their activity, and to be honest I can't remember if I actually saw this, or read about it later on that day, some interesting things happened. The mother eagle took one of its eaglets out of the nest and dropped it in midair. The young eaglet panicked of course and started flapping its wings wildly. Before hitting the ground, the mother swooped underneath and saved the youngster. Then the mother would climb high and do this whole process over and over until the eaglet was able to

means daddy. Incredible, isn't it that God would have us call Him daddy, as I did my father. The same God who created the earth, the universe, the angelic realm, and all of humanity wants us to relate to Him in as personal a way as possible, like a loving, caring, and protective dad.

> *You have received a spirit of adoption as sons by which we cry out, 'Abba! Father!' Romans 8:15*
> *For by Him all things were created, both in the heavens and on earth, visible and invisible, whether thrones or dominions or rulers or authorities—all things have been created through Him and for Him. He is before all things, and in Him, all things hold together. Colossians 1:16-17*

Last Thought

The next time you feel a bit discouraged or rejected by circumstances or life itself, remember the God who made the universe loves you deeply. He is not just looking down upon you from above, but is at your bedside, as a loving dad would be with a sick son or daughter. He is pretty busy with all that is going on in this world, but never too busy to take care of you. So, yes, call Him God, Father, and even Lord, but also call Him daddy, for He is that too.

Scripture References

Mark 14:32, 35-36 *32 They all came to Gethsemane, and Jesus said to His disciples, 'Sit here until I have prayed.' 35 And He went a little beyond them, and fell to the ground and began to pray that if it were possible, the hour might pass Him by. 36 And He was saying, 'Abba! Father! All things are possible for You; remove this cup from Me; yet not what I will, but what You will.'*

September
Week 1

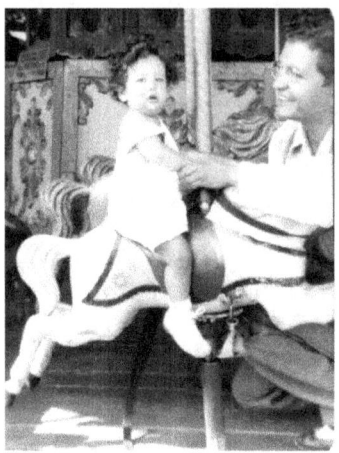

Abba Father

Because you are sons, God has sent forth the Spirit of His Son into our hearts, crying, "Abba! Father", (Daddy)! Galatians 4:6

When I was a young child, perhaps four or five years old, I used to storm into my dad's office at church without knocking. Of course, I wanted to see my dad immediately and probably had some silly questions to ask him. But without hesitation, he dropped what he was doing and listened to everything I had to say. I know others who happened to be in the office that day may have been a bit perturbed at my dad, letting me take preference over them, but he did.

Add to this another time when I was in the hospital a year later. And who was it that came into my room that night after surgery, my dad, of course. As my mother told me later, he came to tell the nurses on duty that he would be staying through the night. They assured him he did not need to stay, because they would take care of me just fine. "No way," said my dad, "I will take care of my son." So, my dad stayed through the night, assisting the nurses, which did not particularly make them happy. He sat by my side, working on Sunday's sermon, and getting me anything I needed.

In a way, my dad, to me, was kind of like Paul's view of God to him. In his epistles, Paul often refers to God as *Abba Father*, which essentially

September

Abba Father
Mid Air Panic
Never Deserted
Wolf and the Blade

August
Vision	*Perseverance*	176
Venus Fly Trap	*Temptation*	178
Just So Many Days	*Omniscience*	180
Green Tomatoes	*Patience*	183

Additional articles
The Oak and the Vine	*Cling to*	186
Surrounded	*Stressed*	188
Palm Sunday	*Relocated*	190
Jesus' Six Trials	*Unfairly treated*	193

Epilogue	198
Photo Credits	200
Last Comments by Publisher	202

February
How Beautiful You Are	*Healed*	85
Valentine's Day	*Loved*	87
Lincoln the Christian	*Endurance*	89
Red Seas in Life	*Worry*	93

March
Emergency Lane	*Irritations*	98
Esteem	*Befriended*	100
Steeper Near the Top	*Tired*	102
Eye on the Sparrow	*Anxiety*	106

April
Silent Saturday	*In-betweens*	110
Jesus' Facecloth	*Unfinished*	115
All Was Lost	*Restored*	119
Breakfast with Jesus	*Repaired*	124

May
Floating with God's Will	*Relax*	129
A Mother to Remember	*Ups & downs*	131
Pebble Beach	*Reformed*	135
Timely Words	*Encouraged*	138

June
A Little Girl's Tears	*Foreknown*	142
Flint and the Fire	*Ask*	147
Father's Day	*Alternatives*	150
Pruned	*Sanctification*	154

July
First Independence Day	*Disappointment*	158
First Days in Heaven	*Reward*	161
Rawhide Marathon	*Encouragement*	168
Lost in the Marsh	*Rescued*	171

Table of Contents

	Theme	Page
Title Page		1
Books by Kent McClain		3
Copyright		4
Dedication		5

September
Abba Father	*Perspective*	11
Mid Air Panic	*Hope*	13
Never Deserted	*Abandonment*	16
Wolf and the Blade	*Criticism*	18

October
Boll Weevil	*Direction*	22
Butterflies	*Contentment*	25
One River, Two Seas	*Discernment*	27
"Mask, Mask, Take It Off!	*Origin of Halloween*	30

November
Ready, Willing, and Able	*Uniqueness*	35
The Shipwreck	*Crushed*	38
The American Colony	*Recovery*	44
Thanksgiving President	*Sovereignty*	48

December
Third Place Trophy	*Sacrifice*	54
Bethlehem Star	*Shine & Show*	58
Silent Night, Holy Night	*Inspiration*	62
Binoculars	*Vision*	66

January
A Word of Gratitude	*Appreciation*	70
Coming and Going	*Departures*	74
A Palm Tree's Core	*Replenished*	78
The Making of a Pearl	*Trials*	80

As my brother and I arrived at the church where my dad's memorial was to take place, there were at least 12 limousines lined up outside with San Diego dignitaries. They, along with more than 1,000 other people, came to pay their respects to my dad. To this day, it is the largest memorial service I have ever attended.

Such adoration makes sense, for my dad had pastored two different churches at the same time while in San Diego and had a radio broadcast that reached over 42,000 people every week. My dad was well-loved, thought of, and respected by many in that part of California.

Even though his early life in the ministry was marred by divorce and a family break up, it did not keep him from doing the best he could with the ministry years he had left.

Therefore, "I devote this book and September's first article to you, dad, and perhaps when I get to heaven one day, we can continue the talks we were just beginning to enjoy before you passed."

Book Dedication

This book is dedicated to my dad, with whom I was unable to spend time growing up. My mom and dad divorced when I was only six years old.

My dad was a Nazarene pastor at the time and was forced to leave his ministry position because of this breakup. He immediately joined the Navy, becoming a naval officer and chaplain on the USS Jason. He eventually recovered from the divorce and entered back into the pastoral ministry in another denomination. Because of my mom's bitterness toward my dad, my brother and I were not allowed to spend time with him. Today, the court system would not have allowed this, but it did back then.

As I entered high school and then college, I began desiring more quality time with him, for I was of age to make this determination. As I got to know him, I grew to love my dad and wished he could have been there for me when I was young. Nevertheless, at least I had some time with him before he died.

He was only 52 years old when he passed away suddenly from a heart attack. I will never forget the night before he died; he called me from his hospital bed.

> He said, "Kent, I love you so much. Do you forgive me for not being there when you were growing up?"
> "Dad, I forgave you long ago for that, and I love you too, I love you very much."

He seemed to be at peace after that, at least that is what a nurse told me later on. He died early the next morning.

Always There to Repair

By Kent McClain

© US Copyright 2021

ISBN: 978-1-938367-59-5.

Publication date: December 2020

Published by Destinee Media (www.destineemedia.com)

Cover design and editing by Myrna Sleath McClain

Primarily the New American Standard Bible is used throughout the book, although other translations are employed and some paraphrasing of my own. When I paraphrase, I keep Scriptures concise, but never at the cost of losing the original meaning or message.

Due to duplication, only single quote marks will be employed within the context of a verse or passage. John 11:25 is an example of this: *Jesus said to her, 'I am the resurrection and the life; he who believes in Me will live even if he dies.'* As can be seen, customarily placed double quotes have been removed.

Books and Articles by Kent McClain

Teachable Moments (Teaching Children How to Remember God's Truth)

Teachable Moments Year One (Memorable and Interactive Lessons with Children to help them Remember God's Truth)

What Was I Thinking? (Learning an Ocean of Grace in a Pond of Legalism)

Revealing God's Design with Love (What Scripture Tells Christians about Homosexuality and Gender Change)

Mission Possible (A Sequential Account of Jesus's Discipleship). Unpublished

Truth Spoken from the Heart of a Sixth Grader. Unpublished.

Articles on the Christian life can be read and downloaded from www.tmoments.com

I picked fifty-two of my favorite devotionals that deal with our need for repair, reinforcement, and restoration, including several stories of encouragement, hope, rejuvenation, and life-changing perspective. The devotionals cover twelve months, four per month, with four extras at the end to complete a fifty-two-week year. These devotionals come from hundreds of articles I have written over the past twenty years, which I called *Teachable Moments*. Most appear on my website www.tmoments.com.

Last Thought

Another article employing the USS Jason, with a different application, appears in November for Veterans Day. I encourage you not to miss this one, especially if you want to see just how unique you are to God!

God speed, and may these devotional articles meet the need of the moment in your life.

Kent McClain

Cover and Title

There arose a fierce gale of wind, and the waves were breaking over the boat so much that the boat was filling up. The disciples were scared and frightened, but Jesus got up and rebuked the wind and said to the sea, 'Hush and be still.' And the wind died down, and it became perfectly calm. Mark 4:37, 39

The book's cover and title (*Always There to Repair*) were inspired by the USS Jason, a repair ship in the United States Navy. My dad was the naval chaplain on this vessel, whose mission was to repair, restore, and give hope to damaged boats while at sea. To bring needy ships to port was either impossible due to their condition or impractical because of the time lost to their mission by towing them.

The USS Jason was an essential and vital ship to the US Navy, commissioned from 1945 to 1995. Its crew, over the years, did exemplary work saving numerous ships for further service.

The purpose of the devotional articles within and the USS Jason are similar, in that they seek to repair, restore, give hope, and even add perspective so that we can navigate the troubled waters of this world. The only difference being that the Spirit of God, unlike the USS Jason, is **ALWAYS THERE TO REPAIR,** for He travels with us everywhere we go. And as promised in Scripture, God never abandons us, no matter the storm or circumstance.

Be strong and courageous, and do not be afraid or terrified, for the Lord *goes with you; He will never leave you nor forsake you. Deuteronomy 31:6*